D0205914

# EQUALITY
# AND
# EDUCATION

# EQUALITY
## AND
# EDUCATION

*Federal Civil Rights
Enforcement in the
New York City
School System*

MICHAEL A. REBELL

*and*

ARTHUR R. BLOCK

PRINCETON UNIVERSITY PRESS
Princeton, New Jersey

Published by Princeton University Press, 41 William Street,
Princeton, New Jersey 08540
In the United Kingdom: Princeton University Press,
Guildford, Surrey

Library of Congress Cataloging in Publication Data will be
found on the last printed page of this book

ISBN 0-691-07692-8

This book has been composed in Linotron Sabon

Clothbound editions of Princeton University Press books
are printed on acid-free paper, and binding materials
are chosen for strength and durability

Printed in the United States of America by Princeton University Press
Princeton, New Jersey

To Josh and Laura,
*may they always value both
equality and education*

and

To Judy Penzer,
*whose political growth has
been an inspiration to me*

# CONTENTS

# ACKNOWLEDGMENTS

In January 1980, we began a study of the broadest civil rights investigation ever conducted in an urban school system, the Federal Office for Civil Rights' New York City Compliance Review. Our research over the next three years profited greatly from the willingness of the major participants in this event to share with us their recollections, perceptions, opinions, and, in many cases, their files.

We are particularly grateful for the cooperation of the persons who were the chief negotiators and policymakers for the board of education and for OCR during the crucial years of the review—Irving Anker, Bernard Gifford, Charles Schonhaut, Michael Rosen, Martin Gerry, David Tatel, and J. Harold Flannery, Jr. Many officials in these agencies during the time we conducted our research provided important assistance by permitting us access to files and documents and by arranging clearances for interviews. These persons include David Wirtz, Frederick Cioffi, and Charles Tejada. We would like to acknowledge, as well, the contributions of the persons on our interview list in Appendix A.

In the early stages of our research, we benefited from two unpublished papers concerning the early history of the New York City Compliance Review: Michael Rosen's "Staff Integration and the New York City School System" (1979) and Margaret Terry Orr's "A Critical Examination of Policy Process: OCR Review of New York City Schools" (1979).

Professor David Filvaroff served us well as a consultant on the legislative history of Title VI of the 1964 Civil Rights Act, and Susan Kantor of Lieber Attitude Research, Inc. gave us valuable technical assistance in constructing our survey.

We would like to thank, as well, those persons who read and commented on portions of the review copy of this report: Professor William Clune, University of Wisconsin Law

School; Professor Drew Days, Yale Law School; Allen Dobrin, New York City Board of Education; Professor Amy Gutmann, Department of Politics, Princeton University; Professor Jennifer L. Hochschild, Woodrow Wilson School of Public and International Affairs, Princeton University; Professor Peter Schuck, Yale Law School; Professor Roger Smith, Department of Political Science, Yale University; and Professor Stanton Wheeler, Yale Law School.

Our study was made possible by a contractual grant from the National Institute of Education of the United States Department of Education. An important side benefit of this grant was the continuation of our working relationship with NIE Program Officer Ronald Anson, whose interest, ideas, and unflagging efforts to spare us from bureaucratic complications have always been appreciated.

During our final year of work, Meryl Macklin, our legal clerk, became singularly important. She performed extensive legal research with distinction and took on many administrative burdens as well.

Finally, we would like to thank our secretaries and other office staff who, over these years, have helped us to produce this manuscript. In particular, we wish to acknowledge Jeanne Hall, who diligently prepared numerous drafts; Nicholas Humez, our indexer; and Ellin O'Callahan, whose mastery of the art of word processing relieved us from the most arduous tasks of manuscript preparation.

MICHAEL A. REBELL ARTHUR R. BLOCK

*New York, New York*
*March, 1984*

THE RESEARCH reported herein was performed pursuant to contract #NIE-G-80-0032 of the National Institute of Education of the United States Department of Education.

Contractors undertaking such projects under government sponsorship are encouraged to express a professional judgment freely in the conduct of the project. Therefore, points of view or opinions stated here do not necessarily represent official NIE position or policy.

# ABBREVIATIONS

| | |
|---|---|
| AFC | Advocates for Children |
| CETA | Comprehensive Employment and Training Act |
| CSA | Council of Supervisors and Administrators |
| EEO | Equal Employment Opportunity |
| EEOC | Equal Employment Opportunity Commission |
| EES | Equal Educational Services |
| ESAA | Emergency School Aid Act |
| ESAP | Emergency School Assistance Program |
| ESEA | Elementary and Secondary Education Act |
| HEW | Health, Education, and Welfare Department |
| MCAT | Medical College Admissions Test |
| NAACP | National Association for the Advancement of Colored People |
| NIE | National Institute of Education |
| NTE | National Teachers Examination |
| NYABE | New York Association of Black Educators |
| OCR | Office for Civil Rights |
| OE | Office of Education |
| OECD | Organization for Economic Cooperation and Development |
| OEEO | Office of Equal Educational Opportunity |
| OEO | Office of Economic Opportunity |
| OMB | Office of Management and Budget |
| PEA | Public Education Association |
| SEC | Securities and Exchange Commission |
| UFT | United Federation of Teachers |
| UTLA | United Teachers of Los Angeles |

# EQUALITY
## AND
# EDUCATION

# A CASE STUDY
# THROUGH THREE LENSES

In 1974, the Office for Civil Rights of the United States Department of Health, Education and Welfare announced that it would initiate a massive, new, computer-based investigative approach to probe patterns of civil rights compliance in large urban school systems. The prototype for this ambitious project was the "New York City Review," which was to become "the largest civil rights investigation of a public education institution ever undertaken."[1] This new investigative technique was expected to open up entirely new possibilities for civil rights enforcement. To some extent it did. But, at the same time, it also revealed fundamental limitations in OCR's institutional functioning and significant ambiguities in the egalitarian statutes the agency was attempting to enforce.

The legal underpinning of the reviews is contained in Title VI of the 1964 Civil Rights Act. In seemingly simple language, Title VI prohibits discrimination on the basis of race, color, or national origin in any program or activity receiving federal financial assistance. At the time this law was passed, Congress's focus was on the elimination of the *de jure* dual school systems in the South that had been declared unconstitutional ten years earlier by the Supreme Court in *Brown v. Board of Education*.[2] Defining *discrimination* in this context was a relatively straightforward task. By 1972, however, after the most blatant violations of *Brown*'s mandate had been eliminated and the civil rights focus had moved on to more subtle discrimination problems in both the South and the North, identifying discrimination became more difficult. Neither the language of Title VI nor its legislative history provided clear standards for this new phase of civil rights enforcement.

In this unsettled legal field, the OCR based its "Big City

Reviews" (as the multicity investigation came to be called) on a set of controversial premises. The idea of a massive, comprehensive investigation of an entire school system made sense only if one assumed that discriminatory practices were deeply imbedded in the system's normal operating procedures. The designers of this model believed that from the investigations would emerge statistical disparities that would establish an irrefutable pattern of discrimination against minority students, much like the sudden appearance of a recognizable figure in a "connect the dots" puzzle.

Specifically, the New York City Review was designed to consider issues such as unequal allocations of resources to predominantly minority schools; racial segregation in pupil assignments to classrooms and "ability" tracks; disproportionate suspensions of minority students; and denial of requisite bilingual curricular and counseling services to Hispanic and other language-minority children. In response to complaints filed with OCR by local civil rights organizations, the review was expanded in 1976 to include sensitive employment issues, such as teacher hiring practices and racial imbalance in faculty assignments.[3]

By the time the Ford administration left office in January 1977, the New York City Review had produced two detailed "letters of findings" cataloguing nearly two dozen charges of unlawful discrimination. These letters were received angrily by high-level school and teachers' union officials and with cautious optimism by local minority group advocates.

Under the Carter administration, OCR jettisoned much of the massive investigative model approach, but it accepted the validity of most of the major allegations set forth in the New York City letters. It pressed ahead with remedial negotiations. Ultimately, these efforts resulted in two "voluntary" agreements, one on the employment issues and another on the student services items.[4] Attempts to implement the agreements thereafter ignited intense political controversy, a renegotiation of one of the agreements under the Reagan administration in 1982, and extensive litigation, some of which continues up to the time of this writing, a decade after the review was first initiated.

The unprecedented scope and impact of the New York City Review would be reason enough to undertake a detailed case study of these events. But because of its magnitude, its unusually extensive documentary data base, and the manner in which its unfolding spanned four presidential administrations (from the civil rights offensives of the late 1960s to the retrenchments and diminished expectations of the early 1980s), the New York City Review also provides a rare and dramatic opportunity to analyze the dynamic interaction of ideology, politics, and law which constitutes the contemporary civil rights enforcement process.

This rich source of issues and insights offers at least three major thematic approaches for case study analysis. First is an ideological analysis focusing on the ambiguity in Title VI's definition of discrimination and on whether the conflicting egalitarian concepts were reconciled in the implementation process. Second, the implementation process itself, given the unprecedented resources OCR devoted to it, provides an opportune framework for an implementation analysis of a major regulatory initiative. Finally, OCR's formulation of egalitarian policy issues left open by Congress raises serious questions about traditional separation of powers assumptions; it thus calls for a comparative institutional analysis.

Rather than press an exclusive—and somewhat artificial—concentration on any one of these approaches, we decided to take a cue from both Graham Allison's study of the Cuban missile crisis[5] and Paul Peterson's approach to policy-making in the Chicago school district,[6] and to analyze the case study data from all three of the basic analytical perspectives:[7] ideology, implementation, and institutional comparison. Like Allison and Peterson, we believe that a multifaceted approach provides a complementary, comprehensive perspective on the data; reconsidering the same series of events from a variety of angles constitutes a more accurate rendering of the significance of what occurred. As Peterson has put it, each perspective, by itself, "is only a snapshot of a multidimensional event. By interrelating the [three], one achieves a more exact interpretation."[8]

Thus, the events which transpired during the New York City Review, recounted in Part Two of this book, will be analyzed in Part Three through three different lenses. Before commencing the case study and discussing its ideological, legal, and legislative background, however, we will summarize briefly, in the remainder of this Introduction, the ideological, implementation, and comparative institutional perspectives, as they will be utilized throughout the book.

## THE IDEOLOGICAL PERSPECTIVE

In popular usage, *ideology* is a vague term, often connoting fanaticism or narrow self-interest. But, in its classical sense, "[i]deology is the conversion of ideas into social levers."[9] More precisely, a political ideology can be defined as "a system of political, economic and social values and ideas from which objectives are derived. These objectives form the nucleus of a political program."[10]

America has developed such a fundamental ideology[11] on equality issues. This egalitarian ideology reflects a distinctly American world view emerging from the nation's liberal heritage, from its unique historical situation as a pioneering "new world" culture, and from its agonizing experiences of slavery and racial confrontation. Thus, egalitarianism in America has roots that are distinctly different from the Marxist and other socialist influences that shaped egalitarian perspectives in the old world European cultures.

America's fundamental egalitarian ideology can best be described in terms of two distinct but complementary ideological "strands"[12]: equality of opportunity and equality of result. The first perspective emphasizes the right of each individual to pursue his or her goals; it holds that any discriminatory obstacles that impede an individual's path should be eliminated. The second perspective shares this basic commitment to individual pursuit, but it is more ready to see pervasive discriminatory obstacles in political and social structures[13];

building on the American tradition of pragmatism, and on the emphasis in contemporary court orders on immediate, effective measures to remedy social ills, the latter perspective calls for efficacious action to ensure prompt removal of discriminatory barriers. Advocates of opportunity, by way of contrast, see in this approach a danger of overemphasis on compliance mandates and numerical quotas which can undermine basic individual initiatives and opportunities.

Because adherents of equality of opportunity often agree that affirmative measures should be taken to eliminate discriminatory impediments, and advocates of equality of result retain a commitment to individualism and competition (after discriminatory barriers are thoroughly eliminated), the differences between the two perspectives, we believe, really represent differing positions on a continuum of an overall fundamental American egalitarian ideology, rather than distinct, contradictory positions.[14] At the same time, however, these differences should not be minimized. The tension between the opportunity and result strands of egalitarian thought is the explosive factor behind controversial civil rights issues such as busing, preferential admissions to college and graduate schools, and affirmative action in hiring.

The senators and representatives who enacted Title VI of the 1964 Civil Rights Act briefly considered, but failed to resolve, these ideological conflicts. The legislative history indicates that they deliberately avoided defining *discrimination* and left the fundamental conflict between equality of opportunity and equality of result to be resolved by the courts or during the administrative implementation process.[15]

The assumptions behind the Big City Reviews' massive investigatory model largely reflected an equality of result perspective, thus setting the stage for conflict with the New York City Board of Education, whose orientation was toward classic notions of equality of opportunity. Viewed in ideological terms, then, a case study of the New York City Review is the story of how issue was joined between organizations reflecting these divergent perspectives and of the way ideological compromise was achieved. As such, the study has important im-

plications for the broad range of opportunity/result controversies which are at the cutting edge of contemporary civil
rights controversies.

## THE IMPLEMENTATION PERSPECTIVE

The increased social reform activism of the federal government
in the 1960s and 1970s was paralleled by a new approach to
the study of public policy by social scientists. A body of literature known as implementation analysis emerged from the
more traditional fields of public administration and policy
analysis.

"Impact studies" were the forerunners to implementation
analysis. These investigations sought to determine whether
there had been effective compliance with particular laws or
policy directives. Typical subjects were problems of compliance with major Supreme Court decisions, such as the ban on
school prayers,[16] and the extent of improvement in student
performance in programs funded under Title I of the Education and Secondary Education Act of 1965.[17]

Many of these studies found that compliance with major
court rulings and statutes was incomplete, and that expensive
social programs were not delivering the anticipated results.
These specific findings, together with a growing popular perception that many of the ambitious social programs of the
Great Society era had not succeeded, led to heightened awareness among social scientists of the distinction between the
formulation of a policy and its actual achievement. By the
mid-1970s, this gap—aptly termed the "missing link"[18]—had
become the focus of a number of scholarly undertakings which
came to be known as implementation analysis.

Many of the implementation case studies, particularly the
earlier ones, "were factually dense accounts, usually lacking
explicit theory or conceptual frameworks."[19] In reaction,
some scholars began to formulate comprehensive theories,
drawing upon a wide variety of social science disciplines,[20]
often complete with complex schemes of variables.[21] These
theoretical schemes in turn have drawn criticism from other

scholars, who note that the "fragmentary and disjunctive nature of the real world . . . [make] a general theory of the implementation process . . . unattainable and, indeed, unrealistic."[22] These critics believe that policymaking should be viewed as an organic and evolutionary process.[23]

The implementation literature provides an important new analytical approach. Its basic methodology, though still in a formative stage, serves to free one from the assumption that an adequately funded government program will fully achieve its stated goals, and it forces one to be sensitive to particular factors—conceptual, organizational, political, environmental, legal—that influence implementation and determine its eventual outcome.

Implementation analysis also complements the ideological perspective. In analyzing events from an ideological perspective, there is a tendency to assume that they can be fully explained by the purposeful actions of unitary actors who are pursuing clearly articulated goals.[24] The implementation perspective, however, emphasizes the "non-rational" factors, such as organizational routines and bureaucratic politics, that will inevitably deflect, modify, or defeat even well-conceived plans and objectives.[25]

Applying this perspective to the New York City Review, we determined that the organic, evolutionary process at work here could best be described in terms of three variables that have been identified in the implementation literature as being most significant for this type of study: goal ambiguity, organizational process, and politics.[26] Goal ambiguity was particularly significant in this situation because of Congress's failure to define the operative standard—discrimination—that was the *raison d'être* of the statute.[27]

The second significant variable, organizational process, as applied here, encompasses both the normal routines of the federal and local bureaucracies and the additional problems raised by the innovative data collection and systems management techniques created for the Big City Reviews.[28] The third significant variable is politics—national politics (such as President Richard Nixon's "Southern Strategy"); local politics (such as historical battles among the New York City Board of Education, the Board of Examiners, the teachers' union, and minority group advocates on teacher hiring and licensing issues); and everyday bureaucratic personality clashes and turf battles.[29]

In short, analyzing the events of the New York City Review in terms of these three major implementation variables not only will provide important insights into implementation problems, but also will place our conclusions in a conceptual framework that will facilitate comparisons with existing or future implementation studies.

## THE COMPARATIVE INSTITUTIONAL PERSPECTIVE

The starting point for any consideration of comparative institutional roles within the American system of government is, of course, the traditional separation of powers model. This model posits a tripartite division of governmental functions among the legislative, executive, and judicial branches. The legislature, as the people's direct representative body, generally is seen in normative democratic theory as the forum for making basic value choices and policy decisions. The executive's role is primarily to "execute the laws" which incorporate these legislative policy decisions. The role of the judiciary, the least political branch, is to apply the legislative policy formulations and intent (and the Constitution) to particular cases and controversies.[30]

Increasingly, it has been recognized that contemporary exercises of governmental authority do not fit neatly into these categories. This is particularly true in the case of administrative agencies. The era of modern administrative agencies began less than one hundred years ago, with Congress's creation of the Interstate Commerce Commission in 1887. Since then, agencies have proliferated in number, variety, and function, and there has been a corresponding increase in the conceptual problems of reconciling their actual activities with democratic theory.[31] In fact, "the development of the administrative agency in response to modern legislative and administrative need has placed severe strain on the separation of powers principle in its pristine form."[32] The actions of administrative agencies, in wielding enormous powers without being accountable to the electorate, raise "legitimacy" issues which are so serious that they have been said to constitute a continuing unresolved "crisis" for the functioning of American Government.[33]

Much of this "legitimacy" problem stems from Congress's tendency to delegate substantial policymaking authority to administrative agencies without providing clear standards as to how such authority should be exercised.[34] Because Congress lacks both the time and the expertise to decide the plethora of policy choices involved in the complex social and economic regulatory process that seems inherent to modern government, substantial delegation of authority to administrative agencies is probably unavoidable. This does not mean, however, that all issues are equally suitable for delegation, from either a legal, practical, or political point of view, or that improvements cannot be made both in the capacity of agencies to exercise such functions and in Congress's ability to obtain ultimate accountability.[35]

Congress's failure to define discrimination in Title VI is a prime instance of such a delegation of fundamental policymaking responsibility. Therefore, it provides an opportunity for a detailed analysis of precisely how one particular type of administrative agency "makes" policy at the grass-roots implementation level and whether such policymaking is—or could be—performed effectively and in a manner consistent with democratic theory.[36]

The problems raised by the delegation of policymaking authority to administrative agencies is part of a broader challenge to the traditional separation of powers model. This challenge is posed by the new, more activist roles being taken on by all three branches of government in the post–New Deal era. We previously studied analogous separation of powers problems in our analysis of the court's new role in contemporary institutional reform litigation, in which judges are called upon to articulate basic remedial social policies and to formulate and implement compliance standards.[37] Accordingly, we believe that the problem of administrative agency policymaking and policy implementation can best be understood from a comparative institutional perspective that compares the actual functioning of administrative agencies with analogous activities of courts and legislatures. For this reason, we will use the findings on judicial and legislative activities discussed in our previous book as a point of comparison for analyzing OCR's institutional functioning in the present work.

In summary, then, we will view OCR's attempt to enforce federal anti-discrimination law in the New York City school system through three different lenses: the ideological perspective, the implementation perspective, and the comparative institutional perspective. Specifically, the study is organized as follows. Part One will set the stage for the case study narrative and the analyses by reviewing American egalitarian ideology (chapter 1) and by describing the ambiguity in egalitarian policy standards as formulated by the courts (chapter 2) and the Congress (chapter 3). Part Two will then recount the story of the Big City Review in New York City (with comparative insights obtained from similar reviews undertaken in Chicago, Los Angeles, and Philadelphia)[38] (chapters 4-6). In Part Three, we will analyze these events in terms of the ideological perspective (chapter 7), the implementation perspective (chapter 8), and the comparative institutional perspective (chapter 9). Concluding comments will be presented in the final chapter.

# PART ONE

## The Ideological, Legal, and Legislative Background

# CHAPTER ONE
# AMERICAN EGALITARIAN IDEOLOGY

## EQUALITY AND THE AMERICAN EXPERIENCE

More than two hundred years ago, the American colonies announced their Declaration of Independence to England and the world by declaring as a self-evident truth "that all men are created equal." In essence, "[t]he equal legal and moral status of free individuals was America's reason for independent existence."[1] The American Republic established the concept of equality as a revolutionary, democratic principle in the eighteenth century, and egalitarianism has remained a dominant concern of American politics ever since.[2]

America's unique role as the midwife of egalitarianism in modern history can be traced primarily to three factors. First was the image and the reality of its geographical location in a "new world." The allure of an unsettled continent of virgin territory, separated by thousands of miles of ocean from the turmoil, the discontent, and the inequities of the European continent made America seem the veritable "promised land" of biblical imagery.[3]

The second important aspect of America's early experience that contributed to the development of egalitarianism lay in its liberal origins. The original American colonists brought with them from Europe a strong commitment to Lockean liberalism, which emphasized the dignity of each individual, his equal role in the establishment of the political state, and the corresponding obligations of that state to promote each individual's self-development. This liberal ideal was able to take root and thrive in the virgin American soil, free from the ideological competition of the feudal heritage of England and other European countries.[4]

The third egalitarian dimension of the original American experience was its strong rejection of the status orderings of European society.[5] Although economic differentials have always marked the American scene, the absence of a hereditary elite class and entrenched privilege has led commentators from early times to the present to emphasize the unparalleled "equality of esteem"[6] that marks social relationships in the United States.

In short, then, America's new world setting, its adherence to the liberal ideal, and its revolutionary break with aristocratic trappings combined to create an egalitarian credo based on the "ideals of the essential dignity of the individual human being, of the fundamental equality of all men, and of certain inalienable rights to freedom, justice and a fair opportunity [which] represent to the American people the essential meaning of the nation's early struggle for independence."[7] This egalitarian credo marked a new era in world history. It symbolized for the nation's citizens, and for the established political orders throughout the world, a radical break with past assumptions concerning the limits of the human condition and the potential of human nature.

Egalitarianism, by its very nature, is a revolutionary doctrine. "Once loosed the idea of Equality is not easily cabined."[8] As Tocqueville put it (not without some foreboding): "It is impossible to believe that equality will not eventually find its way into the political world, as it does everywhere else. To conceive of men remaining forever unequal on a single point, yet equal on all others, is impossible. They must come in the end to be equal upon all.[9]

Despite these predictions however, American society clearly has not achieved the full flowering of equality that Tocqueville and other early commentators had anticipated. To be sure, in certain areas, such as extension of the franchise, egalitarian practices which the founding fathers would have considered radical have been implemented.[10] But these have not been accompanied by equal sharing of political power or by equal distribution of wealth.

The dynamic growth of the American economy has substantially reduced the prevalence of the kind of grinding poverty which was experienced by the masses in traditional European society, and which continues to be the plight of peasant populations throughout much of the world today.[11] However, in terms of the relative distribution of wealth, proportionate holdings of the top and bottom strata of society have remained remarkably constant throughout America's history.[12] And, significantly, despite the promise of America's original egalitarian revolution, the contemporary patterns of economic distribution in the paradigmatic new world society are scarcely different from patterns of distribution in the old world European societies: income differentials in the United States today are roughly similar to those of the European democracies.[13] Such patterns of relative economic inequality, of course, tend to perpetuate political inequalities.[14]

The main reason for America's failure to develop fully and consistently its initial egalitarian potential is apparent: America's liberal vision also incorporated the capitalistic ethic and related goals of economic development—and equality and economic efficiency are not easily reconcilable.[15] Paradoxically, America became the prime locus for the flowering of the capitalistic ethic in the modern world for many of the same reasons that it developed the new egalitarian credo. Its *tabula rasa* environment allowed unfettered development of a Lockean liberal ideal which emphasized the virtues of "equal" opportunity through untrammeled individual self-development. When combined with Calvinist notions of the righteousness of material accumulations[16] in an environment where traditional social and economic barriers to individual enterprise held little sway, Lockean individualism accelerated the development of the capitalistic ethic.[17]

Thus, even at the time of Tocqueville's visit to America, when the expansion of Jacksonian democracy was in its heyday, countertrends of wealth and position stemming from economic enterprise already were beginning to take hold.[18] In the decades that followed, the accession of the industrial revolution further fueled the original capitalistic ethic and caused the pursuit of economic development to dominate the American scene.[19]

The dominance of economic development perspectives, combined with the monopolistic hold of liberal ideology in America, explains why a socialist reaction, which developed after the outset of the industrial revolution in Europe, never seriously took hold in the United States. Ironically, then, America, which had first brought the ideals of equality to world consciousness, divorced itself from the sustained further development of those ideals which occurred in Europe through the socialist movement. The substantial egalitarian pressures of European labor organizations and social democratic parties have had no real ideological counterpart in the United States.[20]

Given these developments, it might well be asked why the egalitarian credo did not become even more submerged on the American scene. Despite a favorable climate initially, the weight of two hundred years of intense capitalistic economic development might have been expected to stifle egalitarianism and result in marked hierarchical social ordering, at least as compared with the European democratic societies.[21] (Centralized trends inherent in advanced industrial economies, of course, create the preconditions for expanded governmental activities and welfare state expectations,[22] but South African history has shown that industrialization and centralization also can lead to an expansion of privilege and hierarchy.[23])

Since America lacked the kinds of working-class movements organized around Marxist and socialist ideologies that had impelled egalitarian developments in Europe, another force must have accounted for the continuing egalitarian thrust in American society. The factor that explains that thrust would appear to be the intense racial dynamic of American history. The confrontation between America's pristine, new world egalitarian ideals and the realities of probably the most oppressive slave society known in post-Renaissance times created a unique "American dilemma,"[24] one which ignited a strong egalitarian spark that, since the mid-nineteenth century, has been a driving force in American history.[25] Indeed, the unfolding of the racial confrontations of the Civil War and Re-

AMERICAN EGALITARIAN IDEOLOGY

construction era led to a revitalization of the nation's egalitarian ideals.[26]

American egalitarianism, while driven by its contradictory liberalism/racial oppression dynamic, also has been shaped by an optimistic economic assumption that unbounded wealth is available in this new world society for all those willing to work to obtain it. As a result, at the core of American egalitarianism is a concept of equality of opportunity which derives from economic development imperatives, but which simultaneously acknowledges a commitment to remove barriers to individual opportunity erected during slavery, the Reconstruction era, and its aftermath. In comparison with egalitarianism in Europe, therefore, American egalitarianism reflects a philosophy of pragmatism more than a theory of social transformation. Its premise is that society needs to be opened up, not remade; its focus is on historically stigmatized racial and ethnic groups, not on wealth-related class divisions; and its prime concern is with practical political remedies, rather than with ideological confrontations.[27]

In sum, the concept of "equality" in the American context is a complex phenomenon that has emerged from two centuries of contradictory, yet complementary, idealistic and racist elements. Accordingly, America's fundamental egalitarian "ideology" encompasses a variety of egalitarian perspectives and meanings,[28] which come into focus only in the political interchanges attendant upon implementation of specific social reforms. Therefore, to understand the dynamics of egalitarianism in America, it is necessary to define more precisely the categories of "equality of opportunity" and "equality of result," the two major analytical poles along a continuum of complex elements that constitute the fundamental American egalitarian ideology.[29]

## EQUALITY OF OPPORTUNITY
## AND EQUALITY OF RESULT

As discussed above, the American liberal tradition was heavily influenced by the writings of John Locke. In contrast to conservative theorists, Locke assumed that all men are endowed with a substantial attribute of reason; they are therefore equally capable of comprehending the laws of nature (which are based on reason) and of agreeing to establish political institutions that will inure to the benefit of all. Reason further shows us, according to Locke, that "God has given us all things richly,"[30] and that each individual in the "state of nature" is assumed to have staked out a fair share of available property. Government institutions, therefore, are instituted as a "convenience" to regulate and promote the natural rights to life, liberty, and property, which were the original legacies of all individuals in the state of nature.

Starting from these premises of fundamental natural equality and open access to nature's bounties, government for Locke can be said to have existed for the purpose of promoting "equality of opportunity" so that each person could continue to develop fully his individual talents and "property." The open fertile environment of the American continent, which had been analogized by Locke himself to his ideal original state of nature,[31] provided a logical locus for the flowering of such equal opportunity.

It is, however, precisely in the pursuit of these individual opportunities that the inherent conflict between the two basic strands of liberal thought, equality and liberty, comes to the fore. In order to enjoy an untrammeled path to the opportunities they sought, those individuals who emerged more successful in the social competition tended to emphasize the inviolability of particular liberties and property rights. They sought ways to assure the primacy of the pursuit of life, liberty, and property and to uphold these values in the face of both envy and the egalitarian pressures of the masses of their less successful fellow citizens. In this connection, John Stuart Mill expressed grave apprehensions about the potential "tyranny of the majority," and he articulated the need to establish certain basic rights, such as freedom of speech, as a bulwark for full development of the creative potential of those capable of outstanding achievement.[32]

In this way, equality of opportunity came to represent a

balancing of the ideals of equality and liberty. Each individual was to be encouraged to develop fully his natural abilities, and both the individual and society as a whole were expected to benefit from the resulting release of talent and energy.[33] Limited governmental interventions (such as antitrust, minimum wage, and occupational health and safety laws) would ensure that over-zealous pursuit of personal gain by one individual or entity did not unduly interfere with the "equal" potential of other individuals to similarly pursue their opportunities. At the same time, certain definitive rights were established to provide bulwarks for the "liberty" of self-fulfillment, so that majoritarian "factions" could not stifle legitimate individual enterprise and expression. The resulting liberal ideal was summarized in 1878 by Ralph Waldo Emerson. "Opportunity of civil rights, of education, of personal power, and not less of wealth; doors wide open . . . invitation to every nation, to every race and skin, . . . hospitality of fair field and equal laws to all. Let them compete, and success to the strongest, the wisest, and the best."[34]

But the equality of opportunity ideal which Emerson toasted has always been tarred by deep-seated disquiet about the fairness of the competitive setting.[35] This problem is often illustrated by analogizing equality of opportunity to a footrace, in which the field is open and those who fairly outpace the others are entitled to their prize. Contemporary advocates of equality of opportunity recognize a need to remove discriminatory hurdles that in the past blocked the paths of some of the runners. Critics of equality of opportunity, however, charge that removal of all the long-entrenched barriers, especially those created by the long history of slavery and state-mandated segregation, is an extremely difficult—if not insuperable—task.[36]

In addition to the problems of eliminating the barriers on the field, an additional and conceptually even more difficult issue is that at the very starting block some of the competitors are disadvantaged, since they come weighted down with unfair handicaps and burdens stemming from prior economic or social position. As President Lyndon Johnson forcefully put it:

You do not take a person who, for years, has been hob-
bled by chains and liberate him, bring him to the starting
line of a race, and then say you are free to compete with
all the others, and still just believe that you have been
completely fair. Thus it is not enough just to open the
gates of opportunity. All our citizens must have the ability
to walk through those gates. . . . We seek not just legal
equity but human ability, not just equality as a right and
a theory but equality as a fact and equality as a result.[37]

To be fully fair, however, society would need to compensate
for these initial disadvantages before the life race had begun.[38]
Traditionally, the provision of equal educational opportunity
has been advanced as the optimal form of such compensation.
Recent research, however, has indicated that the schools, at
least as they have operated traditionally, at the traditional
levels of resource commitment, have not been able to accomplish this enormous task.[39]

Disillusionment with the society's historical failure to provide meaningful opportunities for the underprivileged has led
some commentators to conclude that society must go beyond
providing equal educational opportunities, that it must take
steps to overcome the most basic differentials in family wealth
and other environmental limitations.[40] To be fully consistent
on this point, it would probably be necessary to interfere
massively in private lives by radically restructuring job allocation procedures,[41] constantly redistributing wealth and prohibiting inheritance rights, raising children apart from their
parents, or even tampering with initial gene pools.[42]

In short, full implementation of the ideal of equality of
opportunity seems to imply a social obligation to remove or
compensate for "accidental" handicaps which disproportionately burden certain of the competitors before life's competition has begun. But there is no logical stopping point once
society begins to take seriously the prospect of eliminating
such initial disabilities. Obviously, reasonable lines must be
drawn somewhere. And it is precisely about where to draw
the appropriate lines that fundamental differences emerge be-

tween adherents of equality of opportunity and adherents of equality of result in the American context.[43]

Advocates of equality of result are more skeptical about the degree of meaningful opportunity actually being given to the disadvantaged under current social conditions; they believe that substantial structural reforms are necessary to provide an equitable "starting block." Although tending to be optimistic about the possibilities of human nature, political theorists whose writings support the equality of result perspective do not ignore the obvious differences in natural talents and attributes among individuals.[44] (On the other hand, they do tend to believe that removal of social injustice will permit each individual to develop a much greater range of personal abilities.[45]) But despite their acceptance of the reality that all people will never be equal in their abilities and accomplishments, these thinkers would hold that each individual nevertheless is entitled to substantially equal treatment. " 'All men are created equal' is not a declarative sentence; it is an imperative. It is not a statement but an exhortation. It is not an affirmation or description. It is a command. . . . It says in substance, within certain limits and for certain purposes, that we should treat all men as if they were the same, although we know full well that they are not."[46]

The most influential statement of the result-oriented radical egalitarian perspective in contemporary American thought is John Rawls's much heralded book, *A Theory of Justice*. Rawls builds his theory from liberal social contract principles, rather than from Marxist precepts. He posits an "original position" which might be said to constitute an ideal equal opportunity perspective. In this hypothetical setting, there is a "veil of ignorance" in which "no one knows his place in society, his class position or social status, nor does anyone know his fortune in the distribution of natural assets and abilities, his intelligence, strength and the like."[47] From this perspective, it becomes clear for Rawls that rational individuals, being ignorant of what life may actually have in store for them, will establish a society that attempts to minimize all inequities, whatever their origin.

Specifically, Rawls argues that rational individuals would adopt two basic principles. The first would require full equality in the assignment of basic civil and political rights; the second would permit particular social and economic inequalities only if they would result in increased benefits for all, and particularly for the least advantaged members of society. This second principle means that, "in order to treat all persons equally, to provide genuine equality of opportunity, society must give more attention to those with fewer native assets and to those born into the less favorable social positions. The ideal is to redress the bias of contingency in the direction of equality."[48]

In essence, the equality of result approach, exemplified by Rawls, seeks to rectify the major difficulty of the equality of opportunity perspective by maximizing the ability of each individual to compete on a fair basis.[49] The theory assumes (and asserts as a priority in its first principle of justice) classical liberal values, permitting individual enterprise and wealth and power differentials, but within egalitarian bounds established to promote the general welfare.[50] In short, the "result" sought by Rawls, like most other result-oriented American political theorists, is a realistic fair opportunity—that is, "more equality,"[51] rather than thoroughgoing income redistribution or complete equality of condition. (For this reason, much of the contemporary criticism of the equality of result perspective, criticism which attacks "idealistic" expectations that hierarchical orderings can be eliminated from human society, is misaimed at equality of condition straw men.[52])

It is clear, however, that in attempting to rectify the limitations of the equality of opportunity approach, the equality of result perspective raises additional conceptual and practical difficulties of its own. The first of these stems from the inherent tension between "equality" and "liberty." Attempts to implement egalitarian results, especially through large-scale structural reforms, inevitably impede the liberty of many individuals who are adversely affected by the reforms. (The impact of the affirmative action admissions system on "innocent" white applicants is a frequently cited example.) Some critics have gone so far as to assert that assurance of a thoroughgoing equality of result may require imposition of governmental authority to a degree that is incompatible with retention of traditional American liberty values.[53]

Rawls was not unaware of this problem. Accordingly, he emphasized that his two principles of justice were to be perceived in lexical order, "and therefore the claims of liberty are to be satisfied first."[54] But if Rawls's recommendations for substantial redistributions of wealth, power, and prestige under his second principle are to be taken seriously, it is likely that substantial, continuing regulatory compulsion will be needed to effect compliance with that goal.[55]

The second major problem inherent in the equality of result approach is its failure to provide a consistent theory of economic incentive. The strength of the classical liberal doctrine of equality was, of course, its ability to do just that. In viewing life as a competitive struggle, classical liberalism emphasized motivation, individual incentive, and the consequent potential for enormously expanding the wealth of the society as a whole. Result-oriented egalitarians, by way of contrast, although not advocating socialist distributions, have been more concerned with how to slice the pie than with how to make it larger.[56]

In sum, then, equality of opportunity is most consistent with the tenets of individualism and liberty, and it is believed to promote a dynamic outpouring of energy, enterprise, and accomplishment. At the same time, however, this approach can create serious new inequalities, and it offers no real answer to the gnawing problems of unfair initial starting points and persistent discriminatory hurdles. Equality of result purports to provide solutions for these deficiencies, but, in doing so, it raises other substantial concerns in terms of preserving personal liberties and sustaining economic progress.

The contradictions inherent in American egalitarian thought are serious and, perhaps, ultimately irreconcilable with the liberal tradition. Under these circumstances, theory can provide insights for political action and can sensitize the actors to the problems and possibilities of certain courses of action. But it cannot provide definitive answers to how governmental intervention should be directed to ameliorate fundamental inequities. Perhaps this explains why the courts, whose institutional orientation is to reconcile competing values and interests in the process of applying abstract principles to immediate factual problems, have played a dominant role in the development of American egalitarianism over the past thirty years.[57] Accordingly, we will turn in the next chapter from the realm of egalitarian theory to the realm of egalitarian practice, and we will consider how these egalitarian controversies have been handled by the courts.

CHAPTER TWO

# EQUALITY AND THE COURTS

It has been generally acknowledged that the modern civil rights era began with the Supreme Court's landmark school desegregation decision in *Brown* v. *Board of Education*.[1] Since *Brown*, the courts have, of course, delved deeply into major egalitarian issues on the cutting edge of social controversy. The culmination of this era of intense judicial concentration on egalitarian issues could be said to be marked by the decision in *Regents of the University of California* v. *Bakke*,[2] the medical school preferential admissions case in which fifty-eight *amicus* briefs, the most ever submitted in any Supreme Court case, presented virtually every conceivable legal—and philosophical[3]—argument about equality.

*Brown* and *Bakke*, therefore, are focal points for examining the interplay of the themes of equality of opportunity and equality of result in contemporary equal protection cases. As we shall see, the courts' failure to establish a clear standard or consistent principles[4] on these issues shaped OCR's implementation of egalitarian precepts in the New York City case study.

In linking the preceding theoretical analysis to the court cases and implementation issues in the case study to follow, we will use *equality of opportunity* and *equality of result* as terms with the following meanings:

*Equality of Opportunity*: An emphasis (within the total American egalitarian ideology) upon individual effort and accomplishment which contemplates removal of particular discriminatory barriers so that individuals can advance in accordance with their actual present abilities.

*Equality of Result*: An emphasis (within the total American egalitarian ideology) upon overcoming societally caused economic or social disadvantages by eliminating

the effects of past discrimination through structural reforms, including, at times, the provision of immediate
access for the formerly disadvantaged to certain fundamental social, educational, or economic benefits.*

## SCHOOL DESEGREGATION

The Supreme Court's decision in *Brown* was, primarily, a
strong affirmation of the equality of opportunity credo. Technically, it was a reversal and renunciation of the "formal
equality" holding of the 1896 decision in *Plessy* v. *Ferguson,*[5]
in which the Court had decreed that so long as blacks were
given access to "equal" school resources, segregated facilities
would satisfy constitutional precepts. Emphasizing that "today, education is perhaps the most important function of state
and local governments,"[6] the Court in *Brown* probed beyond
the form of "separate but equal" physical facilities and looked
to the substance of educational opportunities being made
available to black students. Building on a series of prior decisions which had shown that in specific instances "equalizing" physical facilities did not provide true equal educational
opportunity,[7] the Court held that separate education necessarily generates "a feeling of inferiority" in the hearts and
minds of black students and concluded with the ringing state-

* The discussion in the text has emphasized the fundamental American
egalitarian ideology and the sometimes complementary, sometimes conflicting, equality of opportunity and equality of result strands of which it is
composed. It has argued that both the conservative notion of formal equality
and the socialist notion of equality of condition are foreign to the American
context. Strictly speaking, American egalitarianism might be viewed as a
continuum ranging from a conservative "formal access" pole on the right,
through liberal opportunity/result concepts in the middle, to an equality of
condition pole on the left. However, since the extreme formal equality and
equality of condition positions do not command substantial political follow-
ings, and since they influence the political debate occasionally only by exerting
some centripetal rhetorical force on the basic equality of opportunity or
equality of result positions, it is both simpler and more accurate to discuss
American egalitarianism in terms of the basic equality of opportunity/equality
of result dichotomy.

ment that "separate educational facilities are inherently unequal."[8]

In short, the Court's main concern in *Brown* was to guarantee full, fair opportunity[9] which would allow black students to develop their natural talents and abilities. But imbedded beneath the surface of this strong articulation of the classical liberal credo were the seeds of a result-oriented approach to educational equality. Indeed, the *Brown* decision exemplified the close interplay between the two concepts. For in order to ensure full, effective "opportunity" for black students, the Court saw that it could not merely analyze the specific resources which had been, or could have been, provided in separate black schools. Instead, it concluded that at a certain point it becomes counterproductive to focus on the fairness of resource inputs or on the precise causes of differential achievement, and it becomes necessary to look for solutions by insisting on actual results. Thus, integral to the Court's approach in *Brown* was a result-oriented view that the Court must look not at questions of equalizing resources, but "instead to the *effect* of segregation itself on public education."[10]

The significant equality of result implications of *Brown* slowly began to emerge as its desegregation mandate began to be implemented. In the early years, some of the lower courts adopted a narrow equality of opportunity perspective. They asserted that all the Supreme Court had required was for the state to open its schools to children of all races, and "if the schools which [the state] maintains are open to children of all races, no violation of the Constitution is involved even though the children of different races voluntarily attend different schools, as they attend different churches."[11] Because few black students were motivated to face the hostility and community pressures attendant upon enrollment in white schools, only token integration occurred under this standard during the first decade following *Brown*.[12]

However, as it became increasingly clear that a standard of voluntary access to educational opportunity was not achieving meaningful desegregation in most southern school systems, the Supreme Court finally moved in a result-oriented direction to assure that the intent of *Brown* would be effected. Thus, in *Green* v. *County School Board*,[13] when statistics showed that despite three years of operation under a "freedom of choice" plan not one white child had gone to a black school and 85 percent of the black children still attended the black school, the Court held that freedom of choice was "unacceptable." Rather than analyzing the specific impediments to fair opportunity which existed under the freedom of choice plan (such as poverty, psychological reservations, attitudinal pressures, and social inertia), the Court's unanimous opinion emphasized results and required the school board to develop "a plan that promises realistically to work and promises realistically to work *now*."[14]

This move toward affirmative action to achieve results was emphasized again in the Court's next major desegregation pronouncement, *Swann* v. *Charlotte-Mecklenberg Board of Education*.[15] There, the Court upheld the district court's imposition of numerical guidelines (in that case 71 percent white, 29 percent black) for judging the effectiveness of integration in each school in the district. Of equal precedential significance was the Court's affirmance of the use of "bus transportation as one tool of school desegregation,"[16] despite strong arguments that busing and redistricting away from the neighborhood school interfered with the "freedom of choice" and opportunities of white students.

The Supreme Court's strong emphasis in *Green-Swann* on "results that work now" seemed at the time to presage elimination of the traditional *de jure-de facto* distinction in segregation cases. Commentators had long noted[17] that the logic of *Brown*'s holding that separate schools were inherently unequal would call for remedying all segregated schooling patterns, whether these had originated because of "purposeful" state laws and actions (*de jure* segregation) or because of "natural" housing trends and other such developments which could not be attributed directly to any purposeful state laws or actions (*de facto* segregation).

Some cases considering segregation patterns in the North in the first years following *Brown* held that proof of *de facto*

segregation was sufficient to establish a constitutional violation.[18] The Supreme Court's holding in its first major desegregation case outside the deep South, *Keyes v. School District
No. 1*,[19] did not accept such a standard, but it did hold that
school systems that had not operated under statutory segregation mandates nevertheless would be held accountable for
segregated schooling patterns if they had taken actions in the
past (such as zoning and school site selection) which contributed to segregation. The Court further held that a finding of
*de jure* segregative acts in a substantial portion of the Denver
school system would justify mandating effective remedies to
eliminate segregation throughout the entire system, in the absence of countervailing proof by the school board of nonseg-
regative intent system-wide.

A year later, in *Milliken v. Bradley*,[20] the Supreme Court
dramatically shifted direction away from its previous result-
oriented approach. There, the Court refused to uphold the
concept of inter-district remedies, precluding the district court
judge from including fifty-three suburban school districts in
an ambitious cross-busing scheme to desegregate the Detroit
school system. Although the facts strongly indicated that effective desegregation of the predominantly black urban school
system would require integration with the suburbs,[21] Chief
Justice Burger's opinion for a close five-four majority held
that achievement of such a result would not warrant offsetting
other important values, such as local control of education and
avoidance of overbearing judicial involvement in school operations. Reflecting a strong equality of opportunity perspective, the decision emphasized the lack of any findings of intentional segregation by the suburban school districts, rather
than the need to include these districts in a busing plan if any
meaningful desegregation were to be accomplished.

Consistent with the movement away from a result orientation in *Milliken* has been the Supreme Court's emphasis, in
a related series of constitutional decisions, upon the necessity
in constitutional equal protection cases of a finding of discriminatory *intent* by state officials, rather than finding of

mere discriminatory *impact* on affected minority populations.[22]

Under an "impact" standard, a plaintiff need only show that a disproportionate number of minority-group members are being denied the benefit at issue (for example, jobs, schooling, or voting) and that "result" is enough to shift to the defendants a heavy burden of justification which is difficult to establish. Under the "intent" standard, however, it is not the result of the disputed policy which is dispositive, but, rather, the frame of mind of those who adopted or implemented the policy and whether they actually sought to discriminate or restrict opportunities for minorities. The need to prove such a subjective state of mind (even if objective indicia of subjective views are permitted) is, obviously, a more difficult task for the plaintiff.

However, although current constitutional doctrine requires a finding of discriminatory intent, many Supreme Court decisions continue to reflect a result orientation by interpreting the language in congressional statutes or administrative regulations (as contrasted to constitutional precepts) to hold defendants to an impact standard.[23] Moreover, even in its constitutional rulings, the Court, depending on particular circumstances, at times seems to emphasize equality of opportunity by calling for strong evidence of discriminatory intent, while at other times it emphasizes equality of result by accepting minimal indicia of intent. Notable in this regard are two major desegregation cases decided in 1979, *Dayton Board of Education* v. *Brinkman*[24] and *Columbus Board of Education* v. *Penick*,[25] in which the Court held that northern cities which were operating school systems that in fact segregated students along racial lines at the time of the *Brown* decision had a continuing affirmative duty to take steps to eliminate the vestiges of this dual system, or at least to show that current racial practices do not reflect the impact of the pre-1954 policies. Since most northern cities, like Dayton and Columbus, took few affirmative steps after 1954 to affirmatively change basic patterns, the effect of these holdings was to revive the focus on results, despite the ostensible distinction between intent and impact.[26] As Justice White wrote in his majority opinion, "[T]he measure of post-*Brown* conduct . . . is effectiveness, not . . . purpose."[27]

In short, then, in the decades since *Brown*, the law concerning school desegregation may be said to have oscillated from a strong equality of opportunity direction to a strong equality of result direction, and then returned somewhat (although not completely) toward the opportunity pole.[28] Overall, however, the Court's emphasis in the classic southern desegregation cases on plans which "[promise] realistically to work *now*" gave important legitimacy to advocates of equality of result, a legitimacy which continued to add substance to the result perspective even after the Court had moderated its own stance.[29]

## Affirmative Action in Admissions

The fundamental conflict in egalitarian values which was reflected in the evolution of school desegregation law over the twenty-five-year period following the Supreme Court's decision in *Brown* was put into more immediate and sharper focus in the late 1970s in the intense controversy that developed over affirmative action policies in university admissions.[30] In response to egalitarian pressures, many universities had established admissions procedures which either set aside a specific number of places in entering classes for members of minority groups or accepted minority applicants having grades and standardized test scores lower than those of accepted white applicants.[31]

The resulting disputes between critics and defenders of these practices, reflecting the equality of opportunity and equality of result perspectives, were phrased in terms of both "justice" issues (contrasting notions of individual merit[32] with arguments in favor of compensation for past and present discrimination[33]) and "social utility" issues (involving considerations of how the development of talent[34] and overall societal efficiency might best be promoted[35]).

The focal point of this controversy was *Regents of the Uni-*

*versity of California* v. *Bakke*,[36] in which the admissions system adopted at the University of California's medical school at the Davis campus was being challenged. Under the Davis plan, applicants from a number of specified minority groups who claimed to come from educationally or economically disadvantaged backgrounds were permitted to have their applications reviewed by a special admissions committee. This committee would recommend candidates for sixteen of the one hundred places available in the entering class. The minority candidates recommended by the committee generally had substantially lower undergraduate grade point averages and test scores than those admitted under the regular admissions process. Alan Bakke, a white applicant who was denied admission, challenged the legality of this process, which he claimed precluded him from fairly competing for 16 percent of the available places in the entering class.[37]

The Supreme Court's treatment of this issue culminated in a lengthy, complex decision containing six separate concurring and dissenting opinions. Basically, four members of the Court, joining in an opinion by Justice Brennan, stated that the preferential admissions system should be held to meet constitutional requirements, while four other members, joining in an opinion by Justice Stevens, said that Title VI of the 1964 Civil Rights Act precluded any type of race-conscious admissions system, and, since that disposed of the immediate issue in the case, they did not have to address the constitutional issues. The ninth member of the court, Justice Powell, who thus became the swing vote, held that the specific "quota" approach used at Davis was unconstitutional.

At the core of the differing opinions and arguments set forth by the justices in *Bakke*[38] was the basic controversy between the perspectives of equality of opportunity and equality of result. The four justices in the Brennan group, on balance, reflected an equality of result perspective. They emphasized the fact that although blacks represent approximately 11.1 percent of the overall population, their proportion in the medical profession was approximately 2.2 percent; under normal procedures, few blacks would be admitted to medical school, causing this disparity to continue indefinitely.[39] While recognizing the importance of the values of individual desert and individual opportunity in the American political and legal tradition,[40] the Brennan group gave great weight to the need to root out historical patterns of societal discrimination. "Properly construed, therefore, our prior cases unequivocally show that a state government may adopt race-conscious programs if the purpose of such programs is to remove the disparate racial impact its actions might otherwise have and if there is reason to believe that the disparate impact is itself the product of past discrimination, whether its own or that of society at large. There is no question that Davis' program is valid under this test."[41]

Justice Powell's swing opinion gave greater weight to the values inherent in equality of opportunity and to the need for color-blind equal treatment of all races.[42] He rejected the notion of imposing a result-oriented solution to remedy broad patterns of societal discrimination, at least where no court or legislative body had found specific instances of discrimination in the immediate situation.[43] Consistent with his equality of opportunity perspective, Justice Powell refused to accept the two "justice" arguments put forward by the University in defense of its preferential admissions policy (increasing the traditionally low minority representation in medical schools and the medical profession, and countering the effects of past societal discrimination), as well as its major social utility argument (increasing the number of physicians who would practice in currently underserved minority communities). However, adopting what some have called a "Solomonic compromise,"[44] Justice Powell accepted the University's final social utility justification for preferential admissions,[45] the educational benefits of an ethnically diverse student body. This diversity rationale, set forth as an issue of academic freedom under the First Amendment, was held by Justice Powell to provide a "compelling" justification for a race-conscious policy.

Under Justice Powell's approach, a university seeking to diversify its student body could give extra consideration, on an individual basis, to ethnic background, and in assessing the extent to which such consideration would be appropriate, the admissions committee apparently could also give "some attention to [total] numbers."[46] Thus, Justice Powell's compromise would probably allow a university admissions committee to implement an affirmative action program ensuring precisely the same minority representation as did the one at Davis, but in a manner less likely to grate against majoritarian sentiments.[47]

In subsequent cases raising affirmative action issues similar to those in *Bakke*, the Supreme Court majority again has avoided frontally facing the basic equality issues[48] and has issued technical rulings which resolve the immediate controversy without providing consistent precedents on the core issues of egalitarian principle.[49] Thus, in *United Steelworkers of America* v. *Weber*,[50] a procedure requiring that 50 percent of those selected for admission to an aluminum company's apprenticeship training program be minorities was upheld as being a "voluntary" action of a private company which did not violate Title VII of the 1964 Civil Rights Act and did not require consideration of constitutional issues. Similarly, the requirement that 10 percent of federal funds for local public works projects be set aside for minority contractors, the issue in *Fullilove* v. *Klutznick*,[51] was upheld primarily on the grounds that congressional findings of past discrimination in the construction industry justified a remedial approach of this type. The basic constitutional issues and the equality of opportunity/equality of result problems related to them, although discussed at length in the concurring and dissenting opinions,[52] were not reached in the main decision of the court. The majority further indicated that henceforth the Court would leave to Congress and the executive agencies the difficult problem of attempting to articulate basic principles or policies on egalitarian issues.[53]

The Court's deferential attitude in these recent cases is consistent with the contemporary trend toward greater involvement of the legislative and executive branches in the articulation of egalitarian principles and policies; this trend will be a major focus of our case study of executive branch implementation of equality principles. Before the case study is presented, however, a final background perspective, namely Congress's approach to equality issues, must be outlined. The next chapter will discuss the history behind Congress's enactment of equality standards in Title VI of the 1964 Civil Rights Act and related civil rights statutes.

CHAPTER THREE

# EQUALITY AND THE CONGRESS: THE LEGISLATIVE HISTORY OF TITLE VI AND ESAA

The Supreme Court's 1954 decision in *Brown* v. *Board of Education* forcefully established the principle that school segregation is inherently inequitable and unconstitutional. In the decade following *Brown*, however, the judiciary failed to effect the broad changes needed to vindicate this principle. In 1963, over 99 percent of black children in most southern states still attended segregated schools.[1]

Judicial tempering during that era was paralleled by a lack of firm legislative and executive branch initiatives in support of the anti-discrimination principle. Especially striking was the continuation of federal funding to segregated programs in the deep South. Federal money continued to be used to build schools that segregated black children (including the children of black servicemen living on military bases); to build hospitals that excluded black patients and doctors; and to distribute surplus food to whites only. As late as April 1963, neither Congress nor President John F. Kennedy had treated civil rights as a priority issue. Unwilling to risk the South's traditional support for the Democratic party, the Kennedy administration had proposed no significant civil rights legislation, and civil rights advocates in the House could not even muster a respectable minority in support of their bills.

TITLE VI OF THE 1964 CIVIL RIGHTS ACT

*Passage of the Act*

By the summer of 1963, the political equilibrium was altered by a dramatic upsurge in popular opinion. Civil rights demonstrations in Birmingham, Alabama and elsewhere in the South had been met with ugly reactions and chilling acts of violence. Responding to the national mood of moral indignation, President Kennedy directed the Justice Department to draft a new civil rights bill. He announced this effort in an eloquent speech which called for just treatment of black citizens.

Kennedy was now committed to pressing for a landmark piece of legislation, one which would contain meaningful guarantees of equal treatment. But its passage would require political savvy. In order to terminate an anticipated filibuster, it had to be acceptable to the House Judiciary Committee, to the full House, and to two-thirds of the Senate.[2]

The administration began serious consultations with congressional leaders even before putting its bill in final form. Interestingly, neither Kennedy's speech nor the draft bill addressed the issue which was to become the core of Title VI, that is, termination of federal financial support for discriminatory programs. The legislators who were consulted, however, stressed the importance of this issue. Many potentially viable new federal programs (including aid to education) had been killed by Congress in the past because southern congressmen, who might otherwise have supported them, could not accept riders—attached to all such bills by Adam Clayton Powell, Chairman of the House Education and Labor Committee—which would preclude the new federal aid for programs that were found to discriminate. If an omnibus civil rights law were passed which included a "uniform Powell amendment," new programs thereafter could be judged on their merits without repeated fights over such civil rights riders.

Reacting to this concern, the administration added a new section to its proposal—a predecessor to Title VI that would confer upon federal departments *discretionary* authority to cut off funds to discriminatory programs. The administration was opposed to a *mandatory* cutoff requirement, because that might compel termination of funding for programs that provided vital services to the very minority persons whose civil rights it was seeking to protect.

Following these initial deliberations, the administration sent Congress an omnibus bill banning discrimination in voting rights; in access to (privately owned) restaurants, bus stations, and other public accommodations; and in the use of publicly owned and operated facilities or federally assisted programs. In the House, the bill was referred to a subcommittee of the Judiciary Committee.[3] To the dismay of administration officials concerned with the bill's political viability,[4] liberal members of the subcommittee (with the aid of some southern members who hoped to overload the bill) added an entirely new section banning race discrimination in private employment (Title VII), and they made the federal funding cutoff under Title VI mandatory rather than discretionary. ("Discretion," the representatives believed, might well turn into inaction.) The full committee affirmed these changes,[5] and the bill was sent to the House on November 20, 1963.

Two days later, President Kennedy was assassinated. As the shock of the event subsided, newly inaugurated President Lyndon Johnson had to make a fundamental political decision about whether to support Kennedy's civil rights bill, despite his own southern origins. He chose to do so, and he appealed to the public to treat this bill as a memorial to the late President. He bluntly informed congressional opponents that he was prepared to utilize every bit of his formidable legislative skill to overcome any obstacles they might create.

In February 1964, the House passed the Judiciary Committee's bill by a bipartisan vote of 290 to 130. The bill was sent to the Senate, where its supporters had to overcome the opposition of both the Judiciary Committee and Chairman James O. Eastland (who was an implacable foe of civil rights legislation) and the threat of an interminable filibuster. As in the House, exceptional bipartisan cooperation won the day. By unconventional means, the House bill was maneuvered to the Senate floor without the Senate Judiciary Committee's recommendation. On the floor, under the leadership of Senators Hubert Humphrey (Democrat) and Thomas Kuchel (Republican), the case for the bill was explained systematically. Simultaneously, Senate leaders and administration officials formed a quasi-formal, behind-the-scenes negotiating group that hammered out policy compromises.

In the public and private Senate deliberations (as well as in the press), most attention was focused on the sections of the bill dealing with discrimination in public accommodations (Title II) and in employment (Title VII). The general provisions of Title VI, regarding discrimination in federal programs, aroused relatively little concern. Only a handful of southern Senators foresaw the enormous implications of Title VI, which eventually was to prove the most controversial part of the Act.

The Senate debate turned into the longest filibuster in that body's history. It was terminated by a cloture vote on June 10, 1964. On June 19, by a vote of 73 to 27, the Senate approved an amended bill hammered out in the bipartisan negotiations. It was known as the Mansfield-Dirksen Substitute. Just before Independence Day, the House passed the Senate bill.[6] The political strategy had worked. Senator Everett Dirksen shared the credit for a historic civil rights law that could be presented to the public as being firm but moderate.[7]

## The Structure of Title VI

As it emerged from a year of political bargaining, Title VI, the section of the Civil Rights Act[8] banning the use of federal funds in programs which discriminate, consisted of five parts. First, section 601 prohibited discrimination on the basis of race, color, or national origin in programs receiving federal financial assistance.[9] The next two sections delineated the role of the executive[10] and the judiciary[11] in enforcing these equal treatment guarantees. The remaining parts of Title VI set forth certain limitations on federal enforcement powers in regard to employment practices,[12] excluded mortgages and other federally guaranteed contracts from coverage of the Act,[13] and established clearly defined due process procedures for the Act's enforcement.

The limitations on the enforcement powers of the executive and judicial branches were meant to resolve the main problems which concerned Congress during its deliberations on Title VI: executive discretion and the funding termination sanction. These problems were worked out through strict procedural requirements which would maximize political accountability. Executive discretion would be limited by "rules, regulations, or orders of *general* applicability"[14] that the departments and agencies were "directed" to enforce under section 601. The agencies also were required, in formulating their rules, to take into account the policies and objectives underlying the federal programs whose funds might be in jeopardy.[15] Moreover, these agency regulations could not go into effect without the approval of the president. Finally, in individual cases, agencies would have to provide administrative due process—a hearing and findings on the record prior to any fund termination order[16]—and the agency decisions would then be subject to judicial review.[17]

The mechanisms relating to funding termination sanction posed a greater problem. As indicated above, proponents of the Act feared that if a funding cutoff sanction were made discretionary, it might never be used; at the same time, they were wary of mandatory cutoffs that would be detrimental to the very minority groups they sought to protect.[18] Southern opponents of the Act faced a different dilemma. Obviously, they opposed any federal funding terminations. But if some type of enforcement mechanism was unavoidable, they tended to prefer a mandatory standard; such a standard would make it more difficult for enforcement authorities to use their discretion to overlook segregation in the North and apply their enforcement efforts exclusively in the South.

The compromise solution arrived at in the final bill required any actual termination orders to be filed with appropriate congressional committees, along with a "full written report of the circumstances and the grounds for such action." Congress would have no legal authority to override the order, but the order would be stayed automatically for thirty days while under congressional review. This mechanism would serve as a general notice to agencies that Congress was monitoring their enforcement efforts.

Congress also tried to discourage use of the cutoff sanction by providing for alternative compliance mechanisms. First, it required federal agencies to give fund recipients ample notice of alleged noncompliance and to make substantial efforts to secure compliance through voluntary means. Second, if voluntary means failed, the agency could—in lieu of a funding termination—use "any other means authorized by law" to end discrimination. (Ordinarily, "other means" would consist of the agency's referring the matter to the Justice Department, with a request that a suit for an injunction be sought to stop the discrimination.[19]) These intricate provisions added up to a plausible legislative compromise that allowed liberal advocates of civil rights compliance to be satisfied that reasonably strong enforcement and sanction mechanisms would be available where necessary and conservative opponents to believe that the complex mechanisms would rarely be invoked. How these mechanisms would actually work in practice, no one could confidently predict.

## The Drafters' View of Equality

In Title VI, equality and discrimination are two sides of the same coin.[20] Its key section reads: "No person in the United States shall, on the ground of race, color, or national origin, *be excluded from participation in, be denied the benefits of, or be subjected to discrimination under* any program or activity receiving federal financial assistance" (emphasis added). This language in essence means that "no person shall, on the ground of race, be treated unequally."[21] But what does equality mean in this context? The concept was never clearly defined.[22] Both of the perspectives on equality discussed in chapter 1 were acknowledged during the debates in Congress. The proponents of the Act explained its text in general terms suggesting the concept of equality of opportunity. The opponents, however, charged that the statute would lead to governmental imposition of equality of result.[23]

For the liberal sponsors of the bill, Title VI's fund cutoff sanction was a key weapon to assure that discrimination was actually eliminated and meaningful opportunities provided to blacks.

The bill would offer assurance that hospitals financed by Federal money would not deny adequate care to Negroes. It would prevent abuse of food distribution programs whereby Negroes have been known to be denied food surplus supplies when white persons were given such food. It would assure Negroes the benefits now accorded only white students in programs of high[er] education financed by Federal funds. It would, in short, assure the existing right to equal treatment in the enjoyment of Federal funds. It would not destroy any rights of private property or freedom of association.[24]

The proponents also expected, however, that the equality of opportunity promoted by Title VI would work hand in hand with existing and anticipated social welfare programs. Civil rights laws would root out exclusionary practices in public programs and in the private marketplace, and in the long run they would lead to more equal results in the distribution of income, status, and power. But, at the same time, affirmative social programs designed to furnish housing, political organization, job training, and compensatory education would also be necessary to ameliorate major social problems.[25]

The opponents of the Civil Rights Bill, however, insisted that its provisions would necessarily be interpreted to mandate much more immediate equality of results. In the extensive debate over the employment section of the bill, they repeatedly raised the spectre of employers being forced to hire (or promote) less qualified (or less senior) black workers in preference to more qualified (or more senior) white workers. Senator Richard Russell charged: "We may be sure that whether it is imposed in the open regulations or not, in the actual administration of the proposal to provide Federal control of employment in private industry, the end result will be job preference . . . for those belonging to the minority groups."²⁶ The sponsors strongly denied such scenarios, as Senator Humphrey assured in reference to Title VII: "[N]othing in the bill would permit any official or court to require any employer or labor union to give preferential treatment to any minority group."²⁷ Similarly, in the House debates about Title VII, Representative Joseph Minish said: "[E]mployment will be on the basis of merit not of race. This means that no quota system will be set up, no one will be forced to hire incompetent help because of race or religion, and no one will be given a vested right to demand employment for a certain job."²⁸ To ensure that there was no doubt on this point, a specific provision was written into Title VII to preclude any possible reading of the statute that would require preferential hiring and racial balancing schemes.

> Nothing contained in this subchapter shall be interpreted to require any employer . . . to grant preferential treatment to any individual or to any group because of the race, color, religion, sex, or national origin of such individual or group on account of an imbalance which may exist with respect to the total number or percentage of persons of any race . . . in any community . . . or in the available work force in any community.²⁹

In the relatively short Title VI debate, the discussion of racially imbalanced school facilities and student bodies was a close parallel to the extensive affirmative action colloquies on the Title VII employment issues. The supporters of the bill tried to distinguish between officially sanctioned acts of discrimination, which the Act would reach, and conditions of racial imbalance, traced to other causes, which it would not. Representative Celler remarked: "There is no authorization for either the Attorney General or the Commissioner of Education to work toward achieving racial balance in given schools. Such matters, like appointment of teachers and all other internal and administrative matters, are entirely in the hands of the local boards. This bill does not change that situation."³⁰

Two amendments were adopted to satisfy objections regarding such racial balancing. The first explicitly carved out of Title VI's direct coverage all employment practices (except where a primary objective of the federal funding was to provide employment[31]). The second added a limitation on any federal official's authority to issue orders seeking "to achieve a racial balance in any school by requiring the transportation of pupils or students from one school to another," except as required by the Constitution.[32]

Despite these amendments, it is still plausible to assume that the liberal proponents of the Act did not totally preclude the possibility of its being interpreted in the future in a result-oriented manner, depending on future circumstances.[33] The thrust of the drafters' concerns in 1964 was to end blatant denials to blacks of equal access to basic opportunities in, for example, education, employment, and public accommodation, particularly in the face of entrenched resistance to court orders in some sections of the South.[34] Because of this focus on overt discriminatory practices, no significant discussion arose about the more complex methods that would be designed to deal with the next generation of civil rights issues—methods such as affirmative action programs and other result-oriented remedies intended to eliminate the vestiges of past discriminatory conduct and to overcome *de facto* segregatory patterns.[35]

Rather than specifically defining *discrimination* in a way that would anticipate these problems, the drafters assumed that the statutory anti-discrimination standard in Title VI would be synonymous with the constitutional anti-discrimination standard, which presumably would be developed by the courts in their Fourteenth Amendment equal protection decisions in light of future events. This approach, of course, clearly left open the possibility that Title VI would incorporate result-oriented affirmative action concepts if such notions should become part of subsequently developed Fourteenth Amendment equal protection doctrine.[36]

The proponents of Title VI repeatedly stressed that it was a remedy for violations of constitutional standards—nothing

more and nothing less.[37] As mentioned earlier, Representative
Powell had regularly attached riders to federal aid bills prohibiting use of funds to support segregated programs. To a
large extent, Title VI was seen as a uniform "Powell Amendment," affecting all federal aid. No longer would federal tax
money be spent to build hospitals or schools that refused to
admit black patients or students. In this context, *discrimination* was equated with *unconstitutional*.[38] Senator Humphrey stated: "No one can argue with any degree of sincerity
that Federal funds should be administered in a discriminatory
fashion. . . . Such is clearly violative of the Constitution."[39]
Similarly, Senator Abraham Ribicoff declared that in passing
Title VI "we are 100 years behind the Constitution."[40] Senator
Kuchel explained Title VI as a guarantee that federal funds
would not be spent "in an unconstitutional manner." It was
"furthering a policy of non-discrimination, and thus eliminating defiance of the law of the land."[41] "The law of the
land," of course, meant *Brown* v. *Board of Education* and
related precedents.

The representatives and senators also seemed to realize that
constitutional doctrine was in a state of flux and subject to
further development. Senator Humphrey, for example, referred to recent court decisions to assure his collegues that
Title VI would not presently require racial balancing, but he
also left the door open for new equal protection standards
that might evolve in the future. He cited three federal court
decisions that had found racial imbalance to be unconstitutional, but he also noted the opposite holding of the Sixth
Circuit Court of Appeals in a case from Gary, Indiana.[42] Thus,
equal protection doctrine as it "now stands"[43] did not require
correction of imbalance resulting from normal residential zoning. Senator Jacob Javits also noted at another point that "the
qualifications relate to discrimination, and the courts will pass
on the way in which that word is implemented."[44]

In sum, then, Title VI was passed with a clear legislative
intent to remove discriminatory barriers in a classic equality
of opportunity manner. At the same time, however, by incorporating the constitutional equal protection standard into

this component of the bill, Congress apparently intended to ensure doctrinal flexibility by tying the statute to the evolution of egalitarian principles in the courts, even if this evolution should (as indeed it did) move egalitarian concepts in more of an equality of result direction. Such flexibility, of course, had the added advantage of avoiding intense legislative controversy and promoting passage of the compromise bill. However, the lack of a clear definition would prove to present substantial problems at the implementation stage for agencies like OCR, especially since, as discussed in the previous chapter, the doctrinal clarification which had been expected from the courts did not, in fact, materialize.

## THE EMERGENCY SCHOOL AID ACT (ESAA)

Congress' bipartisan enactment of the 1964 Civil Rights Act strongly affirmed the nation's commitment to basic principles of equal opportunity. As noted above, however, Title VI stated these principles in quite general terms. Consequently, in the area of school desegregation it was left to the Department of Health, Education and Welfare and the courts to translate this general notion of equal opportunity into concrete compliance standards. In response to immediate demands from thousands of school districts for clarification of their obligations under the statute, HEW issued guidelines in 1965 (revised in 1966) that became the basis for a burst of enforcement activity by HEW and the courts during the next few years.

The commencement of this enforcement process, however, brought HEW and the courts face-to-face with the hard realities of implementation—resistance to ending openly segregatory practices; creation of new, more surreptitious forms of discrimination; and the persistence of conditions created by past discrimination. These experiences in the South, together with additional enforcement problems encountered as attention turned to segregated schooling in the North, led to a growing realization of the need to reformulate the desegregation guidelines to guarantee better "results."[45]

Two inherent weaknesses in Title VI enforcement had become apparent. First was the dilemma posed by the fund cutoff sanction. It did not allow for graduated pressures. The Title VI sanction, if invoked, would necessitate large-scale funding terminations—amounting to many millions of dollars in large city school districts. Politically, this was not an attractive option for HEW.

The second problem was created by the complex, multilevel enforcement procedures which invited dilatory maneuvers by local school districts. Before its ongoing[46] federal funds could be terminated, a school district was entitled to a statement of charges, a negotiation process aimed at voluntary compliance, administrative hearings, an appeal to the secretary, and judicial review. After exhausting these procedures over several years, the district still could avert interruption of funding by submitting an acceptable plan at the last minute.[47]

The Emergency School Aid Act, enacted into law as Title VII of the Education Amendments of 1972,[48] provided a vehicle for Congress to focus on these school desegregation enforcement problems. The solution the statute incorporated was based on the "carrot" of new money for districts willing to comply with explicit desegregation standards, in contrast to the heavy "stick" of Title VI funding cutoffs.[49] Denial of ESAA funding deprived a school district of substantial sums, but it did not raise the practical (and political) problems caused by a total federal funding cutoff under Title VI. Furthermore, a denial of eligibility under ESAA was fully effective immediately. Due process came afterward.[50]

The origins of ESAA were unusual, and its final form reflected an amalgam of strangely disparate elements. President Nixon had initiated the idea of making large grants of federal desegregation aid, but much of the substance of the bill as it was enacted reflected the input of liberal senators like Walter Mondale, Abraham Ribicoff, and Jacob Javits.[51]

The Emergency School Aid Act was proposed by President Nixon six months before the 1970 midterm congressional elections as a means of consolidating Republican support in the South. Two years earlier, Nixon had captured the White House with a "southern strategy" which included suggestions that he would take steps as president to reduce federal school desegregation pressures. Although by 1968 it was impossible to reverse totally the institutional momentum and public expectations that had been created by *Brown* v. *Board of Education* and by the Johnson administration's vigorous implementation of the 1964 Civil Rights Act, significant changes in civil rights enforcement within the established framework were possible. One step the Nixon administration took in this direction was to slow enforcement of Title VI by the executive branch. Another was to support anti-busing legislation and oppose busing orders in court cases to which the Justice Department was a party. Apparently, ESAA was intended to be a third element in this strategy.

In May 1970, President Nixon told Congress that hundreds of southern school districts needed federal financial assistance to meet the costs of completing desegregation by the following September, as required by court orders and HEW agreements. He asked for appropriations of $1.5 billion in desegregation aid to be spent in fiscal years 1971 and 1972. This money not only would support the dismantling of *de jure* dual school systems—a job that was "largely done"[52]—but it also would support voluntary efforts in *de facto* segregated school districts to reduce racial isolation of minority students, or to provide minority students with compensatory eduction services.[53]

Civil rights advocates in Congress did not trust the administration's intentions.[54] They regarded the terms *quality* and *equality*, as used by President Nixon, as buzzwords intended to cover a retreat from the goal of integration. In the succeeding two-year legislative battle culminating in the passage of ESAA, they tried to limit HEW's discretion over the expenditure of appropriated funds and to promote innovative and aggressive approaches (such as voluntary metropolitan integration) for attaining stable integration and quality education.[55]

Pending full consideration of his ESAA bill, President Nixon asked for an appropriation of $150 million under existing authority to fund a "start-up" program, called The Emergency

School Assistance Program. In August 1970, Congress appropriated $75 million, and ESAP got underway immediately. Most of the money was spent before the November elections. According to two unchallenged investigative reports,[56] these funds were expended in clear violation of the statutory authorization. "[F]unds designed to facilitate the process of school desegregation are granted to districts openly and flagrantly pursuing racist policies which insult and degrade black children."[57] The reports charged that districts receiving federal "desegregation" funds were transferring property to segregated private academies, maintaining segregated classrooms within ostensibly integrated schools, and dismissing and demoting qualified black teachers and principals. The administration's procedures were said to invite these abuses because they contemplated rapid processing of applications (thirty-six-hour turnarounds),[58] making it impossible for regional OCR staff either to judge the merits of proposals or to investigate the civil rights compliance status of the districts.

The allegations of ESAP abuses made a strong impression on Congress. When the Senate resumed deliberations on desegregation aid in 1971, it reached a consensus fairly quickly on adoption of strong measures to limit the discretion of the administration in disbursing ESAA funds. Most critical was the addition of a set of four ineligibility provisions.[59] These provisions, which described practices and conditions that were deemed discriminatory for the purposes of ESAA eligibility, would disqualify a grant application from the competition for awards. They contained strict standards prohibiting (1) the transfer of funds to segregated private schools; (2) the dismissal or demotion of minority staff; (3) the use of student assignment practices that result in classroom segregation; and (4) other practices causing unequal treatment of minority students.

In the areas of employment discrimination and student segregation, Congress adopted an explicit impact test. A school district was to be ineligible for assistance if, after the date of enactment, it "had in effect any practice . . . which *results* in the disproportionate demotion or dismissal of instructional or other personnel from minority groups . . . or otherwise engaged in discrimination based upon race, color, or national origin in the hiring, promotion, or assignment of employees."[60] A district also would be ineligible if it "had in effect any procedure for the assignment of children to or within classes which *results* in the separation of minority group from non-minority group children for a substantial portion of the school day."[61] Because of Senator Ervin's insistence that the above-quoted language on classroom assignment could be used to prohibit all ability grouping, Senator Byrd introduced an amendment, which was adopted, exempting "the use of bona fide ability grouping . . . as a standard pedagogical practice."[62]

The Emergency School Aid Act also provided a procedure by which an applicant's ineligibility under the above standards could be waived. A waiver, however, had to be approved by the secretary (this function could "not be delegated") and only upon a determination that the practice which had triggered the ineligibility had "ceased to exist."[63]

In sum, ESAA was a complex, sometimes contradictory, statute that reflected the crosscurrents of school desegregation views in the early 1970s. Consistent with a strict equality of opportunity perspective, it sought to promote voluntary desegregation through financial incentives, and it explicitly reduced the use of busing as an integration mechanism.[64] But, at the same time, it incorporated explicit eligibility standards, impact tests, and enforcement mechanisms that reflected an underlying equality of result direction which, as we shall see in the chapters which follow, were to come to the fore and promote a result orientation in OCR's enforcement activities.[65]

PART TWO

# Equality and the Administrative Agency: OCR's New York City Review, 1972–1982

The discussion in the preceding chapters has demonstrated that neither the courts nor Congress was able to reconcile the competing strands of American egalitarian ideology. Although the passage of Title VI represented a major political break-through for civil rights advocates, it could not be known until the statute was implemented whether the unresolved, under-lying ideological conflicts and statutory compromises would impede effective enforcement.

Initial implementation of Title VI in the late 1960s was concentrated in southern school districts, where strong ad-ministrative standards, backed up by the courts, substantially accelerated the process of dismantling dual school systems. It was, however, with the "second generation" problems of en-suring that minority students received a meaningful integrated education in formally unitary school systems that the under-lying conflicts between equality of opportunity and equality of result came to the fore.

These conflicts became most clear when Title VI enforce-ment efforts turned in the 1970s to the large urban areas of the North. Consequently, our case study of the implementa-tion of Title VI concentrates on the Big City Reviews con-ducted by the federal OCR. We emphasize the events in New York City, but we place them in comparative perspective with references, as appropriate, to the enforcement activities si-multaneously taking place in Chicago, Los Angeles, and Philadelphia.

The case study of the New York City Review will be pre-sented in the next three chapters. Chapter 4 will set forth the historical background of OCR's nationwide implementation of Title VI in the years after 1964, as well as the events that directly led to the Big City Reviews. It traces the fascinating political-legal history that etablished the conditions for Martin Gerry, as Assistant Director of OCR, to win support within the Nixon and Ford administrations for this massive project.

Chapter 5 will take us into the New York City events,

beginning with personalized understandings of the city school system from the diverse viewpoints of five key participants. The remainder of chapter 5 and chapter 6 will move on to the specific New York City developments: the intense debates and negotiations among OCR, the New York City Board of Education, and various unions, politicians, and advocacy groups; the agreements they reached; and the problems encountered in trying to implement these agreements. These are the events that drove a number of school principals to go to the brink of imprisonment rather than release ethnic data to OCR; that caused local civil rights advocates to accuse the New York City Board of Education of institutionalized racism; and that spurred Senator Daniel Patrick Moynihan to make allusions to Nazi Germany in denouncing the final OCR-Board of Education agreement on the Senate floor. Chapter 5 will focus specifically on faculty hiring and assignment issues, and chapter 6 will focus on student services, particularly ability grouping practices.

CHAPTER FOUR
# THE HISTORICAL BACKGROUND

## IMPLEMENTATION OF TITLE VI IN THE JOHNSON YEARS: 1964–1968

When the 1964 Civil Rights Act was passed, only one-fifth of the school districts in the South had even begun to desegregate, and almost all of the black children in the southern states still attended all-black schools.[1] In this context, it was far from clear how the newly enacted Title VI would be implemented and whether its passage could substantially accelerate the pace of school desegregation.

Title VI called upon HEW to devise regulations and procedures to end discrimination in federally assisted school programs.[2] Within HEW, the key agency was the Office of Education. As an organization accustomed to providing limited financial and technical assistance to local school officials, OE's capabilities as a civil rights enforcement agency were questionable. As Professor Orfield has observed, "It is difficult to imagine any agency less prepared in terms of temperament, tradition, and philosophy to forcefully set in motion a major social revolution."[3]

Not surprisingly, therefore, the initial HEW enforcement stance on school desegregation was quite moderate. The first regulation, issued in December 1964, provided that a school district could establish compliance with Title VI by providing assurances that it would comply either with a court-ordered desegregation plan or with a desegregation plan determined by a responsible department official to be "adequa[te] to accomplish the purposes of the Act."[4] No specific standards for the "adequacy" of such plans were set forth, and no time lines or guarantees of specified results were required.

The next year, however, the atmosphere changed sharply. The key precipitating event was passage of the 1965 Elementary and Secondary Education Act. Because Title VI had eliminated the Powell amendment roadblock to passage of major school-aid legislation,[5] the administration was able to gain passage of ESEA, which became the most massive federal program of aid to education in history.

Enactment of ESEA dramatically enhanced the significance of the Title VI fund termination sanction. So long as federally funded programs had been small and scattered, HEW lacked the basis for a national anti-discrimination program. But the awarding of large ESEA grants to almost all of the nation's 25,000 school districts gave HEW the leverage to compel districts to adopt Title VI compliance plans.[6]

Early in 1965, as passage of ESEA became imminent, state and local school officials, especially from the South, began to pressure OE staff for instructions on Title VI compliance; specifically, they sought information on the criteria that would be used to determine the acceptability of their desegregation plans. These demands precipitated an internal battle at OE between those who thought formal guidelines were essential for effective administrative enforcement and those who opposed guidelines on the ground that they impeded the application of maximum desegregation pressure to school districts on a case-by-case basis.

Using unorthodox methods—the publication in the *Saturday Review* of the "personal" views of a legal consultant to OE—proponents of the former view carried the day.[7] The department officially issued its "1965 Guidelines."[8] These standards cautiously reflected the equality of opportunity premises that underlay Title VI's legislative history. Most notably, in this regard, the guidelines accepted freedom of choice desegregation plans—although the rules did go beyond many of the court cases in spelling out a series of requirements that would make "choice" a real opportunity for minority parents. (For example, parents and students were to receive reasonable notification of available choices.) The guidelines also emphasized requirements for faculty and staff desegregation,[9] apparently at the specific direction of President Johnson, who had strongly condemned wholesale discriminatory firing of black teachers in a number of school districts.[10] Finally, the guidelines designated fall 1967 as the latest compliance date for desegregation of dual school systems.

At the same time that OE's small, overworked civil rights staff was concentrating on applying its school desegregation guidelines to thousands of southern school districts, a major Title VI compliance issue arose in the North. Responding to a complaint from a federation of civil rights groups alleging racial segregation in schooling and housing policies in Chicago, Commissioner of Education Francis Keppel, after a preliminary investigation, announced in a letter to the Illinois school superintendent that OE would defer approximately $32 million in federal funding for Chicago, pending further investigation. The political backlash was immediate and intense. Within five days, Chicago's Mayor Richard Daley met with President Johnson, the President communicated with HEW officials, and HEW reversed itself.[11]

The Chicago incident had two major effects on HEW's civil rights enforcement efforts. First, HEW henceforth would shy away from any significant enforcement activities outside the South.[12] Second, John Gardner, the secretary of HEW, decided to establish a new Office for Civil Rights reporting directly to him—rather than to the OE hierarchy—in order to maximize political accountability. Ironically, however, as the small OCR grew in response to increasing enforcement pressures,[13] the secretary's ability to supervise its activities directly became more difficult; moreover, its separation from OE in time came to strengthen the independent authority of the civil rights enforcers.

The experience of the first year of enforcement under Title VI caused the administrators, lawyers, and investigators in the newly designated OCR to think in more result-oriented terms. Although suitable compliance assurances under the 1965 guidelines had been received from thousands of school districts, little additional desegregation actually occurred. Either the stated plans were violated, or the freedom of choice mechanisms at the core of most of the plans proved ineffectual. To deal with a rapidly growing caseload and increasingly complex enforcement obligations, OCR drew up a new set of guidelines which were issued in April of 1966.[14]

The new guidelines were more detailed and more result-oriented than their predecessors. For example, they established objective criteria to measure school district performance, such as the "positive duty to make staff assignments necessary to eliminate past discriminatory assignment patterns."[15] Furthermore, it was announced that henceforth freedom of choice plans would be judged in terms of their actual results, as demonstrated by explicit statistical improvements in racial balance.[16]

Needless to say, southern school districts strongly opposed these more forceful, result-oriented standards. They challenged in both the courts and the political arena OCR's interpretation of Title VI; OCR won in the courts. The key decision was that of the United States Court of Appeals for the Fifth Circuit in *United States* v. *Jefferson County Board of Education*, which validated the 1966 guidelines, noting: "We read Title VI as a Congressional mandate for change—change in pace and method of enforcing desegregation."[17]

In March of 1968, as its final major action in this field, the Johnson administration issued a new set of school desegregation guidelines. In response to the Green amendment,[18] the guidelines were made more general, for use in all parts of the country. Thus, the previous focus on techniques for dismantling *de jure* dual school systems was replaced by standards aimed at a wide variety of complex discriminatory patterns that were developing in both the South and the North.[19] Despite the omission of some of the detailed criteria of the former guidelines, a fundamental result-oriented approach was maintained: school systems with a history of discrimination were told they were "responsible for taking whatever positive action may be necessary to correct the effects of the discrimination,"[20] and that "compliance with the law requires integration of faculties, facilities, and activities, as well as students, so that there are no Negro or other minority group schools and no white schools—just schools."[21]

By the end of the Johnson administration's tenure, OCR

had proved its efficiency in bringing about desegregation in southern school districts. In the first six years of enforcement of Title VI, six hundred administrative proceedings had been undertaken against school districts, and funding was actually terminated in two hundred of them (in all but four of these districts, the federal aid subsequently was restored).[22] Virtually all southern school districts were implementing school desegregation plans, and, by 1968, 32 percent of black students (compared with 1 percent in 1964) were attending integrated schools.

IMPLEMENTATION OF TITLE VI IN
THE EARLY NIXON YEARS: 1969–1971

Richard Nixon campaigned for the presidency with promises of relieving compliance pressures in the South; indeed, his administration undertook few new enforcement initiatives, and it tried to slow down the desegregation activities of both HEW and the courts. Ironically, however, more school desegregation actually was achieved in the first three years of the Nixon administration than ever before. By 1972, "only 8.7 percent of black students in the states of the 'Old Confederacy' were still attending all (90 percent or more) black schools; the figure had been 68 percent when the Johnson administration left office four years earlier and was estimated at higher than 98 percent when the Civil Rights Act was enacted four years before that."[23] This progress was compelled largely by the Supreme Court's tough mandates in such cases as *Green* and *Swann*, which forced the administration to accept the inevitability of eliminating traditional *de jure* segregation in the South.

The Nixon administration's first major public move to hamstring administrative enforcement of Title VI occurred on July 3, 1969, when Secretary of HEW Robert Finch and Attorney General John Mitchell issued a joint policy statement announcing that HEW would not use the fund cutoff sanction to ensure Title VI compliance. Instead, if HEW could not achieve compliance by voluntary means, the matter would be referred to the Justice Department to consider initiating a court suit for injunctive relief. At the same time, the Justice Department was adopting new procedures, such as substantially increasing the threshold evidentiary requirements for commencing litigation, thereby severely limiting the number of new suits that could be prosecuted with existing departmental resources. At this time, in the arguments before the Supreme Court in *Alexander* v. *Holmes County Board of Education*,[24] the Justice Department also took the unprecedented step of siding with southern school districts rather than with the NAACP Legal Defense Fund on the critical issue of accelerating implementation of desegregation mandates.

The administration's new approach, however, was rebuffed by the Court. First, in *Alexander*, the Supreme Court ordered the immediate desegregation of most southern districts by the fall of 1970. Then, in April 1971, in *Swann* v. *Charlotte-Mecklenberg Board of Education*,[25] it mandated extensive busing to integrate the public schools in a largely urban area. In addition, it generally placed a heavy burden of proof on formerly *de jure* segregated school districts to demonstrate that remaining racially identifiable schools were "genuinely nondiscriminatory."

President Nixon responded to *Alexander* and *Swann* by announcing that he had "instructed the attorney general and the secretary of Health, Education and Welfare that they are to work with individual school districts to hold busing to the minimum required by law."[26] The president also said that the administration was submitting an amendment to the pending ESAA bill to "expressly prohibit the expenditure of any of those funds for busing."[27]

The Supreme Court's actions did not, however, prevent the administration from dramatically curtailing OCR's activities. Although six hundred administrative proceedings had been initiated between 1964 and 1970—an average of one hundred enforcement actions per year—no new proceedings whatsoever were commenced from March 1970 until February 1971. And whereas forty-four districts had been subjected to fund terminations in 1968–1969, only two such terminations were undertaken in 1969–1970, and none were initiated in the three years thereafter.[28]

This pattern of inaction led a group of civil rights attorneys to seek the help of the courts in rescuing the administrative enforcement apparatus from the grip of these policies. They initiated an unusual lawsuit against HEW, charging that the department had violated Title VI by abandoning on a wholesale basis any serious attempt to enforce the statute. In 1973, the United States District Court for the District of Columbia issued a decision in this case, *Adams* v. *Richardson*, upholding their claims. The court described in great detail the extensive pattern of nonenforcement,[29] stating bluntly that HEW had "no discretion to negate the purpose and intent of the statute by a policy . . . 'of benign neglect.' "[30] The court then issued a detailed order requiring OCR within sixty days to commence administrative enforcement proceedings (or other mandatory compliance actions) against all districts that OCR had found out of compliance for the 1970–1971 school year. In addition, for the next three years, OCR would have to submit semiannual reports on its handling of new complaints.[31]

## ORIGINS OF THE BIG CITY REVIEWS: 1972–1974

The Nixon administration's main preoccupation in the civil rights field was with its promises to southern states to slow the pace of school desegregation and to limit the use of forced busing. The administration's posture, however, permitted new initiatives to be developed in the North, initiatives which in time would open major new avenues for civil rights enforcement. In fact, this conservative Republican administration ironically would come to be identified in the North with policies that were more result-oriented than any previously devised under the Democrats.

The civil rights enforcement staff of OCR, ordered to pursue moderate enforcement activities in the South and to avoid the use of forced busing, tended to turn its attention toward areas covered by Title VI which were not affected by these dictates. One such area was discrimination against national-origin minority children with limited English language proficiency. In May 1970, OCR issued Title VI compliance guidelines requiring curricular opportunities to be made available to such children.[32] The United States Supreme Court upheld these guidelines in *Lau* v. *Nichols*,[33] its major bilingual education decision.

A second area of growing OCR enforcement interest was that of "second generation" school desegregation problems which were arising in both the North and the South. These concerns focused on the more subtle patterns of discrimination against students within schools that purportedly had been desegregated. For example, in 1971, it was reported that in a Mississippi school district "[v]isible control of the schools is still white; during the past two years, more than half of all black administrators were fired, demoted, or placed in tangential positions. . . . Inside the schools . . . [is] a new kind of documentation for minor disciplinary incidents. . . . [H]undreds of black children have been expelled or suspended. . . . Over forty percent of black school children attend segregated classes."[34]

In addition to these new Title VI enforcement areas, OCR also was beginning to consider additional enforcement responsibilities required by other new civil rights statutes, specifically Title IX of the Education Amendments of 1972, which prohibited sex discrimination in federally assisted educational programs, and the Rehabilitation Act of 1973, which prohibited discrimination in such programs against the handicapped.

In short, then, prodded by pressures from the *Adams* court to take forceful action, the agency turned its attention to bilingual education issues, second generation race discrimination problems, sex discrimination, and rights of the handicapped. Investigation of these issues in northern school districts where busing would not be a factor was, under the Nixon administration, the most politically viable direction. As a result of this shift in focus, by the mid-1970s most of OCR's efforts were focused on these new concerns, and barely 3 percent of its staff time was being spent working on classic school desegregation problems.[35]

In 1972, Martin Gerry, Assistant Director of OCR, was in a unique position to translate these trends into a new, concrete enforcement model. He had dealt with second generation segregation in the South and with discrimination against Mexican-American children in the Southwest. Perhaps most importantly, he had directed OCR's first major investigation of a northern city since the 1965 Chicago debacle—its review of in-school racial discrimination in Boston. This civil rights foray into the Kennedy family's backyard not only provided valuable practical experience, it also enhanced Gerry's political credentials with the Nixon administration.

Gerry began to think big. He started to develop an investigative model that could be used in any large city. The rationale for this project had four main elements. First, and most simple, approximately 17 percent of all the elementary and secondary black school children in the country were in the five city school systems he first targeted for these reviews,[36] but OCR was using far less than a proportionate share of its investigative resources to ensure that federal funds were not being given to programs that denied these children equal educational opportunity.[37]

Second, because Gerry's previous compliance investigations led him to believe that major problems of in-school segregation and discrimination would be uncovered in any large city, he thought it was time for OCR to take a greater role in addressing these more subtle forms of discrimination.

Third, Gerry argued that uncovering and proving discriminatory patterns set in motion processes that would force large school districts to become more accountable to minority constituencies.[38] However, to achieve this end, investigations of large urban school systems had to be comprehensive, requiring the use of automatic data management techniques.

Fourth, and least explicit (but perhaps most important), was the political element. The administration's southern strategy, as well as the Stennis-Ribicoff bills, created a political climate favorable to increasing civil rights enforcement in the North. At the same time, President Nixon's thinly veiled threat (in August 1971) against any federal official who advocated busing remedies made clear that OCR could accomplish little in the way of inter-school desegregation in big cities. Somehow, a northern strategy had to be developed that would press for equal educational opportunity, but without busing or forced integration.

Through an interesting combination of events, the issue of discrimination against language-minority children facilitated Gerry's creation of a new investigative model. In the summer of 1971, one year after OCR had issued its bilingual education guidelines, the United States Commission on Civil Rights conducted a study of the Puerto Rican population in New York City, focusing in particular on educational opportunities. As a result of the Commission's findings, its chairman, Father Theodore Hesburgh, requested that HEW investigate the denial of adequate educational services to Hispanic children. Senator Javits made a similar request, broadening it, however, to ask for consideration of opportunities for all minority children.[39]

Gerry convinced OCR Director J. Stanley Pottinger to respond affirmatively to these requests, a policy stance aided by the coincidental fact that President Nixon's 1972 campaign committee recently had embarked on a strategy to win the allegiance of Spanish-speaking Americans.[40] Thus, in the summer preceding the 1972 elections, OCR initiated a "national origin review" focusing on the situation of New York City's 300,000 Hispanic children. In August, Gerry broadened the investigation to consider all pending complaints against the Board of Education, including Title IX violations and other types of Title VI violations.[41] By 1973, Gerry had created a task force of staff and special assistants in his Washington office to help create an all-inclusive investigative model. Now, all the elements were on-line to turn the New York City investigation into a pilot project for even broader undertakings.

Thus, in 1973, the New York City Review was maturing into the general concept of what was to become known as the "Big City Reviews" (sometimes also referred to as large-scale "Equal Educational Services [EES] Reviews"), which were to encompass not only New York, but also Chicago, Los Angeles, and Philadelphia. The broad issues to be comprehensively and systematically analyzed under this model were presented in the "Issues Outline,"[42] a 172-page typewritten document which set forth more than 100 questions about education programs in New York City. The paper was divided into the following four areas:

1. Comparability of allocation of educational resources among different racial and ethnic school populations.[43]
2. Inappropriate educational environments for racial-, ethnic-, and language-minority children.[44]
3. Assignment of children to segregatory and educationally inappropriate classrooms and instructional groupings.[45]
4. Discrimination in noninstructional programs, extracurricular activities, and discipline practices.[46]

By 1975, OCR's new director, Peter Holmes, fully endorsed Gerry's plans and was heralding the New York City Review (and reviews planned for Chicago, Los Angeles, Philadelphia, and Houston[47]) as an innovative civil rights enforcement project.[48] Thirty OCR staffers were assigned to the New York City Review, in addition to six employees of contracting firms hired by OCR who were working full-time on the project. Over $1 million already was committed to purchase sophisticated computer and data processing services, and to support the design and implementation of an investigative model applicable to all big cities. Even if OCR's analyses ultimately showed that discrimination had not occurred in New York, he said, this expenditure of resources would be productive because "OCR will have developed a whole new complement of skills . . . [and] the fund of knowledge we acquire with respect to procedures and investigative techniques applicable to large city systems can become a valuable source of information to private civil rights organizations."[49]

According to Holmes, these capabilities were important because compulsory metropolitan-wide desegregation on a massive scale simply was "not in the cards"; therefore, the most OCR could do on behalf of the large numbers of minority children who lived in big cities was to focus on educationally harmful discrimination within the schools. Thus, despite the aura of bold new initiatives conveyed by this massive resource commitment, there was a troublesome underlying tension in OCR's new approach. As one OCR official candidly put it, "It really was a return to Plessy—if blacks could get equal services in their separate location, that would be fine."[50]

These intra-school segregation issues, upon which the Big City Reviews were to focus, were "second generation" issues for southern school districts that had dismantled their *de jure* dual school systems. In the northern cities, however, neither the courts nor OCR had dealt with fundamental problems of segregation in school assignment. (Such first generation issues were still the priority concerns of most civil rights advocates in the North who were pressing for integration regardless of whether existing segregation resulted from *de jure* or *de facto* causes.[51]) The strategy of the Big City Reviews may have been politically ingenious in pressing a major civil rights enforcement thrust against the Democratic-controlled urban centers, without raising spectres of forced integration and busing that would rankle the Republican ranks wherever applied. But it also had an inherent flaw which was to plague OCR's efforts throughout the reviews: without a prior finding of intentional segregation of students, both the school district officials being charged with violations and general public opinion had difficulty accepting the legitimacy of OCR's allegations.

In short, then, the Big City Reviews opened up new directions for civil rights enforcement in terms of geographical locale, issue focus, and methodological approach. In New York City, the massive investigation initially scheduled to last three years would stretch to five, and eventually it would produce two detailed sets of findings alleging pervasive discrimination by the New York City school system, as well as two consequent agreements between OCR and the Board of Education which sought to resolve the issues. However, a decade after the Hesburgh/Javits requests, the results of the investigation were still unclear, as full compliance with the agreements had not been achieved. Moreover, the continuing legal force of the employment agreement had become the subject of controversial political interventions and litigation. The detailed story of the New York City Review will be told in the next two chapters.

# CHAPTER FIVE

# FACULTY HIRING
# AND ASSIGNMENT

New York City, the testing ground for the Big City Reviews project, has the nation's largest and most complex public school system. When the reviews commenced, New York City had over 1 million students, some 60,000 teachers, and a budget of approximately $3 billion. Between 1955 and 1975, minority enrollment as a proportion of the student body had grown from 28 percent to 68 percent.

These rapid demographic changes had political ramifications. In the late 1960s, demands by minority groups for "community control" of schools ultimately led to the passage of a school decentralization law. This law divided power between thirty-two local community school boards, which were given primary jurisdiction over elementary and junior high schools, and a central administration, headed by a "chancellor," which was given jurisdiction over the high schools, special education, and certain city-wide budgetary, teacher hiring, and instructional standard matters. On top of this structure was a politically appointed seven-person central board of education, which had policymaking responsibility for system-wide issues.[1] The ethnic confrontations of the decentralization fight had only begun to move from center stage, and the system was just beginning to adjust to the new governance structure, when, in the mid-1970s, New York City's financial crisis, which brought the municipality to the verge of bankruptcy, exacted its toll on the schools. Thousands of teachers were laid off and services to students were extensively reduced.

It was into this churning sea of institutional restructuring, financial cutbacks, and underlying ethnic confrontations that Martin Gerry proposed to launch his new venture in civil rights compliance investigatory techniques.

## An Overview: The People and Their Politics

Dozens of people played important roles in the New York City Review, but five of them stand out: Martin Gerry, David Tatel, J. Harold Flannery, Jr., Irving Anker, and Bernard Gifford. They are notable not only because of what they did, but also because they represent a spectrum of viewpoints about the condition of minority students and staff in northern urban school systems and about the appropriate role of federal civil rights enforcement.

### Martin Gerry

"The review was Martin Gerry's baby," a high official of OCR told one of the authors early in this study, and the comment became a familiar refrain throughout the interviews.

In 1967, Gerry graduated from Stanford Law School and went to work for Mudge, Rose, Guthrie & Alexander, Richard Nixon's Wall Street law firm. In 1969, he moved to OCR, where he worked as an executive assistant to the director, Leon Panetta, a liberal Republican. When President Nixon fired Panetta for refusing to slow down civil rights enforcement,[2] Gerry remained. He carried out OCR investigations in the South and Southwest, becoming particularly involved in the problems of intra-school discrimination against Hispanic children. He also took charge of OCR's compliance effort in Boston, which laid much of the groundwork for the later Boston school desegregation litigation.[3]

From 1972 until he left the agency in January 1977, Gerry took personal control of the New York City Review. Despite his other duties over these years as assistant, deputy, acting director, and ultimately director, he "ran the investigation from Washington." The local OCR office in New York (Region II) was circumvented. In fact, Gerry rented office space for his Washington task force in the World Trade Center, which towers over Region II's offices one-quarter mile away.

Gerry's leadership of this project was aggressive, enthusiastic, and—to many of the people with whom he dealt—

infectious. A New York civil rights activist, recalling a 1973 meeting Gerry organized with New York civil rights groups to build local support for his plans, said that it was a tremendous morale booster to have someone come from Washington with so many ideas and, most important, with promises of substantial investigative resources. The school officials he accused of discrimination, of course, were less appreciative. Years after the fact they characterized Gerry as having been overbearing and publicity-seeking.

Gerry's personal style went hand in hand with his express theories about the role of OCR. He thought of himself as a prosecutor. From this perspective, the New York City Board of Education represented the forces of deeply engrained institutionalized discrimination against minority group children. He was particularly impatient with board officials' liberal self-images; indeed, he was more struck with what he perceived as the many unrecognized similarities between New York City and, for example, Charlotte, North Carolina, than with the much-touted differences. For example, he noted that ability grouping practices, used by many southern school districts to resegregate *within* schools after the courts had forced them to dismantle their dual school systems, were based on testing and institutional grouping practices that had been developed in the North.

People often did not know what to make of Martin Gerry. Was this young lawyer from Nixon's law firm really a maverick in the administration, someone with the political skills necessary to maneuver a major enforcement project to a successful conclusion? Or was Gerry's New York City Review— even assuming the best of personal intentions—going to become a Trojan horse? Would it hasten the collapse of OCR from within by misdirecting millions of dollars needed for individual complaint investigation and other pressing needs?

### David Tatel

David Tatel came to the directorship of OCR in May 1977 as an attorney with impeccable civil rights credentials and with close associations with organizations that had been fighting OCR's recalcitrant enforcement pace during the Nixon-Ford years. (These groups had won the court decisions, discussed in chapter 4, which held that OCR had violated the civil rights statutes through its inadequate enforcement efforts.[4])

While respectful of his predecessor's motives and personal talents, Tatel saw the New York City Review as a misallocation of resources. The Office for Civil Rights was expending all of its efforts on two activities—complaint processing and the Big City Reviews—but there was little to show on either account. The complaint backlog had piled up to 2,500. And the Big City Reviews appeared to be indiscriminate and extremely expensive. The investigative model was like a "vacuum cleaner"—around the country investigators were collecting incredible amounts of data which were being fed into an expensive computer system. In many instances, the investigators lacked a concrete idea of what they were looking for or how to set priorities. They did not understand, for example, the difference between issues for which a statistical case could hold up in court and ones for which it could not.[5]

Tatel's plan was to set up efficient administrative structures that would eliminate the complaint backlog, as well as to trim back on the Big City Reviews. These reforms would free up resources for special compliance reviews selected on the basis of Tatel's own issue priorities. He was particularly interested in developing reviews that would lead to metropolitan desegregation—an endeavor that the previous Republican administration had prohibited the agency from undertaking. (Tatel's initiatives in this area later were hampered by anti-busing legislation.)

Although Tatel wanted to devote his energies during his first year in office to the nuts-and-bolts tasks of building an efficient national organization, the New York City Review demanded immediate attention. The city's applications for approximately $17.5 million in federal desegregation assistance could not be approved unless Gerry's two sets of findings about violations of Title VI were resolved. Before Tatel took office, Acting Director Albert Hamlin had withdrawn for further investigation Gerry's Second Letter of Findings, on the grounds that its conclusions were not supported adequately by the cited data and legal argument. Local advocacy groups promptly attacked the withdrawal as a political sellout and demanded reassurance that the allegations of discrimination would be dealt with on their merits, and quickly. Tatel, however, agreed with Hamlin's assessment, and he allowed the revision of these findings to be postponed. But he pressed ahead quickly on attempting to resolve the issues raised by Gerry's first set of findings. While participating personally in high-level policy decisions and critical stages of the negotiations, Tatel hired Nick Flannery to be the chief negotiator with the board. Flannery quickly got to work, and an agreement was concluded over the summer.

Under Tatel, there was a shift in tone in the OCR's relationship with the board. A demanding and capable administrator and an able advocate, Tatel nevertheless had a conciliatory attitude. He approached the school officials as someone willing to give the benefit of the doubt to their motives. He wanted to create an atmosphere in which OCR's obligation to help districts solve their civil rights problems could actually become a practical and constructive process.

The transition from Gerry to Tatel turned the review into a hybrid. Gerry conceived and partially executed it as a model of tough urban civil rights enforcement. Tatel saw it as a departure from a sound application of OCR's institutional capabilities, and he sought to complete it on a conciliatory note. In short, Tatel would not have begun the review the way Gerry did; Gerry would not have ended it the way Tatel did.

## J. Harold Flannery, Jr.

J. Harold ("Nick") Flannery was brought into OCR as an outside consultant, to help the agency's career officials and new political appointees reassess Gerry's work product. Initially, Acting Director Hamlin called on Flannery to determine whether the evidence Gerry had marshalled in support of his

allegations of civil rights violations in New York City could
stand up in a vigorous adversary proceeding. Later, Tatel retained Flannery to carry out the negotiations with the board.
    Flannery was one of the nation's premiere civil rights liti-
gators. He had served for twelve years in the Civil Rights
Division of the Justice Department and for five years in public
interest organizations (including a period as Tatel's successor
as national director of the Lawyers' Committee for Civil
Rights Under Law) before joining a prominent Boston law
firm. His career included a three-year stint as principal trial
counsel in the Boston desegregation case.
    Flannery was not eager to take on the OCR project. Con-
sistent with his background as a trial lawyer, he thought that
administrative civil rights enforcement was generally inferior
to judicial enforcement, particularly when an agency like OCR
ran up against a politically powerful or "ultimately intransi-
gent" school district. He contrasted this approach with the
way the Justice Department (which, of course, did not deal
in nearly the volume of cases that OCR did) would overwhelm
its opposition with an exhaustively prepared, well-targeted
case. Together, Tatel and Flannery reshaped the review to look
more like one of these ironclad court cases. They honed in on
the strongest parts of the two Gerry letters and dropped a
number of weaker findings. Rather than put the board on the
defensive on every issue about which OCR had reasonable
suspicions, they wanted to avoid pressing any charges to which
the board might make a rebuttal that would hurt OCR's
credibility.
    Flannery is remembered by the board's representatives as
a trustworthy and extremely skillful negotiator. Flannery, for
his part, concluded that New York school officials (unlike
their counterparts in Boston) were sufficiently sensitive to racial issues and were competent enough as administrators to
permit a significant degree of voluntary compliance. He therefore attached a high priority to establishing an atmosphere of
mutual respect between the parties. To further this end, he
took the chance early in the negotiations of accepting oral
assurances on an important matter when the board's repre-

sentatives said it was impossible to make the statement in a public document. He hoped that if viable personal and professional relationships were established during the bargaining phase they would lay the groundwork for successful compliance with the final agreement.

But Flannery's original misgivings about the administrative enforcement process continued during and after the negotiations. For example, he assessed the first agreement as "respectable," from OCR's point of view, but "only at its best." "If there is any slippage," he warned his colleagues, "it will go from the defensible to the indefensible in a fortnight."

### Irving Anker

From the early stages of the review until the signing of the second agreement, the board of education's chief executive was Chancellor Irving Anker.[6] Anker's experience and beliefs embodied the school system he administered. Over more than twenty-five years, he had worked his way up the ranks of the meritocracy—high school teacher, department chairman, principal, assistant superintendent, deputy chancellor, and chancellor. He was proud that he had tried to organize a new integrated high school in the mid-1950s; he was proud of the board's positive record of good intentions regarding integration as proved by his reading of the decision in the *Andrew Jackson* case[7]; and he was proud that he lived in an integrated neighborhood and had sent his children to integrated public high schools.

Anker acknowledged that some of OCR's allegations did reveal unfortunate problems in the system, and that others, although finally rebuttable, at least deserved an explanation. (The balance of the charges, however, he believed to be totally unwarranted.) But he insisted that the origins of these real or apparent problems were "innocent." The school system was the victim of societal failings—housing discrimination, income inequalities, and widespread prejudices, for example. "It is one thing to say this is a phenomenon in society we should try to change," he said. "It is another thing to say that where we find this phenomenon reflected in the schools, this is an example of discrimination practiced by the schools."[8]

By failing to take these sociological realities into account, Anker reasoned, OCR's policies were shortsighted. Establishing hiring quotas, eliminating ability grouping, prohibiting black communities from accepting a disproportionate share of the system's black professionals, or undoing the imperfect but workable political compromises behind New York City's system for teacher selection in the decentralized community school districts were "reforms" which would merely undermine the school system's public support. Then, white flight would limit any possibilities for real integration, and there would be fewer resources available for quality education.

Anker's basically good intentions created for Tatel and Flannery a possible basis for arriving at a meaningful agreement. But for Martin Gerry, Anker's understanding of the way the school system functioned typified a basic noncomprehension of institutionalized racism. "I wanted to force knowledge," recalls Gerry. "When Irving Anker said he had not known that there were 4,000 racially isolated classes in his school system, I believed him. But why didn't he know that already?"

.

*Bernard Gifford*

Anker's deputy (from December 1973 until August 1977) was Bernard Gifford, a young black intellectual with a doctorate in biophysics and a rapidly growing expertise in policy analysis and program evaluation. Gifford was the proverbial man in the middle. On the one hand, Anker and Gifford shared both a mutual respect and a set of fundamental values. They believed in integrated schools, rewards for individual merit, and equal opportunity without quotas. On the other hand, they could not always agree on how these general values applied to the reality of New York City's school system, especially regarding such issues as whether racial bias (including unconscious stereotypes) permeated decision making by New York City school officials. Also, Anker objected to OCR's investigation, whereas Gifford welcomed it.

The intervention of OCR fit neatly into Gifford's vision of school system reform. Even before the 1975 fiscal crisis disrupted politics-as-usual in New York City, Gifford thought it desirable and possible to establish a new, progressive coalition of educational interest groups and politicians. He required at least two things to promote this change—leverage and data. First, he needed an organization with the financial or legal power to change the system of rewards and punishments affecting the school system. Second, it was important to have a comprehensive, unimpeachable, and up-to-date investigative report documenting pervasive discrimination against minority group children and educators. OCR could provide both.

Not surprisingly, therefore, OCR's requests for information from Gifford led to an ongoing cooperative relationship. Gifford helped OCR and its consultants understand the workings of the New York City schools and he critiqued some of the agency's hypotheses and methodologies. For its part, OCR authorized its consultants to perform computer runs testing out some of Gifford's ideas.

The complexities of the Anker-Gifford-OCR relationship came to the fore, however, when OCR charged New York City with noncompliance in its First Letter of Findings. Anker asked Gifford to prepare an analysis of the findings for consideration by the board of education. Gifford apparently approached this task with the assumption that OCR basically had reached the right conclusions but, in some areas, for the wrong reasons. Working feverishly for three months, he and his staff attempted to outdo OCR. They produced the "Gifford Report," a far-ranging document which went beyond OCR in concluding that, but for discrimination, the New York City teacher corps would have been 22 percent minority in 1972 rather than 11.2 percent. Also, the report challenged the widely held belief among board officials that racial assignment patterns were solely the result of New York City's school Decentralization Law. It even included a detailed legal analysis which generally upheld OCR's interpretations of the applicability of southern school desegregation precedents to New York City.

Several members of the board of education were very displeased with the Gifford Report. Consequently, Anker removed Gifford from the OCR matter and put his counsel, Michael Rosen, in charge of drafting a reply to OCR that would deny fully any legal liability. Anker then gave his diplomatic senior assistant, Dr. Charles Schonhaut, overall responsibility for conducting the negotiations with OCR. Before the board formally replied to OCR, Gifford's internal report was publicized in the press—with special emphasis on Gifford's conclusions that New York City appeared to employ half the number of minority teachers as could have been expected. His report also was used against the board by OCR negotiators at the bargaining table, and by OCR and civil rights groups in later court cases. By this stage, however, although his work product continued to influence events, Gifford's official involvement with the OCR review was ended.

## THE INVESTIGATION

### Setting the Agenda: The Emergence of the Employment Discrimination Issues

Although the New York City Review had been organized to focus on four specific student services issues, two years after the data gathering had commenced, a new issue came to the fore—an issue which ultimately was to dominate the entire process. This was the question of discrimination in teacher hiring, a highly charged, difficult problem that Martin Gerry had considered, but had consciously omitted from his list of core issues at the time of the project's initiation.

For civil rights advocates in the late 1960s and early 1970s, the most critical educational issue in New York City was discrimination against minority educators in basic hiring policies and practices. In 1970, fewer than 1 percent of the principals and assistant principals in the system were black or Hispanic; for teachers, the figure was about 9 percent. By contrast, the student population was predominantly minority. Over the years, numerous studies and commission reports had concluded that many minority applicants were being excluded unfairly from the school system by the licensing examinations administered by the New York City Board of Examiners, a semiautonomous agency established by state law.[9] It was widely believed—and later established in court—that the passing rate for blacks and Hispanics on these tests was lower than for whites.

In 1970, a federal lawsuit, *Chance v. Board of Examiners*,[10] was brought to challenge the tests for supervisors and administrators. In 1974, an analogous suit, *Rubinos v. Board of Examiners*,[11] challenged the teacher examinations. The *Chance* plaintiffs won a preliminary injunction which led to a series of court mandates and consent decrees that radically changed the system for hiring supervisors in New York City and dramatically increased the number of minority supervisors. The *Rubinos* case, however, was largely inactive, and no court orders were issued against the teacher exams.

In 1973, HEW had alleged illegal discrimination against minority teachers when notifying New York City that it was ineligible for ESAA grants. The main basis for that finding was that teachers were assigned in a manner which made school faculties racially identifiable. These charges did not arouse much interest among local civil rights groups at the time. Their priority was discrimination in hiring: which school a teacher would be sent to after he or she was hired was of less concern. Moreover, many minority group leaders favored assigning black professionals to predominantly minority schools so that they would serve as "role models" for the children.

Gerry did not see much point in making an issue out of the distribution of the relatively few minority teachers in the city's schools. He also was unwilling, at first, to take on the activists' main target—the Board of Examiners licensing system. The reason was political. He believed the EES Review would raise enough controversy without risking an immediate confrontation with the powerful United Federation of Teachers (UFT) headed by Albert Shanker. This judgment was reinforced, Gerry says, by a meeting he had with Shanker at the beginning of the EES Review—"one of the most memorable meetings of my career." Shanker, he says, warned him that he would fight the OCR investigation "every step of the way."[12] Avoiding the main employment issues might at least temper the intensity of the union's resistance. Consequently, Gerry's Issues Outline[13] did not raise any questions about possible discrimination in the use of licensing tests.

However, OCR was forced to reconsider this position at the beginning of 1976, when two civil rights organizations independently filed class action administrative complaints with OCR charging the board with employment discrimination. The complaints were a product of the New York City fiscal crisis, which had begun in the fall of 1975. Thousands of teachers were being laid off. The complaints alleged that these layoffs were affecting minority teachers disproportionately. For example, the complaint filed by the New York Civil Liberties Union, *Cheese v. Board of Education*, stated that the layoffs would reduce the proportion of minority teachers from 12 to 5 percent.[14] These layoff problems, of course, could not be isolated from questions about tests and procedures that controlled access to the system in the first place.[15]

These major complaints were received by OCR just as it was close to reaching an agreement with the plaintiffs in the *Adams* and *Brown* cases on a consent order requiring OCR to process all complaints promptly.[16] Hence, a serious response could not be avoided; OCR met in Washington with the New York civil rights groups. Impressed by the importance of their allegations, OCR then reorganized the New York City Review. First, there would be an employment discrimination investigation covering (1) the hiring and layoff issues raised by the complaints; (2) the assignment and comparability issues that had been included in the EES Review; and (3) questions about equality of treatment for female employees, which had become part of the EES Review (based on Title IX of the Education Amendments of 1972). The employment investigation was given top priority.[17] The second part of the review would then concentrate on the original EES issues, except for the employment-related areas (such as resource comparability problems resulting from teacher assignment issues), which were included in the first stage.

The great irony of this dramatic shift in the scope of the New York City Review was that, later, after several months of data gathering and analysis, the Delta Research Corporation (a contractor hired by OCR to provide technical assistance and data processing services) concluded that the complainants' allegations about the effects of the layoffs on minority teachers were incorrect. In fact, after the massive layoffs, minority teachers formed the same proportion of the teaching corps as they had previously. By the time the layoff allegations were discredited, however, OCR had immersed itself in the underlying employment issues.

## The First Letter of Findings

On November 9, 1976, about nine months after reviewing the *Cheese* complaint, and a few days after Jimmy Carter had been elected President, Martin Gerry called a press conference in New York City to announce the issuance of OCR's letter of findings on the employment questions. Although one short paragraph in this fourteen-page letter exonerated the board of the charges of discrimination in layoffs, the bulk of the letter alleged that the system's hiring process was "exclusionary," a problem that had been "exacerbated" by the layoffs. Specifically, Gerry wrote that the school system had, on the basis of race and national origin, "denied minority teachers full access to employment opportunity through the use of racially discriminatory selection and testing procedures and through the use of racially identifiable employment pools in a manner that discriminatorily restricts the placement of minority teachers."[18]

In regard to discrimination in hiring, OCR focused on three components of the licensing examinations that allegedly excluded minority applicants. First was the basic fact that proportionately more minorities failed the exams, and, since the tests had not been validated satisfactorily, it could not be demonstrated that failure on the test correlated with an inability to teach. Second, OCR held that the system of ranking those who passed in order of their test scores placed minorities at the bottom of the list in disproportionate numbers, and that such fine grade point differences between applicants did not reflect actual differences in ability. Third, the requirement that the eligible list of those who passed an earlier examination must be "exhausted" before anyone on a later list could be offered a position was detrimental to minority applicants, who tended to be represented in larger numbers on the more recent lists.[19]

In addition to these problems with the licensing lists, other problems arose from the city's "two-track" hiring system. The "first track" to employment was the regular Board of Examiners testing system. Those who passed were licensed, placed on a rank order eligible list, and appointed in order to vacancies as they arose anywhere in the system. The "second track," known as the "alternative" or "NTE" method, was created by the Decentralization Law and was described as follows in OCR's first letter: "Under this method, persons may be selected either (1) by being taken out of rank order from the existing rank order lists or (2) by achieving a minimum score (as determined by the Chancellor) on the National Teachers Examination (NTE). This method does not require that preference be given by date of examination or score attained."

The second track did not allow a teacher to travel as far as the first did, however. The alternative appointments could be only to elementary and junior high schools in the lower 45th percentile of schools as they were ranked according to the average reading performance of their pupils (the "45th percentile" schools). In other words, these teachers *could not* be appointed to *any* high schools or special purpose schools, nor could they be appointed to any of the top-ranked elementary and secondary junior high schools (unless they were originally appointed through the alternative procedure and later transferred to a top-ranked school). The OCR investigation found that a disproportionate number of minorities were being hired by the alternative method, and that the average minority enrollment of the schools to which they were assigned was over 91 percent. In short, the alternative system tended to funnel minority teachers into minority schools.

In regard to the second basic employment issue, segregatory assignment patterns, Gerry said that the school system had, on the basis of race and national origin, "(2) assigned teachers, assistant principals, and principals in a manner that has created, confirmed and reinforced the racial and/or ethnic identifiability of the system's schools." Essentially, most of the minority teachers were concentrated in virtually all-minority schools, and hardly any minority teachers were assigned to schools having a substantial proportion of non-minority students.[20]

Discriminatory teacher assignment patterns also were said to raise comparability problems. On the basis of race and national origin, Gerry said, the system had "(3) assigned teachers with less experience, lower average salaries and fewer advanced degrees to schools which have higher percentages of minority students." The factual basis for this finding was set forth in a single paragraph, the heart of which read like an excerpt from the original Issues Outline. It stated that there was "a significant correlation between the percentage of minority students and the average teacher experience in years, the average teacher salary, and the percent of teachers with advanced degrees."[21]

## Reactions and Responses

### INTEREST GROUPS

"Last Gasp of Lame-Duck Bureaucrats" was the headline of Albert Shanker's column in the *New York Times*[22] on the Sunday following Gerry's release of OCR's First Letter of Findings. Shanker attacked Gerry's credibility both as a fact finder and as an educational policymaker. "The Gerry report is both illogical and destructive, and it will bring even more chaos, confusion and conflict to our schools—which are still reeling from massive budget cuts." He charged that Gerry had started with his conclusions and then gone out to find supporting facts.[23]

Although Shanker strongly defended the examination system, stating that OCR had produced no evidence that the Board of Examiners' tests were not job-related, he acknowledged that "[t]here should be more minority group teachers and supervisors and more women in supervisory positions." But the way to achieve this, he said, was for the local interest groups to unite to secure more money from the federal government so that additional hiring—now frozen by the city's fiscal crisis—could begin. The Republican OCR's threat to withhold money was an attempt to drive a wedge between the groups that had just united successfully to vote President Gerald Ford out of office.

The American Jewish Congress also took a strong stand against OCR's findings. Stressing its support for integration and its opposition to racial quotas and "benign discrimination," the organization issued a position paper that raised serious questions about the legal basis for OCR's conclusions. This report stated that OCR's reliance on the Supreme Court ruling in *Swann* v. *Charlotte-Mecklenberg Board of Education*[24] was misplaced, because any racially disparate patterns in New York City were caused by good faith educational experiments rather than by purposeful or intentional school board action. Therefore, based on the Supreme Court's more recent holding in *Washington* v. *Davis*[25] that a plaintiff alleging denial of equal protection of the laws had to prove that disparate treatment was intentional, the situation in New York City would withstand constitutional scrutiny.

Although opponents of OCR were the first to react, supporters also mobilized quickly. The Public Education Association reacted to what it characterized as the "angry rejection by the Board of Education and teachers union" of the OCR findings. In a letter to the board and chancellor dated November 12, 1976, the PEA criticized the school officials for seeming to reject out of hand the new federal mandate for reform; for years they had said that just such an intervention was needed to overcome political pressures which were preventing them from reforming the hiring and assignment procedures.

About one month after the PEA's sharply worded challenge to the board of education, a coalition of eight civil rights and education advocacy groups[26] held a press conference in which they endorsed OCR's basic findings but also pressed for more vigorous sanctions. The coalition released a copy of a letter to Martin Gerry which, following a perfunctory statement of congratulations for OCR's efforts, went on to question the accuracy of OCR's conclusion that layoffs had not adversely affected minorities. (The letter did not, however, offer any statistical analysis.) It declared that any minimally acceptable settlement with the board must include "affirmative action retention and recall of minority teachers," constructive retroactive seniority, and affirmative action for women. The coalition strongly urged that its constituent group be "thoroughly advised and consulted about the substance and progress of your compliance proceedings."

The coalition's letter had an implicit message. It challenged OCR to produce more actual reforms than had been accomplished previously by other agencies that had made similar findings. It hinted that if the coalition members had been consulted by OCR during its investigation, OCR might have done a better job of analyzing the layoff issues. In essence, the letter was an offer of support coupled with a warning that, given "the Board's open antagonism" and union opposition, OCR needed the advice and support of local groups so that it would not be misled about the effectiveness of proposed remedies and so that it would have some political counterweight to the anti-OCR forces.

THE GIFFORD REPORT

Chancellor Anker appointed a fourteen-person committee chaired by Deputy Chancellor Gifford to analyze the OCR findings and present a report to the board of education. For all intents and purposes, the "committee" became Gifford and his staff.

Gifford's approach to this project fit a familiar pattern. As one former high official of the board of education put it, Gifford was a "brilliant maverick. . . . [He] would never talk to people as far as I know. Suddenly, a report would come out." In this case, also, the conclusions in the report were unexpected. Several board members angrily rejected Gifford's first draft, seeing it as a brief for OCR's position. The chancellor then transferred responsibility for developing the board's response from Gifford to his counsel, Michael Rosen.

But the draft report did not die. Gifford circulated it privately and revised it. A copy reached the *New York Post*, which played it up as a secret internal document that warned the board that OCR had proven the existence of employment discrimination against minority teachers. Eventually, Gifford published the report under the title, "Race, Ethnicity, and Equal Employment Opportunity: An Investigation of Access to Employment and Assignment of Professional Personnel in New York City's Public Schools" (the "Gifford Report"), and it included a disclaimer that the document "should not be construed as Board of Education" policy. The Gifford Report continued to influence the board of education—its official reply to OCR consisted mainly of expurgated selections from Gifford's draft—and it affected the way issues were treated in the negotiations and in subsequent court proceedings. For these reasons, the report's main conclusions will be summarized here:

1. Based on an analysis of the "labor pool" from which teachers are hired, one would expect that, in the absence of discrimination, the proportion of minority teachers in the New York City school system would be 22 percent, that is, about *twice* the actual percentage.
2. OCR's conclusions about the racially disparate impact and lack of validation of New York City's testing procedures were correct. Whether or not the examination system was illegal, it violated "the most elementary canons of psychometric testing"[27] and represented bad educational policy.
3. The Decentralization Law was not the historical cause

of racially identifiable faculties. Rather, teacher segregation existed *prior to* decentralization, and, at most, decentralization accentuated a preexisting problem.

4. The New York City Board of Education could not be held responsible for the two-track hiring system which was enacted by the legislature as a compromise intended to improve education in minority schools. But the board was not doing everything it reasonably could to mitigate the segregatory effects of this law.

5. OCR was correct in assuming that, under existing law, it could prove a violation of Title VI based on discriminatory impact, without proving actual intent to discriminate.

The basis for these conclusions was set forth in 323 pages of text, appendices, and tables (about 8 times the length of OCR's letter and tables). The report included 100 pages of legal analysis warning the board that it could be found liable on all of the major race discrimination violations. In short, it was an advocacy document basically supportive of OCR's objectives but quietly disdainful of the quality of OCR's analytical work product. In the space of three months, Gifford had undertaken to do a better analytical workup than OCR had accomplished over three years with vastly greater resources.[28]

Notwithstanding its copious and ambitious analytical content, the Gifford Report was largely a political document. Gifford seemed to be trying to bridge the gap between the board of education, the UFT, the American Jewish Congress, and other "establishment groups" on the one hand and the minorities and advocacy groups on the other. His analytical sections would deprive the anti-OCR forces of their decentralization arguments and make it clear that something had to be done to get more minority teachers into the system. His legal analysis was a reply to the legal objections raised in the American Jewish Congress position paper; it might induce the board, and even, perhaps, the UFT, to take voluntary action in order to avoid legal compulsion from OCR or the courts.

At the same time, however, Gifford presented himself as an adherent of the merit system and a believer in equality of opportunity philosophies. He eschewed "quotas" and proposed "goals."[29] His blistering attack on deficiences in the current examination system was repeatedly qualified by assurances that "examinations are a necessary part of the teacher certification process in New York City."[30] In short, the Gifford Report must be seen as both an attempt to set the record straight on several controversial factual issues and to organize a coalition of educational groups around a significant, but philosophically moderate, reform program.

THE BOARD OF EDUCATION

On April 22, 1977, the board of education transmitted to OCR its official response to the First Letter of Findings.[31] This document contained twenty-eight pages of text and ten pages of appendices. The longest section of the report (twelve pages) was the board's proposed "Equal Employment Opportunity Plan."

The brevity of the board's replies to OCR's specific findings, relative to the space devoted to the board's EEO plan, reflected both tactics and substance. The board declared that it "is and will continue to be in compliance with applicable federal laws and regulations." At the same time, however, the Board Response acknowledged that there were "inequities . . . in employment opportunities" in the school system. These inequities were caused by forces outside the control and legal responsibility of the board, but as a matter of sound educational policy, the board nevertheless was "committed to increasing opportunity for minority employment and to avoiding discrimination in appointment or assignment of staff at all levels."

Thus, the EEO plan was the board's way of saying that it was unnecessary to go into a full-scale fact-finding proceeding regarding OCR's allegations, because the board was already prepared to do everything it reasonably and lawfully could be expected to do to rectify the problems.

In content, the Board Response (except to the Title IX issues) was a patchwork quilt built on swatches from the Gifford Report.[32] The pieces were held together by transitional statements that emphasized the board's good intentions and OCR's ignorance of local procedures and politics. For example, the Board Response emphasized that the alternative hiring system was enacted as New York State policy in an effort to improve education in predominantly minority schools. It enumerated statistics from the Gifford Report showing that the alternative system appears to have resulted in gains in the number of minority teachers employed in New York City schools. This discussion led to an edited version of Gifford's criticism of OCR's use of comparisons between New York and other cities with respect to the proportions of minority pupils. However, no mention was made of Gifford's labor pool analysis which, as discussed above, ended up confirming OCR's suspicions.

The board's EEO plan provided an excuse to avoid a detailed refutation of several allegations in the letter. If OCR was interested in results, the board was saying, then it should be satisfied with these proposed remedies. The key proposals in the plan were:

*Increasing Employment Opportunities for New Teachers*

During a period of layoffs, creative ways would be found to induce some current teachers to retire or take leave. Two specific suggestions were pre-retirement programs for older teachers (early retirement or part-time employment) and work sharing programs.

*Improving the Distribution of Teachers and Supervisors*

1. New assignments. The board would use the opportunity created by the layoffs and attendant seniority "bumpings" and recalls to "foster integration of minority and non-minority personnel" and to correct any disparities in experience, salary, and educational level.
2. Voluntary transfer plan. Teachers would be allowed to transfer freely to vacancies when the transfer would help

a school and district move closer to the city-wide racial-distribution index.
3. Selection and assignment of supervisory personnel. The selection procedures approved in the *Chance* case would be "strengthened and improved." Criteria such as "role model," which tend to discriminate based on race, national origin, or sex, would be eliminated. Where feasible, subjective criteria would be objectified or eliminated.

*Teacher Selection Methods*

1. The board would seek legislative changes to eliminate the rank order list system.
2. Some of the teachers in the eligible labor pool might be given preference in hiring based on job-related factors that also would improve opportunities for minority persons.
3. The board would initiate a research and development program to create a new "equitable, valid system for teacher certification and selection."

In making these proposals, the board also specifically rejected some other remedies. It argued that using New York State certification, rather than a separate examination to license teachers in New York City, would be completely inappropriate. Also, its equal opportunity proposals eschewed the use of any "quotas," and in proposing methods for reducing disparities in teacher assignment, the board excluded the use of forced teacher transfers.[33]

THE NEW OCR DIRECTOR'S REPLY

The New York City Board of Education's response to Martin Gerry's First Letter of Findings was received shortly before David Tatel became director of OCR. On July 6, 1977, Tatel wrote a reply to the Board Response, using it as an opportunity to reassess the situation and to clarify his administration's approach to the issues.

Tatel wrote that he wanted to focus the negotiations on certain "essential" issues. The first was teacher assignment.

To comply with Title VI, Tatel said, the board would have to "reassign teachers and other staff so that there is no more than a 5 percent deviation from the system-wide ratio in any school in the system." This reassignment should be completed in the beginning of the approaching school term, he added, "unless impossible."

The second issue was employment tests. Tatel insisted that the Board of Examiners tests and ranking procedures be validated in accordance with the *Griggs* standard.[34] And, as required by the testing guidelines of the federal EEOC, even if the tests were validated but still resulted in disparate impact, the board would have to try to find another selection device that had less of an adverse racial impact.

The third issue was the board's plan to rehire some 4,000 teachers during the approaching term. Tatel said that this recall should be used effectively as a vehicle to eliminate the violations cited in the letter of findings.[35]

For all practical purposes, Tatel dropped three of Gerry's allegations. He did not mention comparability of instructional resources (teacher experience, salary, degrees); comparability of coaching services; or maternity leave policies. Also, he changed priorities. Teacher assignment now was at the top of OCR's list.[36]

Tatel's letter and an accompanying staff memorandum rejected the board's EEO Plan, which was said to lack sufficient detail to make a full response possible. The major difficulty was that it did not predict what results would actually be accomplished through its proposed reforms and how soon they would occur. Tatel also objected to the board's unwillingness to adopt the "alternative" hiring procedure as the basic city-wide procedure.

## THE NEGOTIATIONS

### The Setting

In early July 1977, OCR and the New York City Board of Education commenced an intensive negotiating process that would result two months later in the signing of a memorandum of agreement resolving all outstanding issues raised by the First Letter of Findings. The atmosphere was tense, and at the outset it was far from clear that agreement would be reached and litigation or funding cutoff sanctions avoided.

The Office for Civil Rights was in the process of concluding a difficult six-month negotiating process in Chicago. There, the board of education had reluctantly agreed to accept a mandatory transfer plan that would result in 1,700 forced moves the following September—but only after an administrative law judge had ruled decisively against the board, and after a series of political appeals, including union overtures to HEW Secretary Joseph Califano and the White House, had failed.[37] Compared with Chicago, the issues in New York were even more complex, and the power of the teachers' union (if not the board of education) to resist major OCR demands was more intense.

As in Chicago, OCR had decided to run the negotiations directly from the Washington office, rather than from the regional office.[38] However, in addition to calling upon the expertise of special consultant Nick Flannery, Tatel himself flew up to New York City to take part in the critical sessions.[39]

On July 14, 1977, in the ominous atmosphere of a power blackout, all of the main actors in the negotiations came together for the first time. David Tatel, flanked by his chief negotiator, Nick Flannery, and by several younger staff lawyers and aides, set forth OCR's position and objectives. Representing the board of education was Chancellor Irving Anker; his chief negotiator, Chuck Schonhaut; his counsel, Michael Rosen; his director of personnel, Frank Arricale II; and various staff members.

During the next seven weeks, day-to-day negotiations would be conducted by Flannery and Schonhaut. Tatel and Anker would periodically confer, and Tatel would return for a "climactic" session in early September. At the negotiating table, the Flannery-Schonhaut relationship quickly became one of cordial, professional bearing and mutual respect, as did the Tatel-Anker relationship at the policymaking level. Flannery was favorably impressed by the intentions, administrative competence, and sensitivity to racial/ethnic issues demonstrated by most of the board representatives with whom he dealt (especially in comparison with their counterparts in Boston). However, he also felt that as one moved down the board's hierarchy, problems of administrative incompetence began to surface. The board representatives, for their part, had similar negative perceptions of the OCR personnel below Tatel and Flannery, commenting that they were "self-righteous," "accusatory," and "insensitive to educational needs."

From the beginning, a number of important scenes were played offstage. The morning after the first session, Tatel "marched downtown and briefed Shanker" about the previous day's events.[40] HEW Secretary Califano had wanted the UFT to be at the bargaining table proper, but the board objected.[41] However, Tatel's and Anker's offices kept the union informed on a regular basis about the negotiations. Nevertheless, there came a point about halfway through the negotiations when the UFT became very dissatisfied with this indirect arrangement. Sandra Feldman, one of Shanker's top aides, arrived one morning at the Board of Education Office and "barged right into the meeting and said we just had to be here."[42] "No one tried to move me," said Feldman, whom Flannery later described as a "formidable" representative; from that point on, the UFT was at the negotiating table.[43]

Aside from the UFT's consultative and later participatory role in the negotiations, no other local interest group played any significant part. There were some ad hoc discussions with the civil rights lawyers in the *Rubinos* case, but OCR made no significant effort to provide the minority group organizations with anything like the consulting relationship demanded of OCR in the coalition's letter to Martin Gerry of December 1976. In September, upon hearing that a Memorandum of Understanding had been signed, the NAACP's lawyer immediately wrote to OCR protesting his organization's exclusion from the negotiating process.[44]

## Incentives for Settlement

Both OCR and the board of education wanted to settle. Besides the normal reasons for settling any dispute (eliminating the risk of losing in court and reducing transaction costs) there were also specific historical, political, and institutional factors that strongly pushed both parties in this direction.

The particular incentives for the board were financial and political. The board was not immediately concerned about the possibility of being subjected to the ultimate Title VI sanction, a total cutoff of federal funding.[45] It realized that it could delay a cutoff for months (or years) in administrative proceedings, and then probably still avert the sanction at the last minute by adopting a compliance plan. Moreover, it was hard to imagine any president countenancing the withholding of approximately $365 million from New York City.[46] But Tatel's July 6, 1977, letter referred to a new financial sanction; OCR had declared the central board and a number of community school boards ineligible to receive ESAA grants for the 1977–1978 school term. Through various grant applications, $17 million in aid had been sought. This amount was not overwhelming, but the threat of its loss was immediate. If the finding of ineligibility was not waived by OCR before a September deadline, the funds would be lost irretrievably.[47]

The ravaging effects of New York City's fiscal crisis turned the threatened loss of ESAA grants into a much more formidable sanction than it would have been in years past. On the eve of the negotiations, this is how the school system looked from central headquarters at 110 Livingston Street.

> Programs and courses had been cut back or eliminated; classes were overcrowded for the most part, the teachers who had been laid off were younger teachers, many of whom were minority; in some areas of instruction, even senior teachers had been laid off; as a result of frequent excessing, many of the teachers in each school were new to that school and unfamiliar with its programs and students. For the Board of Education, this presented major problems and had contributed to further deterioration in public confidence in the school system, as parents found their children placed in large classes taught by teachers who were new to the school and as experimental pro-

grams and such "frills" as music, art, and physical education programs were severely cut back.[48]

The view from UFT headquarters was no brighter.

Not only had the union been unable to secure any major salary increase for the teachers during the prior negotiation and strike, it had given up teacher benefits in exchange for a [shortened school day] program which was unpopular with teachers and parents. Finally, the union had been unable to provide its membership with a fundamental and traditional union benefit: job security.[49]

Settlement would also be desirable if it would quickly dispel a cloud of suspicion about the board's commitment to racial justice and equal opportunity. For decades, people like Chancellor Anker and the board of education's secretary and legal counsel, Harold Siegel, had advocated integrationist goals. While there is considerable room for argument about how firmly or competently the board of education had implemented those goals, there can be no doubt that in 1977 these representatives of the board of education deeply resented OCR's accusations. The accusations, nevertheless, carried significant credibility because they came from the federal agency chiefly responsible for ending blatant discriminatory practices in southern school systems. Furthermore, argue as they might that the board was not responsible for the racially disparate teacher assignment patterns, board officials were apprehensive that OCR might prevail on these (and other) issues in court.[50] A settlement could quickly remove the cloud created by the charges and replace them with OCR's certification that the board was fully committed to guaranteeing equal opportunity.

These ideological concerns, of course, had political ramifications. The board presided over a racial/ethnic volcano. Since the early 1950s, it had made considerable efforts to convince minority groups that their interests were the board's concerns. Thus, each time the various commissions rendered findings about discrimination in the school system, the board responded with ringing declarations of its dedication to improving the opportunities for minority children. In the late 1960s the volcano erupted around the issue of community control, and the school system was almost torn apart. These conflicts eventually were channeled into legislative bargaining, producing a compromise decentralization statute that led to a decline in confrontational politics. The OCR charges, however, had a potential for renewing racial and ethnic polarization.

Board officials sought to minimize this risk. It was a difficult balancing act. Minority constituencies wanted remedies for documented conditions of inequality. However, professional organizations and Jewish groups, recalling the widely publicized anti-Semitic incidents during the community control battles, would mobilize political support to prevent changes that they thought would weaken the "merit system." To avoid antagonizing the latter constituency, the board could not agree to "quotas."

For OCR, reaching a settlement with the board was the only practicable way to satisfy several interrelated goals and pressures. To begin with, OCR was under Judge John Sirica's order in *Brown* v. *Weinberger*[51] to resolve promptly the New York City Review, either by reaching an agreement or by initiating enforcement proceedings. David Tatel had close professional associations with the civil rights lawyers who had brought that case. Therefore, the New York City negotiations would be a major test of the new administration's resolve and its ability to distinguish itself from the taint of non-commitment to civil rights enforcement with which the federal district court had tarred its predecessors.

In addition, although Tatel had reformulated the issues in Gerry's First Letter of Findings and was pressing only the key items that were strongly supported by the evidence, the fact remains that he considered Gerry's Big City Reviews a misallocation of resources; for him, the New York City issues were not the most critical items on the civil rights agenda.[52]

Was OCR's position also influenced by political pressure? The agency kept Senators Javits and Moynihan informed about the negotiations, and it sent at least one briefing memorandum to Vice-President Mondale. However, Flannery insists that Tatel insulated him at the negotiating table from any political interference, and Tatel gives credit to Califano for providing him with similar protection.[53]

The perceptions of board of education and UFT representatives confirm these accounts. Rosen concludes, "Despite efforts by the Board to rally support in the Congress against OCR or to put pressure on HEW/OCR, I think there is little evidence that these efforts had any significant yield."[54] Similarly, Feldman says that while the UFT had access to federal political officials "as high up as the White House," the union mainly received "a lot of sympathy," together with the assurance that "the worst" would not happen. It seemed to her that "the Justice Department and the Office for Civil Rights were pretty independent. . . . [T]here were bureaucrats who had been working on this for years and years and you could only affect it so much politically."[55]

In a larger sense, of course, the negotiations had to be considered political. If the political importance of New York City and Albert Shanker to Democratic politicians was not exchanged directly for bargaining chits, it still clearly influenced expectations about how far OCR could push and what effect the outcome would have on HEW's overall standing with the White House and Congress. Schonhaut notes, for example, that when he sounded out Shanker about agreeing to a point that had been part of OCR's Chicago settlement, Shanker simply replied, "No, this is not Chicago."[56] This larger political picture must have contributed to the general sense at OCR that it would be desirable to move on to something that was "less draining, unpopular, and prickly."[57]

### The Agreement

Given that there were strong incentives for settlement on both sides, what were the minimum requirements for the substance of an agreement? For OCR and Tatel, "What I wanted more than anything else was to get an agreement which would begin to move the school system to a desegregated faculty."[58] Also, it was important to OCR that "desegregation" be defined according to the standards set forth in the leading faculty integration case, *Singleton* v. *Jackson Municipal Separate School District*.[59] That holding required the racial composition of faculties in schools within a district to vary no more than 5 percent from district-wide proportions of minority and non-minority teachers.[60] Of course, OCR had vigorously pursued a number of other issues at the bargaining table, but the board negotiators correctly perceived that staff integration was OCR's "bottom line."[61]

The board's instruction to its negotiators was to stay as close as practical to the content (and presumably to the degree of generality) of the Board Response of April 22, 1977. That document, in a significant break from the board's past policy, did contemplate racially conscious teacher assignments, but this commitment had two specific limits. First, the board would not agree to compulsory transfers of teachers to accomplish faculty integration. Second, there could be no racial hiring quotas.[62]

FACULTY INTEGRATION

Faculty integration, the issue laden with sensitive, result-oriented "quota implications," proved to be the easiest question to settle. This issue was dealt with first (before the UFT became an active participant in the negotiations) and was resolved quickly. The resolution, however, proved troublesome in the long run because the language agreed upon—which apparently allowed each side to think it had prevailed in its key objective—was ambiguous and eventually would cause major difficulty at the implementation stage.

The essence of the agreement was that OCR's 5-percent *Singleton* standard was accepted[63] as the faculty assignment benchmark, but the board would be given substantial time and great latitude in methods to achieve the desired ratios. Specifically, the agreement (embodied in a "Memorandum of Understanding") provided that:

1. Not later than September of 1979, the teacher corps of each District in the system will reflect, within a

range of five percent, the racial-ethnic composition of the system's teacher corps as a whole for each educational level and category, subject only to educationally-based program exceptions.

2. Not later than September of 1980, each individual school in the system will reflect within a range of five percent, the racial/ethnic composition of the system's teacher corps as a whole for each educational level and category, subject only to educationally-based program exceptions.

3. The Board of Education will demonstrate to the Office for Civil Rights, subject to prescribed review, that any failure to meet the commitments set forth in paragraphs one and two hereof results from genuine requirements of a valid educational program. In addition, the Board will demonstrate that it has made and is continuing to make special efforts to overcome the effects of educationally-based program exceptions through effective use of such mechanisms as recertification, recruitment and special assignment of teachers.

In the bold print, these provisions were a victory for OCR. In the fine print, however, they substantially met the board's bottom-line needs. Although OCR obtained its 5-percent *Singleton* standard the board won unprecedented flexibility to meet that goal. One high OCR official noted that he could not recall another settlement in which forced transfers were not part of the written agreement.[64] The board also was not to be held expressly accountable for any degree of progress toward the 5-percent standard until after two years, and an additional year was provided to complete integration down to the individual school level. Further flexibility derived from separate treatment of high schools and of special programs operated by the central board.[65] Finally, even at the end of three years, the board could justify noncompliance with the standard by showing that this resulted from "educationally-based program exceptions."[66]

A comparison with the teacher assignment plans negotiated

by OCR in the other three big cities is instructive. In Chicago, Los Angeles, and Philadelphia, OCR accepted a 10-percent deviation ratio rather than the 5 percent it achieved in New York,[67] but in each of the other cities immediate compliance with the agreed ratios was explicitly required. In Chicago and Philadelphia, agreements reached in midsummer required full implementation by September; in Los Angeles, partial implementation (to a 15-percent deviation ratio) was required by September and full compliance one year later. And, most importantly, in each of the other three cities, the agreement explicitly called for mandatory teacher transfers to achieve the agreed-upon goals. The New York City agreement did not deal directly with the critical mandatory transfer issue, and its ambiguity on this point was to become a major sticking point.

While the text of the agreement does not expressly say that mandatory transfers must be utilized, neither does the text exclude them. Clearly, the board would have wanted an explicit exclusion for forced transfers (indeed, according to Rosen, the UFT specifically asked the board to get such an exclusion inserted into the text[68]); conversely, OCR clearly would have liked to include mandatory transfers explicitly, but it agreed to a text that omitted such a reference. Subsequently, controversy arose between the board and OCR as to whether the parties had actually agreed that the text should be interpreted to mean that if the board failed to accomplish compliance with the *Singleton* standards by other means, it would have to resort to involuntary transfers. Tatel and Flannery say there was such an agreement. Anker and Schonhaut flatly deny it.[69]

Tatel and Flannery say that they discussed the possibility of forced transfers with Anker, and he acknowledged that if voluntary means were unsuccessful, the board would have to use involuntary transfers to complete the integration of the faculty. Anker asked for and received a period of three years to meet the standards. They also say that Anker argued that if mandatory transfers were mentioned in the agreement, it would be impossible politically for the board to sign it. Tatel and Flannery say that they relied on Anker's "unequivocal"[70] oral assurances because "it was better to have an ambiguous agreement than to have no agreement at all."[71]

Anker denies that he committed the board to the possible use of forced transfers. To the contrary, he says he was aware of the plans for "wholesale transfers" in Chicago, and "I can consider it a great victory that we did not have to submit to that deal."[72] He points out, as well, that he had to weather criticism from some quarters in order to agree to as strong a faculty integration plan as he did.

Schonhaut says that the possibility of forced transfers was never discussed in terms of commitments. He and Anker believed that integration would be achieved by voluntary means, and OCR accepted their projections. The agency's reasonable expectations under the circumstances, he suggests, would be that in the event the goals were not achieved after three years and OCR wanted forced transfers, then OCR would have to go to court to enforce the *Singleton* standard and to try to convince the court that forced transfers were required. In short, according to Schonhaut, both sides retained their options. Although OCR did not agree to waive forced transfers, neither did the board concede an obligation to use them.[73]

## THE EXAMINATION SYSTEM

The second major area covered in the negotiations was what OCR referred to as "testing" (or "access to employment") and what the board and the UFT called the "merit system." There was a prolonged and intense debate on these issues. Ethel Fitzgerald, chairperson of the Board of Examiners (who was herself black), took part in these sessions and argued vigorously with the OCR lawyers about test validation and methodologies. The changes finally agreed to would have the following new features:

1. Teacher licensing tests would be validated in accordance with "accepted professional standards," as exemplified in the applicable federal guidelines.
2. Eligibility lists by license would be merged.

3. Rank ordering of persons on lists would be abolished.
4. Affirmative action mechanisms consistent with the above reforms, such as giving hiring preference to persons who had previously served on substitute licenses, would be developed and implemented.

The merger of lists and elimination of rank ordering would require modification of existing state law or a court order. To this end, the board committed itself to sponsor and actively support state legislation and, in the event its legislative initiatives failed, to seek appropriate litigation in support of the agreed objectives.

The main goal of OCR in this area was to ensure that the examination system conformed to EEOC standards of predictive validation. But during the negotiations, OCR operated under two main constraints. First, while the OCR lawyers were confident that the teacher examination system violated the legal standards of Title VII of the 1964 Civil Rights Act, they realized that legal precedents did not clearly indicate whether such practices violated Title VI, which was the basis for OCR's jurisdiction in this situation.[74] The long-pending New York City teacher examinations case, *Rubinos v. Board of Education*, was a Title VII case. Tatel was concerned about the lack of progress there, and how that could hinder OCR's efforts. Furthermore, OCR was vulnerable to the argument that these issues should be left to the courts: *Rubinos* predated OCR's findings, and a court would have greater authority to implement appropriate remedies.

Second, OCR was sensitive to charges that it was proposing changes in the name of equal opportunity which actually would destroy the merit system. Gerry had argued that if the board hired teachers for ghetto schools using the NTE, then they could have no objection to hiring teachers for *any* school using the NTE. The board's response was that neither the NTE nor state certification requirements accurately measured teacher qualifications. Tatel felt the board had a point,[75] and he was not going to go to any great lengths to try to get the board to agree to either of those alternative methods.

The position of OCR was strengthened, however, by the somewhat surprising fact that the board of education agreed in large part with the agency's objectives. It reacted to OCR's allegations with "ambivalence approaching guilt."[76] For years, the board had been battling with the Board of Examiners. At various times it had supported legislation to curtail or virtually abolish the functions of the latter, and it already had submitted bills specifically calling for the merger of lists and the elimination of rank ordering. During the negotiations, Mrs. Fitzgerald and the board's executive director of personnel, Frank Arricale, engaged in vitriolic arguments and feuds. Still, the board was mindful of the political sensitivity of changes in the examination system, and it had to place some limitation on its concurrence with OCR. It refused, for example, to agree to changes that were not clearly spelled out by legislation or court order, and it also refused to commit itself to support the plaintiffs in *Rubinos*.

Because the board was in favor of abolishing rank order hiring and merging of eligible lists, the main issue in dispute during the negotiations became test validation. The lawyers for OCR said they wanted teacher tests to be validated by the method of predictive validation.[77] This high standard of validation had been required in guidelines adopted by the EEOC,[78] but a subsequent effort to coordinate federal government standards had resulted in the issuance of somewhat different Uniform Guidelines,[79] which also permitted an employer to satisfy an easier method known as content validation.[80] Feldman and Fitzgerald argued that the existing tests were content-valid. They challenged OCR's staff lawyers to give any example of a teaching test that had ever been shown to meet the standard of predictive validity.[81] The agency, they said, was demanding the impossible. This attitude, said Feldman, was "disgraceful. . . . They didn't care about educational standards or maintaining qualifications."[82]

From this battle emerged another ambiguous provision. The tests would be validated by standards "as exemplified" in the Uniform Guidelines. Also, OCR would have to be consulted in connection with the design and development of proposed validation standards.[83]

### AFFIRMATIVE ACTION IN HIRING

The last major provision to be negotiated surpassed all the previous ones for ambiguity and open-endedness. Paragraph 6 purported to establish an overall goal for affirmative action employment. It was intended to quantify the overall minimum results to be accomplished through the new testing and hiring procedures by requiring that, for September 1980, "the levels of minority participation in the teaching and supervisory service will be within a range representative of the racial and ethnic composition of the relevant qualified labor pool."

This commitment, however, neither identifies the labor pool, describes its composition, nor states how wide a "range" will be considered "representative." These questions all were left to the investigation of an "independent expert acceptable to the parties."

Paragraph 6 becomes more explicit when it turns to actions it does *not* require the board to take:

1. No teacher need be laid off.
2. No teacher need be hired who has not met "appropriate requirements for employment."
3. No "quotas" are established.
4. No liability is incurred by the board if it fails to meet the affirmative action goals but has made "a good faith effort."[84]

The objectives of OCR in this area had been far more ambitious. Because it was familiar with Gifford's labor pool study, OCR sought a specific proportion of minority teachers, close to Gifford's 22 percent. The board, although it was prepared to make some commitment to affirmative action and to increasing the number of minority teachers, was unalterably opposed to any form of commitment that could be viewed as a "quota."[85]

Rosen reports that this issue was one of the few actually debated by the full board of education during negotiations.

Some board members thought that a labor market study would reveal an underrepresentation of minority teachers in the system; others believed an accurate study would show that the board had a good record for minority employment. The board finally agreed to accept an openended labor pool approach if the "independent expert" conducting the study were primarily responsible to the board; the members believed that the results of the study would be determined largely by the design of the study itself.[86]

By the end of the summer, the main elements for an overall agreement were close to being hammered out by the negotiators. It was not clear, however, that their tentative agreements would be approved by the principals. Acceptance of the agreements on the board's side was especially precarious, because the UFT was lodging vigorous protests against the 5-percent faculty assignment ratios that the board's negotiators had tentatively accepted early in the summer, before the union actively entered into the negotiations.

The atmosphere during the tense concluding weeks also was affected by a newly announced federal threat. The Labor Department notified the city of New York that, because of OCR's finding of violations of Title VI, the city could not go ahead with plans to allocate, for use by the board of education, several million dollars of its grant under the Comprehensive Employment and Training Act; it further intimated that the board's "share" might be denied to the city altogether. The board (and the UFT) had planned on using this CETA money to rehire 1,200 new teachers, thereby reversing the tide of layoffs that had so severely affected the school system.[87] This Title VI deferral threat could not be stalled procedurally. Because CETA was a new program, the Labor Department had the authority to defer the funds immediately—in September 1977—and it was expected to take a firm stance. (The Labor Department official who stood behind this possible sanction was Ernest Green, a black who had gone to high school in Little Rock, Arkansas under the protection of national guardsmen in 1957.)

Thus, under the long shadow of the CETA deadline, Tatel

and Anker ironed out the remaining differences and executed the agreement.[88] But that was not the end of it. Because the board had repeatedly emphasized the power of the UFT in the New York State legislature (and thus the need for the union's cooperation on legislative changes), OCR insisted that Shanker co-sign the agreement to the extent of guaranteeing UFT support for the statutory changes on the examination issues. The agreement was sent to Shanker. In a telephone conversation with Tatel, he strongly objected to signing it. Finally, he did sign, but only while penning in the additional phrase, "under protest."

## COMPLIANCE

Implementation of the teacher assignment provisions of the first agreement began in September 1977, only a few days after the final version had been signed. Although no mandatory transfers were to be attempted, the board was in the process of recalling many teachers who had been laid off during the fiscal crisis the year before, and reassignment of those teachers would be done in a manner that would move the system toward compliance with the faculty assignment goals of the agreement.

The board's Office of Personnel set up a new procedure at its "hiring hall." When a teacher's name was called, he or she would walk to the front desk where a personnel officer would visually categorize the individual by race, and then direct him or her to draw an assignment from one of two boxes. The first box contained all the vacancies in schools which were "short" on minority teachers; the second box contained vacancies in all the schools requiring more white teachers.

When descriptions of this hiring hall procedure were transmitted by the press, there were immediate expressions of outrage. Senator Moynihan made an impassioned speech on the floor of the Senate, attacking OCR and the agreement; he likened the mechanism for racial assignments to the practices of Nazi Germany.[89] In his New York Times weekly column, UFT President Shanker reprinted Moynihan's speech.

Minority group representatives had considered themselves frozen out of the negotiations and were less than enthusiastic about the content of the agreement, but they now felt impelled to defend it publicly because of these attacks which, to their minds, were ill-informed and racist. *The Amsterdam News* criticized Moynihan, and the New York Civil Liberties Union sent the senator an extremely detailed explanation of the agreement and what had given rise to it.

In this highly charged atmosphere, a group of community board members, teachers, supervisors, and administrators, who previously had opposed the review through court skirmishes and other actions, began to plan a frontal challenge to the Memorandum of Understanding. At the end of October, they filed their complaint in *Caulfield v. Board of Education*.[90] The UFT and the supervisors' union, the Council of Supervisors and Administrators (CSA), intervened and supported the plaintiffs' main claims.[91] The Coalition of Concerned Black Educators, represented by the NAACP and the New York Civil Liberties Union, intervened as defendants.[92]

In addition to *Caulfield*, a separate spate of federal court cases was filed in connection with disputes between OCR and the board of education about the central board's eligibility for ESAA funds. The board, of course, believed that it should never have been declared ineligible for ESAA funding in the first place, but even assuming that OCR's declaration of ineligibility was justifiable, the board argued that its acceptance of the agreement should have "cured" any deficiencies. However, OCR said it could grant a waiver of ineligibility only if there were a plan for *immediate* faculty desegregation; since the agreement contemplated a three-year phase-in, the board would not be eligible for ESAA funds until 1980.[93]

The *Caulfield* case came to dominate the relationships among the OCR, the board, and the other interested parties for the next two years, and it delayed implementation of the agreement. The first major obstacle occurred when some of the community board plaintiffs asked the court to enjoin the board from conducting surveys of the ethnicity of teachers to gather information needed to comply with the teacher integration goals. Judge Jack Weinstein denied this request,[94] but shortly thereafter he issued a ruling invalidating the agreement itself. His ruling was novel. Without identifying any express procedures in Title VI that had been violated, he found that: "Title VI mandates that drastic governmental action of this nature that affects the lives of hundreds of thousands of citizens cannot result solely from secret, informal negotiations conducted exclusively by a handful of government officials. HEW regulations must provide for some form of public participation in such critical decisionmaking by those whose rights are directly affected."[95] Thus, although he did not rule that the substance of the agreement was unconstitutional or otherwise unlawful, as urged by the plaintiffs, he did enjoin implementation of the agreement pending HEW's holding of due process proceedings.

The board and HEW immediately appealed Judge Weinstein's order. While the appeal was pending, OCR requested that the board of education continue to implement the provisions of the agreement on a voluntary basis. The board, however, declined. Consequently, there was no implementation activity between mid-March 1977 and September 1978, when the Second Circuit Court of Appeals reversed Judge Weinstein's decision and reinstated the Memorandum of Understanding, pending a full trial on the merits of plaintiffs' substantive claims.[96]

During the hiatus in implementation caused by Judge Weinstein's injunction, Frank Macchiarola had become chancellor. The lifting of the injunction at the beginning of the 1978–1979 school term put the focus on the new administration. How vigorously would it attempt to implement the controversial agreement signed by its predecessor? The agreement required the board to prepare a detailed implementation plan and to submit yearly progress reports. In December 1978,[97] the chancellor's office submitted to OCR a document intended to satisfy both of these requirements.[98]

The board's report was an amalgam of descriptions of accomplishments, implementation problems, and plans for the future, with voluminous exhibits attached; OCR was extremely critical of it. It was said to lack the specificity which would enable OCR to measure whether the board was making progress toward achieving the intent of the agreement. Also, OCR said the facts indicated that the board was failing to make progress toward teacher integration, and the agency faulted the board for having no back-up plan to assure compliance with the 5-percent goals if its voluntary efforts failed.[99]

In January 1979, the board took action in three areas. It reinstituted visual/racial assignments of recalled teachers, though it used a more subtle procedure than the hiring hall theatrics of September 1977. It officially began the search for a consultant to do the labor pool study for the affirmative action agreement by issuing a "request for proposals." And it worked on legislation regarding eligibility lists. Chancellor Macchiarola also informed OCR that, if its current legislative efforts failed, the board was committed to commencing litigation to unrank and merge the eligible lists.[100]

In September 1980, the faculty integration deadline passed without the board's compliance with the agreement's requirements. One month later, the board submitted a second progress report which showed that the system-wide percentage of minority teachers in elementary and junior high schools was 20.3 percent, which would permit a minority teacher range of 15.3 to 25.3 percent under the agreement. Only 9 of the 32 community school districts met these standards. Moreover, only 58 of 115 high schools met the 6 to 16 percent range permissible at the high school level.[101]

Despite these figures, the board asserted that it should be considered in compliance because it was acting in good faith in attempting to implement the agreement. In a meeting the previous month with newly appointed OCR Director Cynthia Brown, Chancellor Macchiarola had argued that the board had taken all reasonable steps short of mandatory transfers (including promoting voluntary transfers and monitoring community district "excessing" policies for integrative effect), and that to compel mandatory transfers at this time would cause massive disruption and would be particularly harmful to black faculty and students.

The board's basic position was that, at the time it entered into the agreement, it reasonably believed its goals could be achieved by regulating the natural flow of teachers into vacancies in the system. The board had planned on hiring substantial numbers of new employees over the next few years, but instead there were frequent layoffs. Another problem was that when the board attempted to fill vacancies by recalling previously laid-off teachers, job offers were declined in large numbers. Former teachers had lost interest in employment in the city school system altogether, or else they would not teach in certain "bad neighborhoods." (When trying to fill high school vacancies in the fall of 1979, the board reported, there were many areas in which ten teachers would be assigned before one would accept the job.) Other alleged obstacles to teacher integration which could not be overcome by resorting to mandatory transfers were shortages of teachers in license fields like math and science and objections of minority parents to losing the services of experienced minority regular substitutes.

The chancellor claimed that he also had continued to experiment with new techniques for increasing faculty integration. He adopted a regulation—the "80-20-80 formula"—which limited by race the prerogatives of community school districts to hire teachers under the Decentralization Law's alternative appointment system. He also made an attempt to limit teacher transfer rights under the union contract, but he was overruled by a labor arbitration (which he did not appeal).[102] Other initiatives were the creation of a "district teacher reserve" and directives involving permanent reassignments and "temporary" appointments of regular substitutes by the community school boards.

The chancellor's description of the problems of implementing methods short of mandatory transfers, and of the unacceptability of such transfers, did not convince OCR Director Brown to interpret the agreement to find the board in compliance. Nor did it persuade civil rights activists. Jimmy Meyerson, attorney for the NAACP, reactivated a dormant federal lawsuit against the board and OCR, demanding compliance with the terms of the agreement.[103]

In the wake of President Carter's electoral defeat in November 1980, and the reassessment of civil rights policy by the new Reagan administration, the chancellor made a further, formal request that the board be deemed in compliance or the agreement be formally renegotiated.[104] In June of 1982, OCR responded informally by denying the request for modification and telling the board it would have to implement mandatory teacher assignments. An outcry by the local press and politicians led to a series of prompt negotiations held under the auspices of Republican Senator Alphonse D'Amato. Shortly thereafter, Secretary of Education Terrel Bell announced that the department would reconsider the matter.[105]

The product of this reconsideration was the negotiation of a new agreement on the employment issues; it was concluded in November 1982.[106] The new agreement virtually relieved the board of any further substantial mandatory compliance responsibilities. In the controversial area of teacher assignment, the 5-percent *Singleton* standard was enlarged to 15 percent. This change was also accompanied by a significant redefinition of the benchmark figure for minority representation—instead of the *city-wide* percentage of minority teachers being used as the base, each borough would be treated separately.[107] Consequently, in Staten Island and Queens, where less than 15 percent of the teachers were minority, the new agreement would tolerate school faculties having no minority teachers at all.[108] Finally, even if some schools in the other boroughs did not meet the relaxed standards, the board would be deemed in compliance if it had made "good faith efforts."

Aside from stating that it supersedes "in all respects" the 1977 Agreement, the 1982 Agreement makes no reference to the issues of legislation to merge eligible lists, teacher licensing tests, and affirmative action hiring. As of July 1984, no legislation had been passed to merge and unrank the teacher eligible lists; neither, in light of this failure, had the board initiated litigation, as Chancellor Macchiarola had promised

112 EQUALITY AND THE ADMINISTRATIVE AGENCY

in his letter to Lloyd Henderson of March 1979.[109] As far as validation of teacher licensing tests was concerned, several years of communications among OCR, the board, and outside groups was inconclusive. Finally, very little had been accomplished toward the labor pool study in affirmative action.[110] Thus, the new agreement presumably removed any legal obligation on the part of the board to make further progress in these areas. It remains to be seen, however, whether the *NYABE* case will reinstate the legal requirements of the 1977 Agreement.[111]

# CHAPTER SIX

# STUDENT SERVICES

The original focus of the New York City Review was on relatively novel theories of discrimination. The plan was to use statistical methods of proof (which largely reflected a result-oriented approach toward educational equity issues) to uncover discriminatory patterns in the allocation of educational resources, classroom segregation of minority children, and racial disparties in the application of disciplinary rules.

However, as discussed in the previous chapter, the focus of the review shifted abruptly in 1976, toward more traditional allegations about employment discrimination.[1] Indeed, the very issues Gerry had originally hoped to soft-pedal—if not avoid entirely—came to dominate the negotiations and the implementation process. The double irony of this turn of events is that when OCR and the board finally returned to the original, and conceptually more knotty, student services issues, they fairly quickly reached an agreement that left both parties largely satisfied about the resolution of the most disputed issue (ability grouping in primary grades). This chapter will trace the history of this second New York City agreement.

## THE INVESTIGATION

### The Second Letter of Findings

Martin Gerry's letter of findings on the employment issues was sent in November 1976, just after the Ford administration had been defeated at the polls. Between the election and the inauguration, Gerry and his special New York City Review staff worked on a crash basis to prepare their follow-up letter on the student services issues. When finally issued on January 18, 1977, on the eve of the change in administrations, the twenty-nine-page document represented the culmination of Gerry's efforts and a swan-song attempt to demonstrate a mastery of school practices in this enormous, educational labyrinth. Using statistics, qualitative findings, and anecdotal information to describe dozens of problem areas in the system, the Second Letter of Findings built the case for Gerry's central theme—minority and non-minority students received educational resources on separate "tracks."

According to Gerry, minority children going through the New York City school system experienced discriminatory treatment at every turn. For example, compared with the experience of white children, black children typically would begin their schooling at an elementary school that was in worse physical condition and had fewer or lower-quality teaching materials and equipment. In addition, they would be taught by teachers with less experience. Overall, there simply would be less money per pupil hour allocated to this school. Even when a school as a whole was racially integrated, black children would be likely to find themselves in segregated "low-track" classes because of their poor reading scores (however, they would not be likely to receive significant remedial reading instruction in these classes). In addition, minority children would be plagued with discriminatory patterns in guidance services and in disciplinary penalties.

The specific allegations that comprised this general picture of a tracked system were:

1. Denial of equal educational resources.[2] Growing out of the first and largest section of Gerry's original "Issues Outline," the comparability section of the second letter concluded that New York City's resources were so maldistributed as to virtually constitute a "dual school system." Among other charges, Gerry pointed out that less qualified staff were assigned to minority schools; per pupil instructional salaries at the high school level were 15 percent greater in predominantly non-minority high schools than in minority schools; and the quality and condition of high school science laboratories, audio-visual equipment, textbooks, and basic school buildings

were inferior in predominantly minority schools. Further-more, minority students allegedly had fewer opportunities to be taught in individualized settings, to enroll in junior high school level "special progress classes," and to obtain diverse and advanced-placement high school curricula offerings.

2. Denial of meaningful educational services.[3] Focusing on the elementary schools in the system that had sufficient num-bers of minority and non-minority children to make classroom integration possible, OCR found segregated classes or group-ings in 204 schools (approximately 20 percent of all the schools in the system). In 59 of these schools, there was no indication that the segregated assignment patterns were re-lated to ability groupings. In another 146 schools, where abil-ity grouping was the purported rationale, OCR asserted, based on "information provided by classroom teachers," that "cri-teria to place minority students in low-ability groups are often both vague and subjective."[4] Furthermore, when supposedly "objective (quantifiable) criteria" were utilized, they often were applied inconsistently or inappropriately.[5] Finally, the letter argued that the segregated groupings were detrimental educationally, since low-ability (predominantly minority) tracks neither were designed to remediate academic deficien-cies, nor, in fact, achieved any successful remediation.[6]

3. Restriction of educational alternatives in secondary pro-grams.[7] Based on OCR's special on-site surveys and investi-gations, it was alleged that the system utilized counseling and course enrollment procedures that channeled minority and female students to lower-level and stereotypical courses and non-minority students to special progress classes and elite ac-ademic high schools. Moreover, it was alleged that minority students had many fewer guidance counselors serving them, and that non-English-speaking children had virtually no guid-ance counselors who spoke their language.[8]

4. Discriminatory discipline practices.[9] Analyzing 21,000 reported student suspensions during the 1974–1975 school year, OCR found a "pervasive practice of punishing students on the basis of race and ethnicity." Specifically, the letter concluded that minority students, on the basis of their race

or ethnicity, "(1) have been disproportionately punished more often and more severely for the same offense and (2) have, through the discriminatory application of the suspension sanction, been kept out of school more often and for longer periods of time than non-minority students." (There was no discussion of the alleged causes of this discrimination other than the observation that it was "facilitated by the school system's failure to clearly delineate the severity of the punishment to be applied for a particular offense.")

## The Withdrawal of the Second Letter

Martin Gerry held a press conference on January 18, 1977, to announce the issuance of the Second Letter of Findings. As he informed the press, "Yesterday, I met with Chancellor Irving Anker of the New York City school system to advise him of my conclusion that the school system is violating civil rights laws which prohibit discrimination against minority, female, and handicapped students."[10]

Chancellor Anker reacted angrily to the substance of the letter and to Gerry's method of releasing it. Gerry, he said, was "headline hunting," and his report was filled with "the most egregious sophomoric errors."[11] Anker's angry comments apparently fell on sympathetic ears among the OCR officials who remained after Gerry's departure. Albert Hamlin and Lloyd Henderson were career officials at OCR who, between them, had more than twenty years of experience in federal civil rights enforcement. Neither man had been part of the New York City Review project but they both had become concerned during the frantic concluding days of Gerry's directorship that the student services letter was being issued in haste, and that it may not have been up to normal agency standards.[12]

Now that he was acting director, Hamlin was in a position to have the situation scrutinized more carefully. He set in motion an "independent review" of the second letter.[13] Participating in this process were (1) OCR staff from the national headquarters and from the regional offices in New York and

Chicago; (2) HEW's Office of General Counsel; (3) J. Harold Flannery, the private attorney who later would be called upon to conduct the negotiations; and (4) various interest group representatives who were consulted informally. The key problem that surfaced during this reconsideration was that the New York City task force had not assembled an adequate internal portfolio of evidentiary materials corresponding to the findings. (Preparation of such a packet was a standard OCR procedure which ensured that admissible evidence would be available for court proceedings; OCR normally maintained a careful record of each step in the development of its statistical case—observation recording, compilation, and analysis of data.) In addition, on its face the letter suggested methodological problems and soft data in regard to a number of findings. Finally, the heavy statistical approach of the entire investigation was inconsistent with recent legal trends, notably the Supreme Court's decision in *Washington* v. *Davis*,[14] which seemed to presage increasing judicial emphasis on intent.

There were three choices: to proceed with the letter despite its deficiencies, to abandon it altogether, or to withdraw it in its current form with the intention of revising it. Hamlin was leaning heavily toward the latter alternative by March 1977, and a final decision in favor of withdrawal was reached in May with the participation of OCR's new director, David Tatel. Hamlin explained the withdrawal to Chancellor Anker and, to avoid violation of the time deadlines in the *Brown* order, he secured the consent of the plaintiffs' attorneys in that case.[15]

Tatel placed much of the responsibility for the content of a revised letter of findings upon a team of investigators borrowed from the OCR's Chicago regional office. The team was given computer support through a special contract with Delta Research Corporation. Besides tracking down the data sources used by Gerry's special task force, the investigators attempted to learn about the New York City school system's operations. They asked for help from Advocates for Children (AFC), the PEA, and other local organizations. These groups cooperated, but they also were suspicious. They feared that the reconsideration might be a cover for burying OCR's findings of discrimination in student services (and perhaps also OCR's employment discrimination findings). Informal communications from former members of Gerry's task force fed these suspicions.[16]

## The Revised Second Letter

The revised letter of findings on student services issues is dated October 4, 1977. The manner in which it was released, as well as its content, differed substantially from Gerry's original letter. Despite the intensive involvement of Washington personnel, the revised letter was issued through routine channels, in this case by Acting Director William Valentine of the OCR regional office in New York City. Gerry had held a press conference, Valentine did not. Gerry had charged the board with discrimination in every area he addressed, stating that the board foreseeably had created a system that was pervasively "tracked" along lines of race, national origin, and sex. The revised letter did not accuse the board of overall discriminatory design. Rather, it expressed varying degrees of concern or suspicion that violations may have occurred, but it withheld judgment pending receipt of further information. Whereas Gerry made a blanket demand for submission of plans to remediate alleged violations, in the revised letter OCR listed under each category requirements for remedial plans and/or requests for further information, explanation or monitoring.[17] (Different statistical methods also were used, but in the major areas that were pursued, Tatel's statistics reached conclusions about violations similar to those reached by Gerry.[18])

In terms of its substance, the revised letter totally abandoned one of the major initial issues of the Big City Reviews—denial of equal educational resources—as well as all allegations of discrimination based upon sex.[19] Classroom segregation now became the main concern.[20] (New emphasis also was placed on compliance with the requirements of section 504 of the Rehabilitation Act.[21] Gerry had broached this topic but had not pursued it in detail, because regulations implementing section 504 had not yet been promulgated when his letter was prepared.)

The findings about classroom segregation were clear and disturbing. In October 1975, at least 75,000 students were in 1,998 racially identifiable or isolated classes (approximately 20 percent of those classes having interracial populations with statistical characteristics that made analysis possible), without any apparent justification for why they could not be educated in integrated settings.[22] A second classroom segregation issue involved instructional grouping of blacks and Hispanics in predominantly minority schools. Looking at 7,887 of these classes, OCR found that 1,792 (nearly 23 percent) of them were identifiably either black or Hispanic in schools where integration of these groups apparently was feasible. The agency concluded through statistical analyses that neither the minority/majority racially identifiable classes nor the black/Hispanic identifiable classes could have occurred by chance, given the student composition of the pools from which these classes were organized.

### The Negotiations

#### The Setting

The timetable for the student services negotiations was determined largely by the attorneys and judge in the *Brown* case.[23] Anticipating *Brown* deadlines, the revised second letter called for a response from the board in forty-five days. On November 22, 1977, the board submitted a partial response, but it also requested clarifications and data from OCR in order to reply more fully on a number of points. In mid-December, OCR convinced the plaintiffs' attorneys in *Brown* to consent to extending until March 1, 1978, OCR's deadline for an agreement with the board or, in the absence of such an agreement, for commencing enforcement proceedings.

On January 18, 1978, the board supplemented its November response, and OCR replied to the board one week later.

At least two other submissions were made by the board in the first half of February. Also at this time negotiations began. When the March 1 deadline came, the parties had entered into active negotiations, but no agreement had been reached. On that date, Tatel sent Anker a letter saying that OCR was referring the matter to HEW's Office of General Counsel for consideration of a course of action. Despite the court deadline, the Counsel's Office did not begin administrative enforcement proceedings. Learning of this fact three weeks later, one of the plaintiffs' attorneys in *Brown* sent the general counsel a terse warning that HEW could be found in contempt of court.[24] By this time, Tatel was ready to declare an impasse and to recommend to Secretary Califano that enforcement be commenced. Tatel met with Anker on April 3, 1978, to try one last time to break the deadlock. The meeting failed, whereupon HEW issued a formal Notice of Opportunity for Hearing,[25] which would commence administrative proceedings to cut off funding to New York City. However, before the proceedings actually got under way, subsequent talks broke the impasse and resolved the outstanding issues, and a settlement agreement on the student services issues was signed on June 23, 1978.

## The Bargaining Process

"The employment negotiations started out easy and became difficult, whereas the student services negotiations were just the reverse," recalls OCR's chief negotiator in both instances, Nick Flannery. There were important substantive differences as well. On the employment issues, there was relatively little debate about legal positions, basic facts, or educational policy. There was a consensus that certain conditions existed that were undesirable (whether or not they were illegal as well), and the negotiations were a tug-of-war on how extensive the remedies would be.

The student services negotiations, by way of contrast, were continuing dialogues on basic facts, critical educational policy issues, legal requirements, and, finally, specific remedies. The

flow of reports and documents between the parties, as well
as the negotiating sessions themselves, became a process of
investigation, analysis, and argument, including intense debates on educational policy issues. But at the end of this process, when the student services agreement was signed, neither
the board, the UFT, nor any politician was heard to complain
that the board accepted tough remedies only because it had
a "gun to its head." Rather, the process had raised new levels
of understanding on the issues. Schonhaut and other representatives of the board saw the agreement as one that probably
would bring about some improvement in educational
practices[26] and, in any event, as one with which they could
live.

There were approximately seven meetings (totaling about
fifty hours) between board and OCR representatives prior to
David Tatel's April 3, 1978, meeting with Chancellor Anker.
Relatively early in this process, the parties agreed on the principles for settling (or postponing) all of the issues that OCR
had raised, except for classroom segregation. The most debated issue in the early negotiations was discipline. In Flannery's view, OCR had an "irrefutable case," and he could
understand the board's resistance only as an effort to protect
its teachers and administrators from further paperwork and
protocols. Schonhaut, on the other hand, stated that there
were serious questions as to whether the statistical disparities
actually were caused by discrimination. The result of this debate, in any event, was not a strong corrective remedy or a
new discipline code, but rather a "triggering device"—the
board would be required to keep racially identifiable records
on all student suspensions—which was intended to facilitate
OCR monitoring and to make school principals "think twice"
when recommending that a minority child be suspended.

In regard to classroom segregation, the remaining student
services issue, the board's initial stance was to try to rebut
OCR's allegations. After investigating the pertinent facts regarding each one of the 3,790 classes that allegedly was racially identifiable or isolated in October 1975, the chancellor
summarized the board's responses in several pages of charts.

They showed that "in 96 percent of the cases cited by OCR, the classroom situations were in accordance with either legal requirements and/or valid educational practice."[27] Although OCR accepted the board's argument that almost half of the statistically identified segregated classes were caused by placement of Hispanic students in bilingual settings, pursuant to the federal court decree in the ASPIRA case,[28] it stood firm on challenging the remaining assignments, including those purportedly based on ability grouping practices.

The board's legal position was that racially identifiable or isolated instructional settings would violate Title VI only if they were caused by intentionally discriminatory actions. Then, relying on its own independent survey of classroom organizations, it said that there were, indeed, a small number of instances of unlawful segregation. These amounted to only 4 percent of the classes listed by OCR as racially identifiable or isolated. According to the board, the other cases listed by OCR reflected errors or could be justified. Thus, while the board committed itself to eliminating the ad hoc practices that accounted for the 4 percent, it denied the need for any policy change regarding the remaining classes.

According to Flannery, OCR then tried to convince the board's representatives to look more closely at the actual classroom assignments and to reconsider their legal and educational validity. Aided by representatives of local advocacy groups with whom they conferred informally, OCR staffers prepared questions about particular schools or particular practices to be looked at in more detail. In preparing answers to these questions, Schonhaut not only consulted with the board's central staff, but he also assembled an informal advisory group of community district superintendents representing five districts that had a spectrum of student racial compositions. According to Flannery, this process revealed a much more pervasive pattern of undisputedly invalid practices than the board had recognized. Kindergarten or first grade children often were assigned to classrooms based on whether they could tie their shoes or tell time; older children sometimes were given classroom assignments based on bus routes, which, of course, corresponded to neighborhoods and ethnicity. The negotiators agreed to work jointly on ways to prevent such clearly indefensible practices from recurring.

Other issues proved more knotty, especially the question of whether reading scores were a valid method of grouping children in self-contained classes in which all subjects were taught. Although the board contended that such ability groupings were educationally desirable, its main argument was feasibility. The professional educators who represented the board vigorously asserted that the system's teachers simply would not be able to deliver quality instruction if principals did not have the option to organize classrooms based on ability tracks.[29] The lawyers for OCR did not have a good answer. In mid-March, an impasse developed over these basic ability grouping issues.

A decision about how OCR would proceed now had to be made at the highest levels. Accordingly, Tatel prepared a comprehensive briefing memorandum for Secretary Califano. In his introduction, Tatel put the EES review and the negotiations into this perspective: "The segregated classroom issue is not an abstract civil rights problem. New York's tracking system is destroying the educational opportunities of thousands of black children. It makes no educational sense and can be easily corrected without busing, goals, collection of ethnic data or any other unpopular devices. *It is precisely the kind of urban school problem on which OCR should concentrate during the next few years.*"[30]

Tatel characterized the board's factual responses as "a virtual confession of uncontrolled tracking with the foreseeable result of producing segregation."[31] He found most objectionable in the board's remedial proposal its desire to continue ability grouping of kindergarten and first grade children based on dubious "indicators" and to maintain all-day tracking in grades two through eight.

Tatel informed Califano that OCR's position, based on department regulations, was "more moderate" than the requirements that some courts had imposed in this area. He noted further that OCR's position "adheres to prevailing educational views concerning the proper uses and limitations of racially-defined grouping as explained in two recent NIE publications."[32] Finally, Tatel recommended that if he could not substantially change the board's position in a meeting with Anker, OCR should begin administrative enforcement proceedings.[33]

Califano authorized the commencement of enforcement proceedings. But he also had an idea for breaking the impasse at the negotiating table. He contacted his appointee to the directorship of NIE, Dr. Patricia Albjerg Graham, and asked her to act as an advisor to the OCR lawyers.

Graham saw her role as "brokering the question of what is possible." One could hardly imagine a person better qualified for this task. She was a former teacher who went on to earn a Ph.D. in American history from Columbia University, concentrating on the history of education. From 1965 to 1974, she ran a teacher training program at Barnard College, which kept her in daily contact with the problems of teachers in the New York City school system. She had administrative experience as a former vice-president of Radcliffe College, and now, as director of NIE, she was to be responsible for setting the federal government's research agenda in matters of learning, educational policy, and school governance.[34]

Graham had not previously thought of ability grouping as a civil rights problem, but she had observed the tracking practices in New York City and found that minority children were placed disproportionately in lower tracks and stayed there "forever." The gaps between upper and lower tracks widened with each grade, and teachers assigned to lower-ability groupings did not feel they had the same obligations to show educational results as did teachers in the higher tracks. Graham believed there were no acceptable criteria for organizing entire classrooms in the primary grades on the basis of ability. Moreover, her understanding of the relevant research was that there was no evidence that homogeneous groupings actually improved learning in the elementary grades among children within normal ranges of intelligence.[35]

Schonhaut said he agreed with Graham on these research

findings. However, he emphasized evidence indicating that teachers and administrators resisted efforts to make them teach more heterogeneous classes. If compelled to accept heterogeneous groupings, teachers rarely provided the individualized work arrangements needed to ensure success in such settings.[36] According to Schonhaut, ability grouping had been practiced for many years, even in virtually all-minority schools, and the most successful programs were highly structured.

Graham and Flannery were quick to point out to the board's negotiators the inconsistency of having argued in the employment negotiations that the teacher licensing and selection system was essential for maintaining a highly qualified teacher corps and arguing now that these same teachers were unable or unwilling to teach heterogeneous classes. Nevertheless, OCR had to deal with the reality that New York City was not only the biggest but also probably the most tracked school system in the country. (In Graham's words, New York City was "deeper into the hole and the hole was bigger.") The stage was set for a compromise.

## The Final Agreement

A compromise finally was reached by distinguishing between two basic kinds of ability grouping: the organization of entire self-contained classes by ability and the creation of ability-based instructional units within a classroom. The key questions focused on in the discussions were (1) at what age level each of these grouping practices could be used and (2) by what criteria the ability groups must be defined.

It was finally agreed that ability grouping at the kindergarten level would be totally prohibited. At the first grade level, reorganization of classes would be permitted for reading and math instruction only. This limited ability grouping would be arranged in accordance with three criteria set forth in HEW's ESAA regulations: grouping had to be based on objective criteria, it had to involve no more than 25 percent of the students' school day, and there had to be special efforts to raise the performance of the lower-ability tracks.[37]

Reaching an agreement on arrangements for the second grade proved more difficult. The board sought extensive classroom groupings by ability for all children above the first grade level; OCR was prepared to move closer to the board's position starting at the third grade level, but it stood by Graham's insistence that second graders were still too young to be tracked. A settlement was reached through adoption of a new concept: second grade classes could be organized by ability criteria (if such grouping is "educationally compelled" and based on objective assessment criteria), provided that the group is "stratified, non-contiguous or bi-modal." This meant that if a principal wanted to organize a grade into ability groups, each classroom had to combine "at least two distinct ability groups" reflecting a diverse range of abilities.[38]

With the second grade issue resolved, settlement was quickly reached for grades three through nine. Here, the parties accepted a version (with some additional safeguards) of a provision in a written proposal the board had made in March, which at that time had contributed to the impasse in negotiations. Class-wide ability grouping would be limited to three categories per grade, and classes within each category must reflect the minority/non-minority population of students in that category. Selection would be based on recognized objective, nondiscriminatory instruments, such as standardized reading tests, but for mathematics instruction "categories were to be reorganized based on recognized objective, non-discriminatory *mathematics* tests" (emphasis added). It was also agreed that "teacher judgment" could supplement the objective tests whenever such judgment would result in greater integration. This provision reflected OCR's (especially Flannery and Graham's) belief that teacher judgment, if free of bias, was potentially the best means for grouping students.[39]

In sum, the agreement between the board and OCR on racially identifiable or isolated instructional settings is exceedingly complex and difficult for both the public and the system's teachers and administrators to understand. Requirements differ by grade level. Distinctions among and within the sets of requirements frequently depend on undefined terms (for example, "educationally compelled") or on heavily loaded technical language (for example, "objective reviewable nondiscriminatory criteria"). Important areas of variation in the basic requirements are permitted, as long as they are approved by school officials and based on "documentation."[40]

The sheer complexity of the agreement raises immediate questions about the feasibility of implementing it. However, if the agreement were fully implemented, it would accomplish several aims. First, what was probably the most tracked school system in the country now would eliminate homogeneous groupings of kindergarten and first grade classes and restrict the practice for grades three through nine. Second, the agreement would eliminate the inappropriate use of tests, particularly standardized reading tests. Third, it would allow leeway for teacher judgment whenever it would have the incidental effect of increasing integration. Finally, and perhaps most important, the investigation would cause high-level board officials to reconsider deeply ingrained practices and assumptions about the effectiveness and fairness of multilevel ability grouping. The board already had recognized and begun correcting segregatory practices which it readily acknowledged to have no educational justification (for example, organizing classes by bus routes). And it had taken on a serious commitment "to implement special efforts to raise the achievement level of students in the lower or lowest achievement groups" when the groupings were racially identifiable.

### Incentives for Settlement

Unlike the faculty employment negotiations, the student services negotiations never came close to brinkmanship. The incentives for settlement were more subtle and complex, particularly with regard to the influence wielded by the sanctions available to OCR. The agency's drastic threat of the imminent loss of CETA and ESAA grants was not repeated in this set of negotiations. Tatel had set a tone with the board of fairly consistent optimism that deferral and the threat of a basic cutoff of Title VI funds would be avoided. On the other hand, it was well known that if no agreement was reached by the summer, OCR would have to begin to consider the deferral of $44.2 million.

Nick Flannery's assessment that New York City did not provide an ideal legal setting for extending the southern precedents on ability grouping practices undoubtedly influenced OCR's moderate position. There was more reason for OCR to be concerned in this second set of negotiations that its position might not prevail in court.

Of perhaps greater immediate concern to OCR, however, was its awareness that implementation was the overriding issue in these negotiations. Ability grouping was such a complex and difficult activity to monitor that achievement of significant gains for minority children was highly dependent on the board's acceptance of and serious commitment to any requirements it formally adopted. In various ways, Schonhaut continued to remind OCR that it could not accomplish much by the promulgation of a "Volstead Act."

Although there was a certain amount of resentment on OCR's side toward the board's continual allusion to feasibility arguments, nevertheless OCR had to give weight to the idea, as Flannery puts it, that "perception can be reality." That is, if the school system believed that it was signing an agreement it could not live with, infeasibility would become a self-fulfilling prophecy.[41] Flannery suggests that the experience of forcing the board's negotiators to come up with detailed descriptions of the practices that had resulted in disparate impact statistics persuaded them to agree to more remedial changes than they would otherwise have accepted. For his part, Schonhaut says that the negotiating process educated OCR to the workings of the system and exposed the inappropriateness of much of the agency's position. In the final analysis, Schonhaut says, the agreement was as strong as it could be. Flannery, on the other hand, has lingering doubts about whether more stringent requirements might have been feasible.

## COMPLIANCE

Whereas the first agreement on employment issues was quickly denounced by many teacher and civic groups, the student services agreement prompted angry reactions from the minority group interests. One month after the agreement was signed, AFC organized a meeting which was attended by representatives of about one dozen such groups. The impetus for the meeting was a memorandum Martin Gerry had prepared which denounced his successors' settlement. "The letter of agreement," the memorandum began, "represents little more than a promise by the school system to comply with the law and a tacit acceptance by OCR of both the continued segregation of hundreds of thousands of minority children in low level ability groups and the continued disparate treatment of minority children under the student discipline system."[42] Both in his memorandum and in an oral presentation at the meeting, Gerry particularly attacked the provisions of the agreement relating to racially identifiable instructional settings. He alleged that it was unprecedented for OCR to accept a plan that neither compensates for widespread past discrimination nor establishes meaningful procedures to prevent future discrimination.[43] Gerry's memorandum ended with a call to arms for the public interest bar: "The OCR-Board of Education letter of agreement sanctioning massive civil rights violations within the schools of New York City, if unchallenged, is likely to destroy much of the legal progress made in the last fifteen years to eliminate racial discrimination within the nation's schools. The agreement represents, in short, *Plessy* v. *Ferguson* at the classroom level with an added guaranty of curricular inequality." There are no indications, however, that there was any substantial or sustained follow-up to this call.[44]

Since 1978, OCR's regional office has conducted somewhat routine monitoring of the classroom segregation and discipline provisions. In both areas, a full yearly cycle of monitoring should have included the following phases:

1. Board of education gathers school level data.
2. Delta Research Corporation processes data.

3. OCR forwards Delta report to board.
4. Board responds to OCR regarding problem areas identified in the Delta report.
5. Through interchanges and meetings, OCR accepts explanations of statistical disparities and/or the parties agree on corrective actions.

OCR has never fully completed this anticipated annual cycle, although it has gotten further along in some years than in others. The high point was between September 1979 and September 1980[45]; during this period, several communications were exchanged and OCR met both with board staff and (separately) with minority group advocates to try to systemize its assessment of the responses prepared at the school level and to obtain a better understanding of problems which might be indicated by the discipline statistics. The low point in monitoring was reached in the 1980–1981 school year, when OCR did not even renew its contract for automatic data processing services; consequently, data gathered by the board of education was never analyzed.

The statistical information that has been accumulated in the past few years, although perhaps not fully analyzed, still is informative. The numbers indicate that the agreement may have led to significant improvements in the area of classroom integration. At the same time, however, the discipline statistics indicate that there may be widespread discriminatory patterns in student suspensions.

### Ability Grouping and Classroom Segregation

The revised letter of findings on student services issues had found that during the 1975–1976 school term there were more than 1,900 racially identifiable classrooms. According to the Delta Research Corporation report for 1978–1979, the first school year following the agreement, this number had been reduced to 365. In the following year, Delta reported a further decrease to 142.[46] Taken at face value, these statistics represent a dramatic decrease in within-school segregation. Nevertheless, surprisingly little attention has been paid to this issue by either outside organizations or the press; OCR's regional office has received few, if any, pertinent inquiries.[47]

These favorable statistics, of course, did not free OCR from its obligation to investigate the causes of the remaining suspected instances of racial isolation. It appears, however, that the regional office has not had the resources necessary to digest the voluminous and rather unsystematic reports prepared at the school level to justify the remaining isolated classrooms.[48] Its difficulties in this regard are, of course, exacerbated by the problem of an ever-changing educational environment. Although the original data are based on ethnic surveys conducted at the end of October, by the time the information is processed by the central board, sent to Delta, and tabulated, it is April or May. Still later, when the schools send explanations about questionable patterns, the school year is over or nearly over, and instructional groupings have been disbanded. Obviously, this process does not allow time either for follow-up visits by OCR or for application of specific remedies.

### Discipline Practices

As noted above, the agreement on student services issues established a new reporting mechanism for student suspensions, which was set forth in a board policy statement.[49] The statement explained that the board and OCR would undertake statistical reviews of suspension data, and "(w)here there is a disproportionate rate of suspension . . . an explanation will be required from the schools."[50] On a semiannual basis, principals would record suspensions on a "School Tally Sheet and Report."

The first report generated by Delta Research Corporation under this system revealed marked statistical disparities in the suspension rates of minority students as compared with nonminority students. During the first semester of the 1978–1979 school term, it was found that 126 junior and senior high schools and 61 elementary schools fell into the suspect range. In September 1979, the chancellor sent a letter to officials responsible for suspensions in these 187 schools, asking them to review the OCR data and to inform him (1) whether the statistics were correct and (2) if so, why the disparities occurred. If the official determined that "the discipline policies and practices operational in the district at present might possibly produce discriminatory patterns of suspensions," he or she was expected to provide a corrective plan.[51]

At the end of November, the board sent OCR an official response to the first Delta report. The response took issue with OCR's statistical methodology, complained that the explanatory information received by the board from the community district and high school superintendents was "anecdotal and extremely comprehensive," and then described ten main categories of responses.[52]

The issue of suspension practices, unlike ability grouping, was of keen interest to local advocacy groups, particularly AFC. At AFC's request, three of its staff members met with OCR's Regional Director Charles Tejada and members of his staff early in December 1979. Tejada gave AFC a copy of the board's response and criticized it as inadequate in several respects.[53] However, he explained the limited leverage available to OCR as long as it was operating under the monitoring provisions of the agreement, as contrasted with a compliance investigation or enforcement proceedings. Tejada invited AFC to provide further input in this area, and he reminded the AFC representatives that outside parties could act independently of OCR by bringing a private court suit.[54]

In January 1980, an OCR regional staff person met with several board staff members to try to bring to bear some of OCR's (and AFC's) criticisms of the board's response. The focus of the meeting was to establish categories of acceptable responses to data showing disparate impact.[55] Throughout this meeting and in its correspondence with the board, OCR never claimed that the suspension statistics established a legal violation. However, it insisted that its statistical methodology was, under the agreement, valid as a triggering mechanism; if disparities could not be explained adequately, the board was obligated to take corrective action.

There is no record of any substantial follow-up after the January 1980 meeting. Required follow-up reports and data analyses were not completed systematically.[56] An additional complication was indecision in Washington. In 1975, Martin Gerry had raised an uproar among state and local school officials by issuing a national policy directive on reporting of disciplinary actions.[57] Ever since, discipline reporting had been "under a cloud" at OCR. When the Reagan administration took office, with its philosophy of minimizing federal regulation, the discipline reporting issue was put strongly "on hold." Under these circumstances, OCR's regional office in New York lacked policy guidelines and political support for following up problems that might be revealed by a complete analysis of discipline statistics in New York City.[58] Thus, compliance monitoring of the agreement remained problematic. The implications of these implementation difficulties will be analyzed in detail in chapter 8.

# PART THREE

*Analytical Perspectives*

The story of the New York City Review, as recounted in the preceding chapters, is a mosaic of complex issues, intriguing personalities, and dramatic political developments. In and of itself, the narrative is a useful record of school reform initiatives on egalitarian issues in New York City over the past decade. In addition, as indicated in the Introduction, the New York City Review, if subjected to a tripartite analysis, can advance understanding in the areas of egalitarian ideology, implementation, and institutional comparisons. And, by interrelating these three distinct, but complementary, analytical perspectives, we can attain a more profound understanding of the complex social reform process.

Accordingly, our analysis and conclusions concerning the significance of the events recounted in the preceding chapters will be set forth in four separate chapters. In chapter 7, we will subject the case study data to an ideological analysis. Specifically, we will consider the extent to which the OCR negotiation process succeeded, where legislative and judicial attempts had not, in reconciling the conflicting equality of opportunity and equality of result strands of the American egalitarian ideology.

The implementation analysis of chapter 8 discusses why an apparently successful reconciliation of ideological elements in the written agreements was not consistently achieved in practice. The discussion will focus on how problems of goal ambiguity, organizational processes, and political factors affected implementation. Comparative data from the other cities included in the Big City Reviews will also be utilized to develop hypotheses on how successful implementation of an agreement of this sort can be effected.

In chapter 9, the comparative institutional analysis will further probe the significance of administrative policymaking by approaching the administrative policymaking process as a form of "pragmatic-analytic policymaking," in contrast to the "rational-analytic policymaking" of the judicial process and the "mutual adjustment policymaking" of the legislative process. Comparisons among administrative agencies, courts, and legislatures in the areas of interest group representation, fact-finding abilities, and remedial mechanisms lead, in the final section of the chapter, to proposals for new conceptual approaches to separation of powers issues.

Finally, in chapter 10, the three lenses through which the case study was viewed will be brought into common focus through an assessment of the extent to which the Big City Reviews can be considered an overall "success" or "failure."

# CHAPTER SEVEN

# THE EGALITARIAN
# IDEOLOGICAL PERSPECTIVE

Egalitarian ideology in America, as noted in chapter 1, reflects a dynamic tension between opposing ideological poles. The equality of opportunity pole is rooted in the basic American commitment to individual liberty. But, especially in the last twenty-five years, counter pressures pushing for practical remedies to overcome entrenched patterns of discrimination have bolstered the equality of result view. Neither Congress nor the courts have either reconciled these competing ideological strands or provided consistent egalitarian policies or principles to guide OCR's Title VI compliance review activities.

Thus, a key question this study has sought to answer is how may an administrative agency enforce civil rights laws when the egalitarian mandate at the core of those laws is undefined? Will the agency develop greater ideological coherence than Congress and the courts? If so, what will be the content—and implications—of that ideology? The detailed case study of the New York City Review provides direct answers to these questions. The administrative implementation process in this instance did produce greater ideological consistency—and this consistency reflected significant blending of opportunity and result components.

We noted in chapter 1 that the equality of opportunity and equality of result positions constitute differing, yet complementary, strands of a fundamental American egalitarian ideology. In most situations, the political dynamic tends to enhance temporarily the influence of adherents of one of the schools, sparking a counter reaction from the opposing camp and raising the level of confrontation and controversy accordingly. In such circumstances, a legislature or a court normally must take a policy or principle stand favoring one side or the other—or, as discussed in chapters 2 and 3, it avoids deciding the highly charged aspects of the issues altogether. Rarely are the conditions ripe for balanced accommodation between the two camps. They were here. The New York City Review's administrative process produced a balanced ideological result because it promoted an open dialogue between adherents of the opportunity and result perspectives and allowed the complementary aspects of the ideological strands to merge into two compromise agreements.

The New York City Board of Education had articulated a classic equality of opportunity point of view. Unlike some southern school districts, whose motives in arguing for freedom of choice could be considered tainted, New York City's commitment to the removal of barriers to individual advancement was deep-rooted and strongly articulated over the years. Chancellor Anker, the board's chief spokesman, represented the best of the equal opportunity school: he took pride in having lived in an integrated neighborhood, in having sent his children to integrated schools, and in having been principal of an integrated high school. Especially in the absence of any judicial findings of discriminatory intent, the New York City officials forcefully pressed the equality of opportunity position in the negotiating process.

By way of contrast, OCR tended to reflect a basic equality of result perspective. As a "line" agency which deals on a daily basis with practical mechanisms for remedying discrimination, it tended naturally to move in a result-oriented direction.[1] The persistence of this tendency throughout various changes of personnel and political administrations is indicative of an inherent institutional orientation. Once an agency like OCR has turned its attention to an issue, it cannot easily retain its institutional legitimacy if it routinely deals in the kinds of generalities, inconsistencies, or avoidance behaviors that frequently are utilized by Congress and the courts.[2] To carry out its nationwide enforcement functions, it must articulate uniform, relatively consistent ideological standards— and standards that can prove effective in practice.

The particular legal mandate of OCR strongly magnified these institutional tendencies. It was charged with enforcing civil rights laws—the most ideologically charged regulatory responsibility imaginable. Unlike Congress and the courts, which were accountable to a mélange of interests, OCR's constituency was essentially civil rights advocacy groups, which tended "to invest every claim with the moral aura of a constitutional right."[3] Operating in such a climate, OCR personnel could not help but be imbued with some degree of moral intensity and ideological fervor. Furthermore, this ideological momentum was not offset by an ongoing interrelationship with the institutions being regulated, an important factor that, in other regulatory agencies, serves to temper regulatory zeal with a sensitivity to the interests and problems of those being regulated. As a distinct civil rights enforcement agency separated from HEW's program divisions, OCR was strictly accountable for eliminating discrimination promptly and effectively. Consequential effects on educational programming—including services provided to minority and disadvantaged students—were of concern, but fundamentally they were "somebody else's" responsibility.

Thus, the initial stances of OCR and the New York City Board of Education reflected strongly contrasting ideological positions. However, as the discussion in the previous two chapters has indicated, by the time the negotiating process got under way, a variety of incentives for settlement induced both sides to engage in serious bargaining. The setting was ripe for achievement of compromises that could reconcile the competing egalitarian perspectives: neither side had disproportionate leverage to compel a full capitulation from the other, and both sides knew that an agreement had to be reached. Analysis of the substance of the compromise agreements on the two main issues involved in the New York City Review, faculty assignment and student ability grouping, will reveal the extent to which such an ideological reconciliation was achieved.

## FACULTY ASSIGNMENT

It is ironic that racial balance of school faculties, one the few areas potentially subject to Title VI's jurisdiction in which

Congress explicitly sought to limit administrative oversight, became the major issue in the implementation process of the Big City Reviews. Section 604 of the Act precluded Title VI enforcement of employment practices, "except where a primary objective of the federal financial assistance is to provide employment." However, it was recognized, even in the congressional floor debates, that this limitation on jurisdiction would not apply where racial discrimination in the employment or assignment of teachers had a direct, detrimental impact on the educational opportunities of students.[4] In practice, this "exception" came to consume the whole rule.

In the deep South, where a failure to integrate school faculties would impede the achievement of any valid freedom of choice plans and would in itself constitute a flagrant perpetuation of a dual school system, faculty segregation practices clearly "infected" student opportunities in this manner. Maintenance of segregated faculties perpetuated the image (and the fact) of "black" and "white" schools and denied students of each race access to role models and individual talents of teachers of the other race.[5] However, in northern school systems, which did not have a history of state-supported *de jure* segregation, the legal significance of patterns of racial imbalance in faculty assignments was far from obvious. Nor were the educational policy implications obvious—some minority advocates, after all, argued in favor of assigning black "role model" teachers to black schools.[6]

Nevertheless, OCR's Big City Reviews did not distinguish between patterns of *de facto* segregation in the North and patterns of *de jure* segregation in the South. In 1972, when OCR commenced the initial stages of what was to become the Big City Reviews, its position was in keeping with the decisions of a number of courts which had ruled that *de facto* segregation in the North was a constitutional violation, no different from *de jure* segregation in the South.[7] However, by 1974, when the reviews officially got under way, the Supreme Court had announced in *Keyes* v. *School District No. 1*[8] that some indicia of discriminatory intent would be necessary to find a constitutional violation in a northern school district.

And by 1976, when the First Letter of Findings was issued, the Court's decision in *Washington v. Davis*[9] had strongly emphasized the distinction between *de jure* (intentional) discrimination and *de facto* (disparate impact) discrimination.

Despite these important developments, Martin Gerry's 1976 letter of findings under Title VI focused almost exclusively on statistical patterns of racial imbalance and the need to remedy them. His sole citation of legal authority for the radical remedies he sought was the Supreme Court's earlier ruling in *Swann*, in which faculty desegregation requirements evolved as part of the overall remedies for eliminating classic southern *de jure* segregation.[10]

If the statistics on faculty imbalance cited in the first letter (82 percent of the minority teachers were assigned to schools having 84 percent or more minority enrollments; 15 percent were assigned to schools where minority enrollment was under 35 percent) had been presented in the context of a classic student desegregation suit against a northern city,[11] they would have constituted important evidence of possible discriminatory intent, and, if a constitutional violation had been found, they certainly would have justified a faculty reassignment order.[12] But there had been no such case in New York City. Neither OCR nor the Justice Department would initiate a student desegregation suit, of course, because any effective remedy in New York City would have required busing, in violation of Nixon administration policies. Consequently, neither OCR nor the board could confidently predict whether these teacher assignment statistics, if examined as a separable issue, would be found by a court to establish a *prima facie* case of violation of Title VI or the Constitution.[13]

Under these circumstances, although OCR certainly had plausible grounds for alleging legal violations,[14] its neglect of the *de jure*/*de facto* and intent/impact distinctions was striking. A major explanation for this posture could be that OCR's fundamental result-oriented approach, growing out of its experiences in dismantling southern school desegregation, became so firmly entrenched as a firm agency ideology that it was little influenced by major shifts in constitutional doctrine.

The consistent result-oriented perspective of OCR was strongly evident in the remedies it insisted upon for rectifying the racial imbalances in faculty assignments. Both Gerry and Tatel[15] sought to apply the 5-percent *Singleton* standard on an immediate basis with mandatory transfers of however many teachers would be required to promptly meet that goal. It was not considered relevant that the *Singleton* remedies were devised by a Mississippi court in response to a flagrant attempt to resist the Supreme Court's mandate to dismantle a dual school system, whereas in New York City the faculty assignment patterns resulted, at least partially, from preferences of the minority communities and from the workings of the alternative hiring system devised by community control advocates.[16]

The fundamental equality of opportunity perspective of the New York City Board of Education[17] was in direct contrast to OCR's result orientation. Chancellor Anker deeply believed that the differences between racial imbalance patterns in the South and those in New York City were fundamental and significant. He maintained that the New York City Board of Education had sought for years to promote, rather than impede, racial integration. Whatever inequities existed were caused by forces outside the board's control.[18] Because Anker and the board members thought they had no legal or moral responsibility for these patterns, they had difficulty understanding how OCR could seek to hold them responsible for ensuring immediate statistical results, results which might have a detrimental impact on faculty morale and on the educational stability of the system.

The board's formal response to OCR's First Letter of Findings reflected a classic equality of opportunity perspective. It would not be pinned down to "specific guaranteed results." Nevertheless, it was willing voluntarily to take steps that might remove certain unintended barriers that were impeding minority employment or the transfer of minority teachers to predominantly white schools. Specifically, the board was willing to implement a new voluntary transfer program, to increase the pool of available positions in predominantly white

districts by speeding up retirements and leaves, and to eliminate use of subjective criteria, including "role model" concepts, in the assignment of supervisory personnel. The board
also offered to explore possibilities for improving the validation of teacher examinations and to seek legislation to eliminate rank ordering of eligible lists,[19] as long as no hiring
quotas were involved.

The final agreement that emerged from the intensive negotiations on these issues compromised the disparate oppor-
tunity/result ideological perspectives of the board and OCR
into a package which, we believe, constituted rare balancing
of the competing ideological strands. The integrity of both of
the ideological positions was maintained.

In chapter 2, we defined "equality of result" in terms of
overcoming societally caused economic or social disadvantages by eliminating the effects of past discrimination through
structural reforms. The faculty integration agreement clearly
was result-oriented in this sense. The linchpin of the agreement
was the 5-percent *Singleton* standard, which had been the key
mechanism utilized in the South to ensure the implementation
of major structural reforms that would dismantle the established segregative patterns in faculty assignments. Adoption
of the 5-percent *Singleton* standard here meant that the New
York City Board of Education also would need to implement
major structural reforms in its hiring and transfer practices
to achieve compliance—or show reasonable good faith movement toward meeting these numerical goals. Similarly, the
commitment to validate licensing exams, to merge examination lists, to eliminate rank ordering of eligible lists, and to
undertake a labor pool study which would form the basis for
judging affirmative action hiring efforts in the future constituted thoroughgoing remedial devices which, if implemented,
would lead to prompt, statistically measurable results.

At the same time, however, the agreement also reflected the
core definitional hallmark of "equality of opportunity," that
is, an emphasis upon individual effort and accomplishment.
Most notable in this regard was the fact that, unlike all previous OCR faculty integration agreements, there was no pro-

vision explicitly requiring mandatory teacher transfers in New York City.[20] Although acceptance of the *Singleton* standard would commit the board to adopt a number of major changes in its hiring and assignment practices, there would be no direct compulsion of individual teachers. The board would be allowed to implement a variety of "voluntary" mechanisms, such as recertification, recruitment, and special assignment, some of which would provide incentives for transfers by enhancing individual opportunities for teachers of all races. On the testing issues, although major reforms were to be undertaken, the core commitment to a meritocratic examination system was maintained; in fact, improved validation of the testing procedures would improve the system's ability to measure and promote in accordance with individual competence.

In essence, then, the faculty integration agreement in New York City adopted an approach based on numerical guidelines that held substantial promise of achieving significant results without becoming a rigid quota system. Confrontational buzzwords were avoided, and the provisions of the agreement focused instead on practical commitments which would protect individual advancement and merit-oriented selection, while simultaneously ensuring significant structural reform and meaningful affirmative action to overcome the effects of past discriminatory impact. In sum, each party felt that its minimum goals were satisfied, without its being forced to yield critical principles.[21] For these reasons, the New York City agreement can be said to represent a successful reconciliation of the competing opportunity/result strands of American egalitarian ideology.

### STUDENT ABILITY GROUPING

Classification practices that place children in separate tracks for instructional purposes, purportedly on the basis of their abilities, have been, and continue to be, widespread throughout the United States. By and large, the practice has had segregatory effects, with minority children tending to cluster in the lower tracks and white children in the upper tracks. Like busing, a challenge to tracking is a sensitive political issue, because it is perceived to threaten the access of white middle-class students to "quality education."

The classic court decisions banning such tracking practices arose in the deep South at the height of judicial involvement in the dismantling of dual school systems. In this context, ability grouping practices were a transparent subterfuge to maintain racially identifiable classrooms within a technically "desegregated" school.[22] Only in one reported case have the more complex student tracking practices prevalent in northern and western cities been scrutinized.[23] This was the 1967 case, *Hobson v. Hansen*,[24] in which Judge Skelly Wright banned the ability grouping practices in Washington, D.C. on the grounds that the tests used to classify the children had not been validated, and that the purported remedial aspects of the tracking program were not working. No court, however, has applied the *Hobson* precedent to invalidate any other major school tracking system, although (as the New York City Review case study has shown) similar patterns of non-validated student classification practices that have a detrimental impact on minority children undoubtedly exist in many other urban school systems.[25]

These issues were pursued by OCR, however, in its New York City student services review.[26] The statistics that had emerged from Gerry's extensive investigations, and that were reaffirmed in the new administration's revised letter of findings, were disturbing: thousands of minority children were being relegated to lower tracks on the basis of vague or subjective criteria, and without any apparent educational justification. Although there were under Title VI no direct legal precedents for assessing these practices, OCR referred to the standards set forth in its ESAA regulations,[27] and it insisted that any student ability grouping be justified by "clear and convincing evidence" of educational necessity, the results of which could be "validated by test scores or other reliable objective evidence."

This result-oriented emphasis on compelling educational justifications (which would eliminate most tracking) was countered by the board of education's insistence that its ability grouping practices were based on "merit" considerations geared to maximizing opportunity for students at all ability levels. Having conducted a detailed survey of all the classrooms whose groupings were questioned by OCR, the board initially claimed that 96 percent of the assignments were educationally justifiable, and the 4 percent that were questionable, which would be promptly eliminated, hardly provided a basis for a finding of intentional segregation.

These student ability grouping issues were resolved with less confrontation than the faculty assignment issues were. This was undoubtedly because investigations undertaken during the course of the negotiating process led the board to admit that a much more pervasive pattern of invalid practices existed than it had realized: children were being assigned to separate tracks based on bus routes, their ability to tell time, or other extraneous factors. Furthermore, the board's own negotiators tended to admit the validity of research findings indicating that, at least in the elementary grades, homogeneous grouping patterns had little apparent connection with enhanced student achievement. In short, the equality of opportunity perspective was difficult to defend after it had been demonstrated that traditionally defined "opportunities" were not really being made available.

The final agreement reached by the parties largely incorporated the burden-shifting, result-oriented approach of the ESAA regulations, but with specific, individualized adaptation to the local situation. Reflecting OCR's skepticism about the educational benefits of tracking and its detrimental impact on racial minorities, separate grouping was totally eliminated at the kindergarten level and minimized in the first and second grades. However, extensive ability grouping was permitted to continue in the upper grades, consistent with the board's educational view that this practice promoted individual achievement.

The ability grouping agreement as a whole, and in each of its specific details, represents an artful balancing of the opportunity/result perspectives. Individual opportunity ability grouping would be permitted—but it would be limited to three categories per grade, with each class reflecting the racial proportions of students in that category. Selection would be based on meritocratic tests, but these must be objective, nondiscriminatory, and directly related to the subject area being tracked. Individualized exceptions would be permitted based on "teacher judgment,"[28] but only where such judgment would result in greater integration.

The ability grouping agreement, then, like the faculty assignment agreement, represented a significant reconciliation of opportunity/result egalitarian concepts. In this case, the result proponents (OCR) were able to convince the opportunity proponents (the board) that their abstract commitment to individual opportunity was belied by the facts. The board, therefore, agreed to tighten its standards in a way that would both promote greater minority representation in the higher tracks and allow for statistical monitoring; for its part, OCR accepted a pragmatic approach and did not press for the radical "result" of totally eliminating the tracking system, which had been the upshot of the *Hobson* case.

The fact that the ideological inconsistencies in anti-discrimination law left open by Congress and the courts were, to a significant extent, reconciled through the administrative enforcement process in the New York City Review can be seen as having either broad or limited significance for the fundamental issues of American egalitarianism. On the one hand, maintenance of the integrity of both the equality of opportunity and the equality of result strands in a compromise agreement substantiates the point, discussed in chapter 1, that there is an overarching American egalitarian ideology: our case study findings indicate that, as compared with the more stringent ideological divisions of European cultures, the opportunity/result perspectives in America are, indeed, distinct but complementary aspects of an overall total ideology.

On the other hand, the very uniqueness of the achievement of this ideological reconciliation raises serious questions. Both of the New York City agreements involved issues that were peripheral to the core desegregation concerns of civil rights advocates. Inter-school student desegregation, not faculty integration or intra-school student assignment, historically has been the major concern of civil rights advocacy groups. Indeed, it might well be said that the success of the New York City agreement can be traced precisely to the fact that there was less political controversy and less partisan confrontation engendered by these "peripheral" issues. Although mandatory teacher transfer plans and the elimination of student tracking elicit serious opposition from some school system professionals and some parents, these issues clearly do not generate the level of intense confrontation raised by forced integration or busing of students.[29]

Is the ideological reconciliation reflected in the New York City agreements, then, an isolated phenomenon of little general significance? We think not. The fact that ideological reconciliation can be achieved if highly charged partisan pressures are moderated is a significant finding.

Further consideration of how such propitious political conditions can be promoted, however, will involve additional analytical perspectives. The moderate ideological synthesis emerging from the OCR/New York City experience was directly related to the implementation process through which it emerged. Thus, an implementation analysis of that experience also is necessary to aid us in understanding the extent to which the tenuous ideological balance reflected on paper in the New York City agreements led in practice to meaningful compliance and effective reform. Such an implementation analysis will be provided in the next chapter.

# CHAPTER EIGHT
# THE IMPLEMENTATION
# PERSPECTIVE

Implementation has been defined as "the process of creating or attempting social change through law."[1] Social science analysis of implementation is premised on an assumption that the precise policy goals set forth in a statute will not necessarily— or even probably—be fully realized in practice. Thus, for the implementation analyst, careful case studies of what happens *after* a law goes into effect are as important as understanding the law's stated purposes. The outcome of the New York City Review dramatically illustrates this point. Clearly, the drafters of Title VI could not have anticipated that the statute, written with an eye on classic *de jure* school desegregation problems in the South, would lead to innovative approaches to integrating faculties and reducing intra-school tracking practices in the North.

Implementation is an ongoing interactive process that can be viewed as encompassing virtually every event and action that influences a legal outcome. To organize this complex field, and to provide findings that can be usefully compared with those of other relevant case studies, we have, as discussed in the Introduction, organized our implementation analysis around three critical variables suggested by previous writings in this field, namely "goal ambiguity," "organizational process," and "politics." This chapter, therefore, will analyze the history of the New York City Review and the agreements it produced in terms of these three key variables; it will then conclude with some reflections on the factors which appeared to promote or impede "successful" compliance with the terms of the remedial agreements.

## GOAL AMBIGUITY

In their classic study of implementation, Jeffrey Pressman and Aaron Wildavsky summarized the implementation process this way:

> A new agency called the Economic Development Administration (EDA) is established by Congress. The EDA decides to go into cities for the purpose of providing permanent new jobs to minorities through economic development. ... Congress appropriates the necessary funds, the approval of city officials and employers is obtained, and the program is announced to the public amidst the usual fanfare. Years later, construction has only been partially completed, business loans have died entirely, and the results in terms of minority employment are meager and disappointing. Why?[2]

The focus of their study was on understanding why EDA's specific statutory goal—to develop new jobs for minorities—had not been accomplished. Although numerous intervening factors and their interrelationships had to be considered, the EDA study, like most other implementation analyses, at least began with a clearly defined, fundamental policy goal against which later developments could be measured. Such a baseline policy goal was lacking, however, in the case of OCR civil rights enforcement in northern cities.[3]

The agency's Title VI enforcement responsibility was to ensure that all beneficiaries of federal funding programs were receiving "equal" educational opportunities. The congressional debates had reflected clear policy standards for southern school desegregation; "equality" in that context meant the dismantling of dual school systems and the prompt integration of white and black students. Operating under this clear standard, OCR formulated explicit desegregation guidelines which, used in conjunction with the strong stance of the courts in *Swann, Singleton*, and other cases, achieved impressive results: in the years between 1964 and 1972, the proportion of black students attending all-black schools in the states of the "old confederacy" declined from almost 100 percent to less than 10 percent.[4]

In regard to the more conceptually problematic segregatory patterns in northern urban areas, however, Congress articulated no clear policy goals either on the face of the statute or in the legislative history.[5] Such "second stage" concerns were simply too speculative at the time of the passage of Title VI. Given this leeway, and the additional, fundamental ambiguity in the underlying equality of opportunity/equality of result ideologies, OCR had no clear policy parameters for approaching Title VI compliance issues in the North. In this regard, the Big City Reviews model could be seen as an attempt to develop a comprehensive approach to the issues. In fact, however, the model was more eclectic than comprehensive. Compliance standards were derived from OCR's desegregation guidelines and judicial mandates in the southern cases; congressionally created eligibility criteria under the ESAA funding statute; guidelines and court decisions in bilingual and employment testing areas; and innovative new concepts that took into account the politics of busing and the administration's "southern strategy."

This eclectic package of standards and methods did not prove viable in practice. By the time serious negotiations got underway in New York (and the other big cities), most of the issues identified in the original investigative model had been sharply modified or eliminated altogether; others were dropped by the wayside en route to the agreements.

The disintegration of the Big City Reviews issue agenda in New York City is charted in Table 1, which juxtaposes the main investigative categories in which allegations of discrimination were made with the areas actually covered in the two agreements.

Table 1 shows that of thirteen original issue areas (which included about fifty subareas), the major New York City agreements[6] provided remedies only for racially identifiable settings (ability grouping) and for discipline problems. Also striking is that the bulk of the time, effort, and controversy in New York City revolved around employment issues—

TABLE 1
## Issue Changes in the New York City Review

| Original Issues[a] | Issues Covered by First Agreement | Issues Covered by Second Agreement |
|---|---|---|
| *Comparability* | | |
| Instructional expenditures | | |
| Nature and extent of instructional services and programs | | |
| Allocation of state and local funds | | |
| Allocation of human resources | | |
| *Student Assignment* | | |
| Racial identifiability of instructional groupings | | Elimination of clearly inappropriate criteria for classroom organization and limitations on use of "ability grouping" criteria |
| Racial impact of special education classification practices | | |
| *Access to Educational Opportunities* | | |
| Criteria and practices regarding availability of and admission to specialized classes and high schools | | |
| Appropriateness of instructional approaches and curricular materials for language-minority children | | (Remedies parallel to *ASPIRA* Consent Decree set forth in separate agreement[b] with OCR) |
| Sex stereotyping in vocational programs | | |
| *Non-Instructional Activities* | | |
| Disciplinary practices | | New record keeping and monitoring |

| Original Issues[a] | Issues Covered by First Agreement | Issues Covered by Second Agreement |
|---|---|---|
| | | procedures concerning racial impact of suspension |
| Guidance services (channeling by race, national origin, sex) Psychological services Access to extracurricular activities | | |
| | | Handicapped students on waiting lists to be offered placements promptly. |
| | Faculty integration (5-percent range) Validation of teacher licensing exams in accordance with "accepted professional standards" Commitment to seek changes in state law on merger of eligibility lists and abolition of rank order appointments Commitment to achieve minority representation consistent with minority proportion of qualified labor pool Affirmative action program to increase number of women in supervisory service | |

[a] The "original issues" as defined here are a synthesis of the main issues raised in the original Issues Outline and the statement of findings in the EES letter of January 18, 1977.

[b] "Plan to Comply with Title VI CRA also Submitted as Part of Application for Waiver of Ineligibility" (Board of Education of the City of New York, September 15, 1977).

teacher hiring and assignment—which had not even been part
of the original model. This pattern was repeated in Chicago,
Philadelphia, and Los Angeles.[7]

Why did Gerry's attempt to fill the statutory policy void
with an innovative policy agenda fall so short of the stated
goals? It is tempting to attribute this occurrence to the change
of presidential administrations and to the fact that Gerry was
forced to depart before his project could be completed.[8] But
even during Gerry's tenure, the original issue agenda had begun to disintegrate as attention shifted from student services
to employment issues. (In Los Angeles, serious investigation
of the original issues was never even initiated.) Thus, a fuller
explanation is needed for this striking and consistent pattern
of extensive concentration on faculty assignment issues that
had not been part of the initial Big City Reviews model.

Some factors were particular to New York City. Originally,
Gerry had consciously rejected inclusion of the sensitive employment issues in order to avoid a head-on confrontation
with the teachers' union. These issues were added to the New
York City investigation after the NAACP and the Civil Liberties Union had lodged formal complaints about the impact
on minority teachers of layoffs resulting from New York City's
fiscal crisis. These complaints were filed at a point in the
*Adams* and *Brown* cases when OCR needed to show sensitivity to its complaint-processing responsibilities; consideration of these claims was dictated further by Gerry's implementation strategy of enlisting the support of local civil rights
groups. (Personality factors also may have been relevant—
Gerry apparently was outraged when he learned the details
of the New York City hiring system.)

Yet, the dominance of the employment issues in all four
cities still requires a more fundamental explanation. We believe the critical factor was Title VI's basic goal ambiguity.
Although one might expect that this ambiguity had left an
open field for ambitious policy innovation, in fact, the void
could not be filled by new initiatives which lacked strong
precedent or political support. Instead, the implementation
process gravitated to more familiar, well-entrenched policy

IMPLEMENTATION PERSPECTIVE

grounds. In contrast to the novelty of many of the issues on Gerry's initial agenda, there was a long history of successful integration of teaching staffs pursuant to policy standards delineated in southern desegregation guidelines, ESAA regulations, and court decisions.[9]

The availability of clear policy standards in the southern desegregation guidelines and ESAA regulations provided a center of gravity for OCR's operations, despite changes in political administrations. This dynamic explains Tatel's follow-up on the employment issues, as well as his emphasis on classroom segregation problems from among the numerous student services issues. Classroom segregation was an area in which there was substantial judicial experience in the South and detailed administrative criteria in the ESAA regulations.[10]

In short then, the experience of the Big City Reviews indicates that if a deliberate policy perspective is not engrafted into the statute by the legislature, the administrative agency charged with the implementation of that policy tends in practice to emphasize the issues, priorities, and compliance approaches with which it is most familiar. In other words, the legislative decision to leave basic policymaking to the enforcement agency had, at least in this circumstance, the rather surprising effect of promoting the continuation of established issue priorities, rather than of creating a viable open field for new policy concepts and initiatives.

ORGANIZATIONAL PROCESS

The organizational structure of OCR in the early 1970s was not designed for comprehensive, agency-initiated investigations of major cities. Consequently, Martin Gerry decided to create a new organizational structure for this project. Basically, the Big City Reviews team was an executive level operation reporting directly to Gerry in the Washington headquarters and circumventing the regular regional OCR structure. Additional independence from existing organizational routines was effected by obtaining extensive services from outside data processing and consulting firms. Gerry also sought to build direct contacts with local constituency organizations (which he hoped to merge into a permanent network) that might fight at the grass-roots levels for OCR-initiated reforms.

Gerry's organizational structure also incorporated a heavy "systems management" approach to implementation. The Issues Outline and the exacting protocols drawn up in conjunction with data processing experts established a hierarchical information structure which would channel investigative activities, perceptions, and the accumulated data into predetermined analytical models established by the central plan.

This heavily structured systems management approach may, to some extent, have fallen of its own weight. It is questionable whether an enforcement agency like OCR could sustain a capability to pursue simultaneously thirteen substantive issue areas and fifty subareas, even if other factors had not modified or deflected the initial goals. (Goal ambiguity, of course, exacerbated this problem; if the review had been based on strong, consistent policy standards, a higher level of commitment by the staff to the new approach may have been sustainable.)

Multiplicity of issues diffuses attention and makes it difficult to communicate a plausible set of findings and remedial proposals, both to school boards and to the general public. And, since effective implementation requires long-term involvement and sustained commitment both by OCR and by local advocacy groups, it may well have been self-defeating to adopt an agenda that would exceed the probable long-range resources and attention span of OCR and these groups.

Therefore, it probably was inevitable that after Gerry departed (and perhaps even if he had not) more normal organizational routines would begin to reassert themselves. Indeed, prior to the appointment of a new director in 1977 and a clarification of political direction from the new administration, Acting Director Albert Hamlin, a career professional in the office, initiated a reconsideration of both letters of findings

and called upon outside experts to provide an objective overview of the state of the review.

When Tatel took office as director, he intensified these efforts toward organizational normalcy. His orientation was
nearly the opposite of Gerry's. Whereas Gerry had tried to
carve out a special Title VI enforcement project in an agency
that was otherwise operating under political pressures to slow
down its enforcement efforts, Tatel began with the assumption
that he was part of a pro–civil rights administration, and that
all enforcement activities should therefore be integrated into
the regular channels of a revitalized agency.

The expenditure of resources by OCR on the Big City Reviews had to be brought into line with other priorities. A
decision was made to limit the number of issues to be pursued
and to press as expeditiously as possible those which remained. It may well be that some of the issues that were
dropped from the second letter or that were deemphasized in
the negotiations could have been reworked into convincing,
substantial allegations. But Tatel would not allocate OCR's
resources and its political capital to pursuing the myriad EES
issues.

The extended time frame of the monumental Big City Reviews project created additional problems. The longer it takes
an implementation process to unfold, the greater the number
of "decision points" that have to be crossed, and the more
opportunity there is for variables to deflect the process from
the original goals and expectations.[11] In this case, four years
passed between the initiation of the Big City Reviews and the
promulgation of the first New York City letter of findings.
Six years passed before the New York City negotiations were
completed. During these time intervals, new factors (including
the political developments discussed in the next section) interfered with a straight pursuit of Gerry's original issues
agenda.[12]

The legal orientation of a civil rights enforcement process
further exacerbates the problems caused by delay in implementation, because the compliance concepts with which the
agency is dealing are highly susceptible to shifts in doctrine

or emphasis in newly decided court decisions. Martin Gerry's letters of findings and his testimony in the *Caulfield* case indicate that he was heavily influenced in the initial stages of the Big City Reviews by the Supreme Court's decisions in *Lau* v. *Nichols*[13] and *Griggs* v. *Duke Power Co.*[14] In both of these cases, the Court held defendants liable for discriminatory impact regardless of their intent. At that time, the Court seemed to be moving in a result-oriented direction. As indicated in chapter 2, however, a countertrend began to emerge shortly thereafter. In *Keyes*,[15] *Milliken*,[16] and *Davis*,[17] the Court increasingly emphasized a need to establish proof of discriminatory intent. Gerry tried to resist the implications of these cases, and his continuing insistence on a statistical/impact approach, despite a changed legal atmosphere, created additional tensions with the board of education and the teachers' union.[18]

The changed legal climate, however, did strongly influence David Tatel. Sensitive to the implications of *Davis* and the recent school desegregation cases, he became skeptical about Gerry's emphasis on statistical proof of disparate impact for establishing legal liability in the broad variety of issues involved in the Big City Reviews. He insisted that the proof accumulated on all these issues be reconsidered from the perspective of whether sufficient evidence existed to establish discriminatory intent in a court case. Apparently, despite the enormous amount of evidence accumulated during the four-year investigatory process, OCR's data on many of the initial issues failed to meet the more demanding standard, and OCR thereafter did not pursue them vigorously.[19]

In addition to providing insights as to why the Big City Reviews methodology and agenda could not be sustained throughout the enforcement process, factors related to organizational process help to explain OCR's result-oriented ideological stance, as discussed in chapter 7. The predominant thrust of Title VI's legislative history, as discussed in chapter 3, reflected equality of opportunity perspectives. The ESAA, by way of contrast, was largely result-oriented, since it provided monetary rewards to school districts that would commit themselves to achieving specified integrative results. Because the same agency was vested with enforcement responsibilities for both statutes, the standards of the two Acts virtually became merged in the field. Neither OCR investigators nor school district respondents focused on the differences between the two statutes during the day-to-day enforcement activities. Practically, if not legally, compliance with Title VI often came to mean compliance with the detailed ESAA standards.[20] Thus, ESAA's specific, result-oriented standards tended to compensate for Title VI's policy ambiguity, pulling OCR's priorities in their direction.

## POLITICS

Political factors strongly influenced the origins and the substance of the Big City Reviews approach. Not surprisingly, as the political environment changed, the direction and the content of OCR's position were modified. The Big City Reviews were, in large measure, a response to administration and congressional pressures during the early Nixon years for "even-handed" civil rights enforcement in the North. The seemingly incongruous posture of the Nixon administration pushing for strong result-oriented remedies becomes readily understandable when one considers that the targets of this affirmative action thrust were New York, Philadelphia, Chicago, and Los Angeles, the Democratic-controlled, major urban centers whose "hypocrisy" on civil rights issues might thereby be exposed.

The Ford administration's de-emphasis of Nixon's "southern strategy" and the Carter administration's reversion to more classic civil rights concerns necessarily caused major shifts in both the manner and the substance of the issues being pursued in the big cities. Tatel surely had no interest in "embarrassing" the urban centers controlled by the Democratic Party. On the contrary, he knew that because of their political ties (including those of the teachers' unions) any positions OCR staked out must have strong legal, evidentiary, and political justification.

Consistent with the new administration's commitment to pursuing classic student integration issues on a nationwide basis (and despite continuing congressional anti-busing strictures), Tatel decided to reorient the compliance thrust in Chicago and Philadelphia, where no letters of findings had yet been issued, toward preparing for possible student integration suits. Accordingly, regional OCR officials were advised that the remaining student services issues were now of low priority. In New York City, where the Second Letter of Findings had already been issued, OCR continued, after reconsideration and review, to pursue those items for which there appeared to be substantial evidence that could hold up in court. Those issues with less compelling evidentiary (or political) substance, however, were quickly dropped during the negotiations.

The change in political administrations also influenced the manner in which the negotiations were conducted. In both New York and Chicago, the cities where the issues were most complex and the boards offered the most resistance, the new Democratic regime hired experienced private civil rights attorneys as special consultants to represent OCR in the negotiations. This decision apparently was informed both by a desire to resolve quickly these long-festering matters with an infusion of high-level talent and by lingering suspicions about the loyalty and/or competence of the local OCR staff people inherited from the Republicans. The consultants' position outside the normal agency lines of command and their professional reputations gave them a semi-independent status that insulated the negotiating process from day-to-day political pressures. This insulation appeared to have a salutory effect (at least from OCR's perspective) in that it maintained the momentum of the process and the pressures toward a quick conclusion.

Political factors also were highly significant when problems of noncompliance with the terms of the negotiated agreements came to a head under the Reagan administration. In June of 1982, the Department of Education indicated that it was prepared to take a firm stand to support enforcement of the 1977 Agreement, despite the board's claim that it was unworkable and unfair. This decision apparently reflected a continuing, long-term institutional commitment, despite the various changes of administration, to enforce strongly faculty integration mandates in all parts of the country. Senator D'Amato's intervention at this point was forceful and effective. He publicly claimed credit for using political leverage to bring about a withdrawal first of OCR's enforcement actions and, five months later, of the agreement itself, in favor of a dramatically weakened new document.[21]

Local political factors also were important throughout the review process. The prime such factor in New York City was the influence of the United Federation of Teachers, probably the most powerful teachers' union in the country. New York City was the home base for Albert Shanker. As national president of the American Federation of Teachers and a vice-president of the AFL-CIO, Shanker's influence on major educational policy issues in New York City was enormous.

Shanker's presence provides the most direct explanation for why New York City's faculty assignment agreement permitted a gradual phase-in period and omitted any specific references to mandatory teacher transfers, the highly controversial requirements that OCR managed to force on the boards in the other three cities. As Shanker himself reportedly said in declining to consent to a proposal found acceptable elsewhere, "New York is not Chicago."[22]

In Chicago, the teachers' union also had initially opposed the mandatory transfer concept, and it tried "to deal on every level"[23] to block it. In the end, however, the union backed off from its opposition to the transfer policy and concentrated its efforts on ensuring that the final agreement would protect the fundamental seniority concepts it had won in its contract.[24] (On these seniority issues, its views did largely prevail.) In both Los Angeles and Philadelphia, the teachers' unions were not even involved in the initial stages of the negotiations.[25] They were advised of the basic plans only after the fundamental points, including mandatory transfers, had been decided. Both the United Teachers of Los Angeles and the Philadelphia Federation of Teachers then accepted the forced transfers as a given and concentrated on working with the boards on implementation methods that would protect seniority and other prerogatives of their contracts.[26]

Developments in New York City also were influenced by the board's political sensitivity to allegations of civil rights violations. Although Gerry charged New York City with deeply engrained institutional patterns of discrimination verging on racism, the board's attitudes toward civil rights issues cannot fairly be equated with those of southern school districts which actively opposed school desegregation efforts. For decades, the New York City Board of Education had prided itself on being in the vanguard of liberal civil rights reforms, and board officials deeply resented OCR's charges of racial discrimination. The board's sensitivities also were influenced by a fear that racial tensions, which had erupted in the late 1960s around the issues of community control and school decentralization but which had diminished over the course of the interceding decade, might be activated again. For these reasons, the board was inclined to seek an accommodation with OCR,[27] if at all possible.

The board was particularly willing to be conciliatory on the hiring/examination issues which, for a number of years, had been an embarrassment to it. New York City's woefully low proportion of minority teachers and supervisors had become a focal point in recent years for investigative committees, advocacy groups, and court decisions. In the early 1970s, in comparison with cities like Chicago, Los Angeles, and Detroit, where 30 to 50 percent of the teachers were minorities, only approximately 10 percent of New York's teachers (and 1 percent of its supervisors) were black or Hispanic. The New York City Board of Education tended to blame the quasi-independent Board of Examiners for this situation, and it supported a variety of legislative and litigation efforts to reform or eliminate the Board of Examiners system. Thus, on the examination issues, the board's position was not far from OCR's; it was the teachers' union and the Board of Examiners which put up most of the resistance to OCR during the negotiations.

A final political factor that should not be overlooked was the influence of the particular individuals who played the major roles. The New York City Review case study illustrates that the outcome of any implementation "game" is strongly affected by the views and personalities of the main actors.[28]

Gerry's influence was, of course, paramount. As already noted, it was universally acknowledged that "the review was Martin Gerry's baby." He created a unique project in terms of the strongly result-oriented egalitarian approach that skirted the busing problem and the new applications of systems analysis and automatic data processing to civil rights compliance monitoring. Gerry's intense commitment to this project persisted throughout his tenure: the Big City Reviews, and especially its New York component, was run directly from Washington because of Gerry's personal interest in overseeing every aspect of its operation. To ensure that his project could not be fully abandoned by the new administration, Gerry worked feverishly to issue the Second Letter of Findings almost as President Carter was marching down Pennsylvania Avenue in his inauguration parade.

David Tatel's background as an experienced civil rights attorney and advocate also had important implications for the outcome of this process. He recast the issues into a more traditional civil rights framework. At the same time, he added a new dimension of professionalism and separation from day-to-day political pressures through his decision to retain experienced civil rights attorneys as outside consultants in the negotiations. Tatel and his consultant for the New York City negotiations, Nick Flannery, placed a high priority on establishing an atmosphere of mutual reliability and goodwill between the parties. They believed that a successful agreement needed to be based more on personal relationships and mutual commitments than on mandatory compulsory pressures. The structure of the final agreements (and their strengths and weaknesses at the compliance stage) clearly reflected these perspectives.

On the board's side, Irving Anker's personal commitment to equal opportunity/integration causes explains much of both his initial resistance to Gerry's charges, which he considered inflammatory and unfair, and his willingness to respond to the Tatel administration's more moderate stance (especially on the ability grouping issues), by working cooperatively with OCR to overcome admitted flaws in the system.

The outcome of the first agreement, however, was probably more influenced by the personality of Bernard Gifford, the system's black deputy chancellor. Gifford influenced the process both through his personal role in the early stages and through the substance of the evidence and arguments he amassed on the compliance issues in his famous report, some of which, like his statistics on the NTE alternative hiring system, tended to refute the board's major defenses.

Gifford basically saw OCR as an ally in his long-standing attempt to achieve civil rights reform from within the school system. Although he, like the chancellor and the board, was committed to a basic equality of opportunity outlook, he was sympathetic to OCR's allegations about hiring and faculty integration; indeed, he had been a leader of the forces within the board which had been attempting to reform the Board of Examiners system. Gifford's advocacy within the ranks of the board of positions supportive of OCR clearly had the effect of neutralizing much opposition which otherwise might have been generated. For example, the legal analysis contained in an appendix to the Gifford Report tended to accept Gerry's readings of the major cases, his assumptions that southern precedents automatically applied in New York City, and his discounting of the significance of *Washington* v. *Davis* and of the shifting legal trends in 1976. If a separate legal analysis had been undertaken by the board's Office of Counsel or the city's Corporation Counsel, the board might have taken a firmer line and even risked going to court on some of the issues.

In sum, then, it was perhaps inevitable that most of the issues delineated by Martin Gerry at the outset of the Big City Reviews process would fall by the wayside because of their inherent lack of policy substance and because of the complexity of the organizational processes put into play. The fact that agreement was reached, nevertheless, on some major substantive issues, including faculty integration and student ability grouping, may be attributable to two factors: the strongly established policy standards, derived from southern precedents and ESAA guidelines, which OCR was able to invoke on these issues and the play of various political issues, including the board's civil rights sensitivities, its relationship with the UFT (and with the Board of Examiners), and the influence of various individual personalities. The fact that agreement was reached on these particular issues, however, was not the end of the story. The extent to which the particular reforms anticipated by the agreements were actually put into practice is a further critical part of the implementation process, to which we will now turn.

## COMPLIANCE

A federal civil rights enforcement agency like OCR is limited in its long-range ability to monitor compliance agreements by its resources and by the consistency of its political support. For these reasons, intervention by OCR can be expected to result in significant, permanent reforms[29] only if the compliance agreement is (1) a mandate for immediate, statistically definable changes or (2) a mutual commitment with the school district to common reform objectives (especially when qualitative educational reforms are involved[30]).

The faculty assignment agreements in Chicago, Los Angeles, and Philadelphia were examples of agreements of the first type; the New York City agreement on student ability grouping to a large extent reflected the second model. By and large, these agreements can be said to have been implemented successfully. By way of contrast, the first New York City agreement, which fit into neither mold, still was substantially unrealized five years after it was signed; at that point, it was "renegotiated" in a manner that essentially formalized the reality of noncompliance. On the other hand, OCR's negotiators in Chicago, Los Angeles, and Philadelphia seemed well aware of the elements needed for a successful agreement. Repeatedly, they told the boards of education and the unions that they would accept almost any plan or any methods for achieving faculty integration—as long as the agreement guaranteed immediate compliance with OCR's specific statistical goals. Indeed, the agreement actually adopted in Chicago was almost precisely the same plan that the board of education had proposed and OCR had rejected ten months earlier. The critical difference in the final version was that the accepted faculty ratios would be put into effect at the start of the 1977 school term rather than over a period of years—and on a definitive mandatory basis. Similarly, in Los Angeles and Philadelphia, OCR made clear that any mechanisms for seniority, voluntary inducements, and educational programming exceptions on which the board and the union could agree would be acceptable, as long as the requisite ratios were achieved immediately at the start of the next school term.

The agency's firm attitude prevailed in each of the three cities, and massive mandatory teacher transfer operations were quickly put into place. In both Chicago and Philadelphia, during the short interval of the summer vacation months, intensive computer programming of the relative seniority rights of all teachers in the system had to be accomplished, letters of reassignments sent out, and appeals against the reassignments processed.[31] In all of the cities, the mandatory transfer process created chaos, confusion, and substantial resentment. Joan Raymond, the assistant superintendent in Chicago, called the process "a monstrosity."[32] In Los Angeles, "parents marched, teachers resigned, people cracked up. There was a big rise in workman's compensation claims."[33] According to an official analysis, prepared by the Los Angeles Unified School District, of the impact of the faculty integration plan over a five-year period, the OCR agreement (which resulted in the transfer of more than 8,500 teachers, including both voluntary and mandatory transfers) led to a doubling of teacher resignations and retirements in 1977–1978, a tripling in 1978–1979 and, between 1976 and 1978, a doubling of attrition among teachers being transferred and a rate of teacher turnover at mid-city schools averaging 35 to 40 percent.[34]

Yet, whatever the cost in terms of teacher morale and systemic stability, OCR clearly accomplished its goals of realizing specific proportions of faculty integration in the three cities where the mandatory transfer policy was promptly put into effect. Substantial compliance with these statistical norms also has been maintained in these cities in subsequent years.[35]

The New York City faculty integration plan, of course, permitted a three-year phase-in, and it did not specify mandatory teacher transfers. Five years after the signing of the agreement, the established goals were far from being met. Only nine out of thirty-two community school boards, for example, had realized the *Singleton* standards.[36] Lack of effective implementation probably cannot fairly be attributed to any pervasive pattern of board of education intransigence or noncooperation. To the contrary, Chancellor Macchiarola and his staff devoted a considerable amount of effort and ingenuity to devising new mechanisms, such as a teacher reserve system, to promote integration.[37] Rather, consistent with the basic tenets of implementation analysis theory, it appears that the very passage of time permitted a large number of events to interfere with the compliance process and to render the original goals and expectations (if they could ever have been met without mandatory transfers) almost impossible to achieve.[38] With the passage of time, resistance to a possible mandatory transfer fallback substantially increased—to the point that political pressures finally led to the renegotiation of the entire mandate.[39] And OCR's inability to sustain consistent and effective monitoring procedures also tended to undermine the likelihood of success.[40]

In contrast to the strong pattern of noncompliance with the first agreement, however, the indications are that there has been at least some success in achieving the goals of the ability grouping provisions of the second agreement.[41] The latest figures show a decrease in unjustifiable racially identifiable classrooms from over 1,900 to 142. This rapid reduction appears to reflect the fact that the ability grouping agreement was based on a consensus on goals among OCR and board of education officials, a consensus which has been accepted as an operating premise of the system. The lack of political visibility of and controversy over the issue, and the relatively straightforward manner in which monitoring can be conducted by statistical reviews also undoubtedly has aided compliance in this area.[42]

In the final analysis, ten years after initiation of "the largest civil rights investigation of a public education institution ever undertaken," the expenditure of millions of dollars and thousands of man-hours and the deflection of attention from numerous alternative enforcement areas seem to have resulted in successful reforms in New York City in only one of the thirteen original issue areas (and, in the other three cities, in effective compliance with established faculty integration ratios). Do these results justify the costs involved?[43] Or is it unfair to measure success only in terms of immediate "objective results"?[44]

It is difficult to answer these questions definitively, especially from the perspective of implementation analysis of a single case; such an analysis can lead to conclusions that are either too grounded in the facts of the particular case, on the one hand, or too abstract if they are taken as broad generalizations, on the other. We believe it important, therefore, to evaluate OCR's performance from an additional perspective, by relating it to that of other governmental agencies which have undertaken similar attempts at egalitarian reform of large-city schooling practices. Such a perspective will be provided by the comparative institutional analysis presented in the next chapter, after which we will return to the problematic issue of evaluating "success" in the concluding chapter.

# CHAPTER NINE

# THE COMPARATIVE INSTITUTIONAL PERSPECTIVE

The comparative institutional perspective is based on the premise that the traditional separation of powers model of the functioning of American government no longer fully reflects reality. Legislatures, courts, and administrative agencies all play unprecedented roles in the expanded governmental activities of the post–New Deal era. In regard to the executive branch, Douglas Yates has written: "Bureaucracies assume a legislative role when they interpret weak congressional mandates. . . . They play an executive role as they make substantive decisions about the innovation and implementation of public policies. They play a judicial role, especially in the regulatory sphere, when they try appeals of their own decisions and hold hearings to resolve conflicts about administrative law."[1]

Our case study of OCR's New York City Review provides a fertile data base for analyzing the actual contemporary functioning of one important type of executive branch agency—the regulatory enforcement office—from a separation of powers perspective. It allows us to consider the extent to which the agency carries out functions that would be considered legislative or judicial under the traditional model, as well as the implications of these new functions. In our previous work, *Educational Policy Making and the Courts*, we devised a methodology for making empirical assessments of the functioning of the legislative and judicial branches.[2] In this chapter we will utilize that framework to evaluate OCR, an executive branch agency.

The EPAC methodology categorizes the separation of powers issues under four headings: (1) policymaking, (2) interest group representation, (3) fact-finding, and (4) remedies. This approach provides both a comparative institutional perspec-

tive on the "legitimacy" of each branch's activities in relation
to the traditional separation of powers model and a functional
analysis of each branch's "capacity" to undertake certain
tasks. Further discussion of the meaning of each of the categories will be provided at the beginning of each of the sub-
sections which follow.

## POLICYMAKING

A central issue in the contemporary separation of powers
debate is whether the legislature's core traditional function,
the making of policy, can be shared with or delegated to the
other branches. Classical democratic theory holds that the will
of the majority expressed through legislative deliberations
must be the exclusive repository of the "popular sovereignty,"
and that any attempts to remove the fundamental policymaking prerogative from the people assembled, or their elected
representatives, would be a violation of the social contract.
Thus, policymaking by activist judges in the interpretation of
the laws, as well as policymaking by activist administrators
in the execution of the laws, creates serious problems from
this perspective.

In our study of the role of the courts in educational policymaking, we concluded that in the overwhelming majority
of cases, judicial decision making was undertaken in accordance with established constitutional or statutory "principles,"
rather than in accordance with the policy preferences of the
litigants or of individual judges. We did note, however, that
the domain covered by constitutional and statutory principles
has expanded dramatically in recent years, because of both
the broadened scope of the constitutional principles enunciated in interpretive decisions of the Supreme Court and social
trends affecting society as a whole.[3] From a functional perspective, we also concluded that judicial deliberations tended
to reflect a "rational-analytic" decision-making mode (defined
in terms of judgments reached and supported by fact and
analysis in the light of explicit standards of judgment), in
contrast to the "mutual adjustment" processes (defined in

terms of the reconciliation of positions of competing interest groups through political bargaining) that tend to predominate in legislative decision making.[4]

Clearly, in the New York City Review, OCR carried out substantial policymaking functions that were at odds with traditional separation of powers notions. Because of the lack of clear egalitarian principles or policies in Title VI or in the applicable court cases, OCR was, in essence, "delegated" with the responsibility of defining basic egalitarian concepts in the course of its enforcement of Title VI. Although this delegation was indirect (in that it stemmed from a definitional void in the statute, rather than from an express congressional mandate), the significance of the equality issues at stake and the fact that the standards were formulated at the operational level, free from the constraints of traditional administrative rule making or adjudication, greatly enhanced OCR's policymaking role, as compared with that of traditional administrative agencies[5] or even of other civil rights enforcement agencies.[6]

A key question that must be considered, then, is what type of policymaking was conducted through such an administrative implementation process? Did it closely resemble the legislative mutual adjustment process, in which competing political pressures are balanced to reach compromise solutions? Did it resemble the more focused, deliberative rational-analytic process of the courts? Or did the OCR experience reflect a conceptually distinct policymaking approach?

From one perspective, the OCR policymaking process appeared similar to the legislative mutual adjustment model.[7] The basic agreements were hammered out in lengthy negotiations that exhibited many of the political accommodations, logrolling, and give-and-take of the legislative process. Indeed, the balanced accommodations that simultaneously gave OCR its 5 percent *Singleton* standard, the board of education its avoidance of mandatory transfers, and the UFT assurance of continuation of the merit appointment system could be said to reflect a paradigmatic mutual adjustment model.

However, on closer analysis, the divergences from the mu-

tual adjustment model seem more significant than the similarities. Unlike a classic legislative setting, the parameters for
decision making here were relatively fixed. The parties were
not free to advance their own priorities and to move the deliberations in accordance with their relative political influence
and savvy. The issues on the agenda were established by
OCR's principled perspectives, the participants in the process
were those invited by OCR, and the political pressures that
could be exerted were indirect and attenuated, reflecting primarily episodic national political influence rather than direct
ongoing local political input.[8] In addition, the focused nature
of the administrative negotiating process required a definite
outcome within a finite time period, a factor which affected
both the relative positions of the parties and the nature of the
ultimate outcome.

Was OCR's administrative policymaking closer, then, to the
principled, rational-analytic decision making of the courts?
Clearly, OCR's initial stance was to enforce basic principles
and to apply consistently to local fact patterns the basic compliance standards that had been developed from national judicial precedents (like *Singleton*) and prior OCR "cases" (Chicago, Los Angeles, and Philadelphia).[9] The agency's
commitment to the strict rational-analytic application of established principles to the case at hand might be said to have
been even stronger than that of the courts, in that OCR's
leaders tended to have an intense commitment to basic ideological goals which was not easily subject to modification or
compromise.[10] As Jeremy Rabkin has put it, "the civil rights
perspective seems to preclude the weighing of countervailing
claims."[11]

Yet, the analogy to judicial rational-analytic processes cannot be carried too far. In this case, principle was accommo-
dated to practical, grass-roots realities in a manner that differs
significantly from what tends to occur in the judicial process.
Although in institutional reform litigations there is much practical input in the negotiation of remedial decrees, these negotiations usually take place only at the remedial stage, after
the basic principles have been defined by the judge's initial

liability decision.[12] With OCR, however, the basic "law of the case" was developed during the negotiating process itself. This introduction of grass-roots considerations at the basic policymaking stage provides a further understanding of how, as discussed in chapter 7, the equality of opportunity and equality of result ideological strands could, in the OCR process, be balanced pragmatically in a manner that does not tend to occur in court cases.

The ability grouping negotiations and ultimate agreement illustrate the differences in the formulation of policies between administrative and judicial processes. The legal requirements of the tracking issues were formulated through a relatively non-adversarial negotiating process, which was heavily influenced by considerations of both general educational theory and specific practices in the field—as well as by anticipated grass-roots reaction to proposed remedial mandates. Although OCR did not compromise its principled commitment to end the disparate impact of tracking practices on minority students, it was able, unlike the court in *Hobson v. Hanson*,[13] to understand and accept "educational justifications" for the continuation of a flexible ability grouping system, and it was even able to moderate the strict requirements of its own ESAA regulations to permit exceptions to "objective" placement assignments on the basis of "teacher judgment."

In essence, then, OCR's administrative/regulatory process formulated principles and policies in a manner that is distinct from both the prototypical legislative and judicial modes. It was more ideologically consistent and more committed to solving the problem at hand than the "unstructured pulling and hauling" of the legislature, but it also was more politically sensitized, pragmatic, and flexible than the "structured process before a neutral decision arbiter" of the courts.[14] The term *pragmatic-analytic* can best be used to describe this type of administrative policymaking and to contrast this decision-making process with the mutual adjustment decision-making mode of the legislature and the rational-analytic decision-making mode of the courts. The pragmatic-analytic mode proved well suited for reconciling highly charged egalitarian policy issues in this case.

## INTEREST GROUP REPRESENTATION

A key question concerning the legitimacy of a policymaking process is whether the interests of all those likely to be affected by a decision are sufficiently taken into account. Traditionally, the legislature has been viewed as the prime arena for articulating public policy issues, because all affected parties and interests are thought to be represented in its deliberations.

Although opponents of judicial activism often assert that few of the concerned parties participate in the judicial process, our EPAC study did not support that view. Rather, we found both a great breadth and a broad variety of interests represented in court proceedings. Furthermore, our comparative legislative/judicial case studies indicated that on similar public policy issues virtually the same parties that appeared before the courts also participated in the legislative deliberations, and all of the viewpoints raised in one forum also were raised in the other.[15] Thus, the courts as policymakers appeared to be as open to broad, varied citizen input as was the legislature.

By way of contrast, a striking aspect of the OCR compliance process in all four of the locales included in the Big City Reviews was the absence of direct participation by representatives of the myriad groups that clearly had a stake in the outcome. In New York, the teachers' union was the only additional participant in the negotiations.[16] In the other cities, not even the union representatives were permitted to take part directly in the bargaining.[17]

The issue of interest group involvement in OCR policy deliberations is complicated by the agency's multiple roles. In its role as a governmental regulatory agency, OCR can be viewed as having an obligation to act impartially, and not on behalf of any particular interests. But as a civil rights enforcement agency, OCR is, to some extent, expected to act like a prosecutor. The traditional prosecuting model would hold that a complainant who initiates a case should not expect to participate further in the investigation, presentation of charges, settlement negotiations, or trial. Thus, even in its prosecuting role, OCR would not feel bound, like a legislature or a court, to involve affected interest groups directly in its policymaking process. However, OCR's primary reference groups, the minority group beneficiaries of federally funded programs, would not easily accept either of these models. On both the local and national level, the representatives of these groups expected OCR to act as a direct advocate for their interests.

Given the complexities of these role expectations, it is not surprising that, over the course of the New York City Review, OCR became estranged from every significant educational interest group in the city. In the beginning, the Big City Reviews model, although condemned by national civil rights organizations as a diversion from higher-priority enforcement activities, was greeted by New York City minority representatives with some interest. Gerry indicated that he wanted OCR to relate to the local groups as would a public interest law firm. The high point in this relationship came when Gerry responded to administrative complaints from the NAACP and the New York Civil Liberties Union and added to the agenda the employment discrimination issues that, until then, he had scrupulously avoided.

From that point on, however, minority interest groups became increasingly dissatisfied with their access to the process. They were shocked by Gerry's finding that the layoffs were not discriminatory, and they claimed that they had not been consulted by OCR in its data analysis. After Gerry left office, the local advocacy groups experienced one disappointment after another: the withdrawal of the student services letter, the exclusion of minority advocates from the employment negotiations, the dropping of many issues in the revised student services letter, and the failure to enforce vigorously the employment agreement.[18]

An integral part of this deteriorating relationship was a basic disjunction between the issue priorities of OCR and the local groups. Historically, hiring, rather than staff assignments, had been the main concern of the New York City civil rights groups. They had repeatedly instituted lawsuits and legislative action to reform the Board of Examiners; they had never raised faculty racial imbalance issues or challenged the assignment implications of the alternative hiring system (which, in fact, they favored). Similarly, no local advocacy group had ever raised the issue of student ability groupings.

Under these circumstances, there was a virtual consensus among the interest groups that their representation in the process was inadequate, and that their points of view were not fairly considered during the negotiations.[19] These perceptions of unfairness were intensified by the knowledge that the teachers' union had become a participant in the negotiations. In response, some of these organizations sought out the courts. Opponents of the teacher agreements began the *Caulfield* case and proponents, the *NYABE* litigation.

If, despite the traditional separation of powers model, administrative agencies like OCR are to continue to engage in fundamental policymaking, it would seem that more participation by affected interests, comparable to the opportunities available in the judicial and legislative processes, must be permitted. This, in essence, was the view of Judge Weinstein in the *Caulfield* case. He initially issued an order which would have invalidated the first agreement precisely because it had resulted from "secret, informal negotiations conducted exclusively by a handful of government officials."[20] Although Title VI and the HEW regulations nowhere specifically provided for participation by affected interest groups or for hearings regarding the terms of the proposed voluntary compliance agreement, Judge Weinstein ordered HEW to provide an appropriate procedure for public comment. He believed that "the huge power concentrations and the bureaucracies of our governments must not be permitted to be exercised secretly and arbitrarily. No matter how benign and well intentioned, those government officials who can, in practical effect, turn on or off the source of hundreds of millions of dollars, must conduct themselves with scrupulous regard for procedural protections . . . if people are to retain their faith in government."[21] On appeal, however, the Court of Appeals for the Second Circuit reversed Judge Weinstein's order. There was no basis, it held, for creating the right to a due process hearing where Congress had not provided for one.[22]

Even if later court decisions or statutory changes could reinstate Judge Weinstein's approach, a further practical problem which must be faced is precisely how increased interest group participation might be accomplished in this kind of process. Most interest group representatives in the OCR case study have recognized that granting them full "party" status had the danger of turning the negotiations into a "circus."[23] Consequently, they have spoken in terms of a more limited, ongoing consultative role.[24]

Such a consultative role might have served a number of purposes during the New York City Review. First, the groups could have provided otherwise unavailable information and perspectives on the specific issues under negotiation. Second, involvement would have lessened the level of misunderstanding and estrangement by acquainting groups on both sides with the hard choices and the considerations that went into the ultimate compromises. Third, participation might have promoted a commitment of the interest groups to the implementation process, and that, in turn, might have increased the chances for successful compliance.[25] Finally, at the least, participation might have avoided some or all of the *Caulfield* litigation, which consumed substantial time, energy, and resources at a critical period in the implementation process.[26]

## FACT-FINDING

Effective policymaking is dependent upon specific facts concerning the particular problem, its likely causes, and the probable impact of proposed remedies. Defenders of the traditional separation of powers model tend to assume a legislative competence in this area, emphasizing the broad scope of legislative hearings and the lawmakers' access to data and expert consultants. Courts, by way of contrast, are assumed to be limited in their ability both to gather all the relevant facts and to comprehend such complex social science data. Our EPAC data indicated, however, that the judicial discovery process (by which lawyers can request or subpoena any relevant documents) constituted an effective information gathering technique, and that judges tended to develop a variety of effective techniques for dealing with complex social science data. The comparative judicial/legislative case studies further revealed that the evidentiary records accumulated in the court cases were more complete and had more influence on the actual decision-making process than did the factual data obtained through legislative hearings, which tended in practice to be "window dressing" occasions organized to justify decisions made primarily for political reasons.[27]

If it is true that the judicial fact-finding capability is more extensive than that of state legislatures, the OCR/New York City case study indicates that the administrative fact-finding capability can be even more substantial than that of either of the other branches—at least when a commitment is made to undertake a major compliance investigation, as in New York City.

Unlike both the court and state legislatures, OCR did not depend primarily on attorneys or interest groups to generate its information. It mounted a substantial and impressive data gathering operation of its own. This operation included considerable manpower commitments and technological resources,[28] as well as significant powers of legal compulsion to require extensive record keeping and reporting by school districts.[29] Data gathering and information assessment was carried out in a variety of ways: original field investigations, collating of publicly available data sources, responses in negotiations, and preparation of and responses to findings and position papers.

Although it is difficult to fault the extensiveness of OCR's fact-finding processes in the New York City investigation,[30] criticisms were lodged concerning the quality of the data gathered and OCR's objectivity in its analysis. Clearly, OCR initially approached its data analysis tasks from a prosecuting perspective. The fundamental premise of the Big City Reviews methodology was that an urban school system controlled by white constituencies made decisions, consciously or not, that caused minority children to receive inferior educational opportunities. Since northern school systems—especially New York City—were adept at articulating nondiscriminatory policy reasons for programs which had discriminatory effects, the reviews were designed primarily to ferret out and correlate "objective" evidence of disparate treatment. In this way, the very methodology of the reviews reinforced the initial ideological perspectives of the OCR officials.

OCR investigators also were criticized for a tendency to approach the issues in overly abstract terms. As one Los Angeles school official put it: "They collect mountains of data. Especially computer programs. But their approach is like throwing material against the wall. What sticks, they look at."[31]

Despite these allegations, the actual use of the data in the pragmatic negotiating and decision-making process appears to have tempered any adversarial bias, and the data analyses that actually affected the decision-making process seemed to be objective and accurate. Indeed, in the *Caulfield* litigation, in which OCR's evidentiary findings were strongly attacked, its findings were corroborated by both the Gifford Report and by the reports of Stephan Michelson, an independent expert hired by the Justice Department. They also were accepted uncritically by an experienced judge with a national reputation as an evidentiary expert.[32] Specifically, the New York City Review undertook complex social science data analyses and supplied definitive answers to a number of significant, controversial educational questions (many of which had not been clarified during previous legislative and judicial encounters with these issues). Among OCR's evidentiary findings were the following:

1. The massive teacher layoffs caused by the fiscal crisis did not disproportionately affect minority teachers. This finding contradicted the common-sense view that minority teachers generally were "last in" and therefore

also "first out," a belief widely held by minority group advocates and school board officials alike.

2. Thousands of school children were placed in racially identifiable instructional settings. Many of these placements were unjustifiable on their face. Many others were the result of ability grouping practices that were educationally dubious at best. Although the board originally attacked OCR's findings, investigations by its own advisory panels caused it to accept many of OCR's determinations.

3. There were no striking disparities in the allocation of educational resources among predominantly minority and non-minority schools. This finding surprised Gerry and contradicted OCR's own expectations, as reflected in the detailed design of the comparability methodology.[33]

In short, it would appear that the fact-finding capability of the administrative agency is potentially superior to that of the legislature and the judiciary. However, it is not clear how often resources will permit this extensive investigative capacity actually to be mounted, or whether an inherent adversarial bias may, at times, distort the accuracy of its findings.

## REMEDIES

From the traditional separation of powers perspective, the area in which comparative competence of administrative agencies—and especially that of a civil rights enforcement agency like OCR—could be anticipated would be their remedial compliance mechanisms. Legislatures do not purport to engage in such activities (although oversight hearings and modification of statutory provisions in light of events could be said to constitute analogous functions). Courts do directly take on such responsibilities, especially in institutional reform litigations. Our EPAC study concluded that judicial remedial involvement in school district affairs was both less intrusive and more competent than is generally assumed, largely because school district officials generally participated in the formulation of reform decrees, with the courts serving as catalysts and mediators.[34] Also, we found the degree of compliance with these court orders to be relatively high.[35]

Comparing OCR's remedial capabilities with these prior findings about the courts, we would conclude that OCR's approach to remedies tends to be more comprehensive and effective when the agency obtains agreements which call for immediate, statistically measurable implementation (as in Chicago, Los Angeles, and Philadelphia). However, when an OCR remedial agreement permits phased-in implementation over a period of years (as in New York), its "staying power" appears to be significantly less than that of the courts; consequently, the degree of its compliance success is diminished.

Active participation by school district officials in the drafting of a court decree substantially enhances the remedial abilities of a court, which on its own lacks the institutional tools and expertise to undertake educational reform. Even better results are possible when an agency like OCR can supplement the input of local school personnel with its own resources and extensive experience in dealing with complex educational/civil rights problems. Moreover, as discussed previously, since pragmatic implementation considerations will have shaped the compliance standards adopted at the negotiated policymaking stage, those standards already are likely to be flexible and adaptable to the needs of the "field." Requests for modification of the decree or for a reconsideration of the "law of the case," which can create substantial delays or impasses in the remedial phases of court cases,[36] should occur less often with an administrative agreement.

Both of the remedial agreements which emerged from the New York City Review reflected these characteristics of sophisticated educational policy substance and flexible implementation sensitivity. The faculty integration agreement specified in advance the "educationally based program exceptions" which would be permissible, but it also set forth the types of supplemental mechanisms the board would be required to institute if it invoked such exceptions. The ability grouping agreement was structured in a complex, grade-by-grade fashion to respond to anticipated feasibility concerns; OCR's negotiators candidly acknowledged that they were influenced in this difficult area by a realization that perceptions of infeasibility could become a self-fulfilling prophecy if the concerns of those responsible for implementation at the school building level were not directly addressed.

Despite this sensitivity to the realities of implementation, the actual extent of compliance with the negotiated remedies in New York City was far from anticipated, especially in regard to the faculty integration agreement. This degree of compliance was in marked contrast to the substantially complete implementation of the comparable agreements in Chicago, Los Angeles, and Philadelphia. As was discussed in more detail in the previous chapter, the differential success rate of analogous agreements by the same enforcement agency must be attributable, at least in part, to the fact that the New York City agreement allowed for a three-year phase-in, while the understandings in the other cities required prompt compliance through immediate forced teacher transfers. The comparative institutional perspective can provide some further insights on this point.

Because of the court's perceived relationship to fundamental constitutional principles, its decrees—even when they are largely pragmatic, compromise documents—have an aura of principled legitimacy that promotes sustained compliance. Of equal importance is the court's functional staying power. Simply stated, courts, through their ponderous procedures, tend to maintain an active presence in a case over an extended period of time.[37] (This is one of the reasons why courts involved in institutional reform litigations are perceived as being highly "intrusive."[38]) As long as a court retains jurisdiction of a matter on its docket, attorneys for any of the parties may request a hearing to complain about implementation delays or unanticipated problems that may arise.[39] In addition, judicial decrees normally contain extensive reporting requirements which not only call for periodic data submissions by the defendent school districts, but also provide regular opportunities for ongoing judicial scrutiny.

An administrative agency like OCR lacks such inherent staying power. Its "docket" is greatly influenced by changes in political priorities and by shifts in the allocation of resources to new issues and new crises. In the New York City Review, OCR delayed taking any concerted action regarding noncompliance with the faculty integration agreement for years after it was clear that New York City would meet neither the 1979 interim goals nor the 1980 final goals; by 1982, when noncompliance had become blatant, the agreement was "renegotiated" to the point of virtual abandonment.

In regard to the second agreement, although there was a certain degree of ongoing monitoring of the ability grouping and discipline provisions by OCR's regional office, it lacked the resources and capability to analyze in any systematic way the data and explanatory information it had gathered. To the extent that the statistics obtained reflected improvements that had occurred, the process had been successful, but OCR did not demonstrate the required capacity for analyzing and acting upon the accumulated data.

Futhermore, even if OCR officials had been more diligent and effective in their monitoring activities, they could not have moved as promptly as a court to modify the agreement or to require the school district to comply promptly. The agency had no direct contempt powers comparable to those of a court. Its closest option would have been to request that the Justice Department commence a litigation to seek enforcement of the compliance agreement as a contractual obligation,[40] and the only alternative course of action would have been to recommence a lengthy process of investigation and threatened reinvocation of the Title VI deferral and fund termination proceedings.[41]

In short, then, a court, as compared with OCR, is better able to monitor compliance on a long-term basis and to respond to unforeseen developments that arise during the implementation process. An administrative agency's institutional capacities seem better geared to enforcement of reforms that can be effected on a quick, single-stroke basis.

If these conclusions are accepted, the question naturally arises as to when an agency like OCR is able to impose the type of immediate remedial mechanism that tends to maximize its remedial effectiveness. Agency officials apparently are aware of the superiority of such mechanisms: in Chicago, Los Angeles, and Philadelphia, school district pleas for more time to implement massive mandatory transfers in "an orderly fashion" were rejected by OCR officials, who appeared to recognize that delay would reduce the likelihood of achieving full compliance. Why were similar immediate measures not required in New York? Differences in the political climate, the personalities of the key participants, and other such factors clearly were involved, but we believe the critical point was the degree of leverage available to OCR to obtain its preferred approach, or, more specifically, the extent and credibility of the sanctions it could threaten.

There are two major sanctions available to OCR under Title VI:[42] to cut off all funds for existing federally supported educational programs (after completion of various compliance proceedings) or to defer new federal funding pending completion of compliance proceedings. Both of these sanctions were applied effectively in the South between 1964 and 1968.[43] In the North, however, these Title VI sanctions had less credibility. The failure of Commissioner Francis Keppel's earlier attempt to impose the deferral sanction in Chicago made a lasting impression on OCR officials. And the fund termination sanction, which could involve tens of millions of dollars (and would cause most harm to the very minority group students OCR sought to help), was perceived by most OCR officials (and also understood by many school personnel) as being too much of an "atom bomb" realistically to be put into effect.[44] By the time the Big City Reviews had gotten underway, in fact, OCR had not attempted to terminate funding for any school districts, North or South, for several years.[45]

One of the most interesting aspects of the Big City Reviews was the manner in which OCR essentially compensated for its practical inability to invoke the Title VI funding termination sanction by utilizing the more credible threat of denying eligibility for the lesser, but still significant, funding available under ESAA.[46] The power to declare districts ineligible for ESAA grants was transformed by OCR into a supplementary sanction which was relied upon repeatedly in Title VI negotiations. (Ironically, therefore, ESAA, which Congress had intended as a "carrot" to induce voluntary desegregation, became OCR's main "stick" for enforcing prompt compliance with Title VI orders.)

There is little doubt that the imminent threat of a loss of ESAA funding was the main sanction that led to acceptance of the strong mandatory teacher transfer agreements in Los Angeles and Philadelphia, and it was also a substantial factor in Chicago. In New York, the situation was otherwise. Both our interviews and questionnaire responses indicated that ESAA sanctions were more significant in New York City than the remote threat of a Title VI funding termination, but even the possible ESAA deferral or loss was not viewed by officials there as a calamity that had to be avoided at all costs. Because the New York City school system was decentralized, many of the community school boards who had applied for ESAA grants were able to obtain their funding by promising to meet the *Singleton* standards immediately. Thus, the New York City system, as a whole, was able to defuse much of the effect of the ESAA sanction by obtaining partial funding. A threatened loss of CETA funding, funding which was expected to permit the rehiring of 1,200 teachers, did influence the New York City board's willingness to reach agreement with OCR, but its impact was less significant than that of the ESAA sanctions in the other cities.[47]

Thus, to the extent that it may be judged desirable to enhance the ability of enforcement agencies like OCR to ensure prompt thoroughgoing remedial compliance, consideration must be given to providing the agency with plausible—not theoretical—sanctions comparable to a court's power to impose immediate, effective injunctive and contempt powers.[48] Of course, it is possible that enhancement of an administrative agency's sanctioning leverage may affect the pragmatic-analytic flexibility of the agreements it negotiates.[49] Assessing the comparative advantages and disadvantages of specific institutional functions and the impact of attempts to modify them is obviously a difficult endeavor, especially given the paucity of available empirical data. Nevertheless, because of the critical importance of these issues, we will offer in the next section some perspectives on the conceptual issues involved.

## SUMMARY PERSPECTIVES

Comparative institutional analysis attempts to confront head-on the problem of relating the traditional separation of powers model to contemporary realities. Although, even in its classic form, separation of powers was not meant to connote an absolute, rigid division of authority among the three branches of government,[50] critics argue that contemporary judicial and administrative agency activism exceeds any reasonable degree of "blending" intended by the founding fathers. Defenders of these new roles would argue that enhanced judicial and administrative activities are inevitable concomitants of expanded governmental activity in the post–New Deal era.[51]

However, unless a defender of contemporary judicial and administrative agency activism takes the position that the constitutional separation of powers framework is totally outmoded, we believe it incumbent upon him or her to justify these new roles in terms of a legitimacy theory that would fit current practices (or a modified version of them) within a conceptual framework that remains faithful to the founding fathers' basic institutional power-sharing concerns.[52] Comparative institutional analysis, which focuses on the actual functioning of contemporary institutions, would appear to be the logical starting point for any such undertaking.[53]

A theoretical framework for comparative institutional analysis has been provided by Neil Komesar in a recent article, entitled "In Search of a General Approach to Legal Analysis: A Comparative Institutional Alternative."[54] Komesar argues that all legal decision making involves a choice among imperfect decision-making institutions. Consequently, "in all cases, legal decision makers must consider the relative merits or attributes of the alternative institutions."[55] The resulting "comparative institutional approach" is defined specifically in the following terms: "The determinants of legal decisions can best be analyzed when legal decision makers are viewed as though they were concerned with choosing the best, or least imperfect, institution to implement a given societal goal."[56] Further development of comparative institutional analysis is hampered at the present time, however, because "[l]ittle formal information is available about the relative merits of alternative social decision makers."[57]

Our empirical study in EPAC of sixty-seven federal court cases and the present case study of OCR's activities in its Big City Reviews are attempts to fill that gap. Taken together, and using the categories of policymaking, interest group representation, fact-finding, and remedies our two studies can be said to have systematically compared the functioning of the three branches of government in very similar educational policy areas. The conclusions we reached concerning the comparative functioning of the judicial, legislative, and administrative branches, as well as the extent of their deviation from the classic separation of powers model, are summarized in Table 2.

What light can these findings shed on the ultimate separation of powers questions? Clearly, they show patterns of institutional capability that belie many of the assumptions of the classic separation of powers model. Courts and state legislatures (but not administrative/regulatory agencies) tend to promote full participation of affected interests. Courts and administrative/regulatory agencies (but not state legislatures) tend to utilize social science data effectively in their decision-making processes. Judicial remedial mechanisms have more compliance monitoring "staying power" than those of administrative agencies, but their content is less comprehensive and less sensitive to implementation realities.

These findings, if they can be verified by further empirical research, provide significant insights for functional decisions

TABLE 2
Summary of Findings on Comparative Institutional Functioning

| | Assumptions of Classic Separation of Powers Theory | Findings on State Legislatures | Findings on Courts | Findings on Administrative/ Regulatory Agency (OCR) |
|---|---|---|---|---|
| Policymaking | Exclusive legislative policymaking prerogative is necessary to ensure popular sovereignty | Partisan mutual adjustment decision-making mode. Effective for reflecting and promoting broad political compromises | Rational-analytic decision-making mode. Effective for articulating fundamental principles | Pragmatic-analytic decision-making mode. Effective for reflecting grass-roots implementation needs |
| Interest Group Representation | Legislature considers input from all affected interests. Other branches are incapable of effective interest group representation | Input from all interests sufficiently involved in the issue and sufficiently well organized to exert political pressure is considered | Input from all interests sufficiently well organized to seek formal legal representation is considered. Representation of minority group interests is more effective | Limited input from affected interests. Participation is specifically discouraged |

| | | | | |
|---|---|---|---|---|
| Fact-Finding | Legislative and administrative agencies—but not courts—are effective in gathering data and applying it to social policy considerations | Fact gathering is "window dressing" with little relevance to actual decisions | Fact gathering is relatively efficient. Facts tend to influence decisions | Fact gathering is most efficient. Facts tend to influence decisions |
| Remedies | Administrative agencies are most effective | Legislative oversight and statutory modifications have some influence on remedial enforcement | Relatively effective formulation of remedial plans when resources of affected parties are utilized by the court. Significant compliance monitoring "staying power" | Most effective formulation of comprehensive, feasible remedial plans. Relatively ineffective compliance monitoring "staying power" |

NOTE: The reader should keep in mind that these empirical findings are based on a limited number of case studies. As such, they must be considered tentative hypotheses which should be tested and refined by further studies.

based on comparative institutional capability. Thus, if maximum interest group participation is to be sought, the legislative or judicial forums would be preferred; if data gathering or remedial efficiency is the concern, the courts or administrative agencies would appear most suitable. Moreover, if a particular activity is, for historical, political, or other reasons, lodged in a branch that has a comparative deficiency in a relevant function, comparative institutional analysis can indicate where changes in established approaches might be pressed (for example, opening the administrative process to greater interest group representation).

But these insights into functional capacity still leave unanswered the critical "legitimacy" questions: When is it appropriate to allow or encourage a branch to undertake new activities that are inconsistent with or not contemplated under the classic separation of powers model? When is the courts' rational-analytic policymaking mode or the administrative agencies' pragmatic-analytic policymaking mode to be preferred to legislative mutual adjustment?

In our prior work on the role of the courts, we took a cautious approach to these issues, outlining the problem but leaving unanswered the ultimate question of when "particular aspects of social problems should be handled through the principled, analytic judicial process or through the instrumental, mutual adjustment patterns of the legislature."[58]

Professor William Clune criticizes this approach in a recent essay review of *Educational Policy Making and the Courts*.[59] Clune uses our data to support a theory of comparative institutional advantage which unabashedly advocates judicial involvement whenever "careful factual analysis" ascertains a "defect in a legislative process," and which further argues against the "formalism" of judicial reluctance to accept political methods for dealing with the issues involved in the cases over which courts have taken jurisdiction.[60]

In essence, Clune's approach deals frontally with the sensitive "legitimacy" issues by standing them on their head: courts are said to be acting "legitimately" whenever they take on a function that they can perform comparatively well. Furthermore, once a court appropriately becomes involved in a case, any reasonable steps that are taken to deal effectively with the issues are considered to be *per se* "legitimate."

There are, however, several difficulties with this approach. First is the question of who defines relative competence. How do we know when there is a "defect in the legislative process?"[61] If legitimacy becomes solely a function of capacity and all "formalistic" limitations on institutional functioning are scrapped, there is serious danger of subjectivism at best and partisanship at worst in assessing relative institutional capabilities. As Clune himself acknowledges, "comparative institutionalism converts politics directly into doctrine."[62]

Second, such a political perspective on institutional functioning may undermine the basic notion of institutional legitimacy to a degree that could threaten not only theoretical rectitude, but also practical institutional functioning. The authoritativeness of the courts, for example, is related to society's need for finality in settling public values and to the legal system's perceived continuity with traditional values, as well as its ability to enhance the stability of the larger political system.[63] This authoritativeness is based on an underlying public acceptance of the inherent legitimacy of the courts' role in this context. Should the courts' functions come to be perceived as being interchangeable with those of the other branches, depending on relative capability on particular issues, there are serious questions as to whether the traditional deference to the courts' authoritative pronouncements will continue—especially when those pronouncements are controversial.[64]

In short, then, we believe that some formal limitations must be maintained, although these limitations should be reconceptualized to reflect contemporary realities. This formidable task can be approached, we believe, by considering the original purpose of the separation of powers doctrine and then assessing the extent to which any contemporary proposal that deviates from the traditional model supports or undermines that basic purpose. In other words, we would agree with Justice White's note in his dissenting opinion in *Immigration and Naturalization Service v. Chadha*, that the appropriate way

to frame the legitimacy issue under current conditions is to
ask "whether the act in question raises the dangers the Framers
sought to avoid."[65]

The crucial "danger" that concerned the framers clearly
was excessive concentration of power in one political branch.
As James Madison put it, the key issue is whether "the whole
power of one department is exercised by the same hands which
possess the whole power of another department."[66] From this
perspective, the critical point is whether power is being concentrated within one political branch to such an extent that
there are no effective checks and balances from the other
branches, not whether any particular traditional, formal
boundaries have been crossed.

Specifically, in terms of the policymaking power, the standard would be whether power delegated to the courts or administrative agencies results in exclusive policymaking with
little or no effective accountability by the legislative authority.
Under this standard, some delegations of policymaking authority by Congress to administrative agencies or the courts
would clearly be appropriate; that is, those that do not transfer
all policymaking authority and that retain substantial, active
oversight functions in the Congress. Under such circumstances, excessive accumulations of power in the judicial or
administrative branches, and the potential danger of frus-
trating the popular will expressed through the people's legislative representatives, would not arise.[67]

We believe that the indirect delegation of Title VI policymaking authority to OCR in the present situation met this
standard, since Congress's original and continued involvement
in the issues was active and substantial,[68] and since the statutory scheme provided for significant judicial oversight. Assuming that delegation of policymaking authority by Congress
was appropriate here, we would assert further that the administrative implementation process was the most suitable
alternative forum. As was indicated in chapter 2, the complexities of the opportunity/result dynamic of American egalitarian ideology were not easily reconcilable through a stroke
of principled analysis by the courts; rather, they required an

ongoing balancing of the differing ideological perspectives, as sensitized by a particular constellation of facts and political inputs. This is precisely what pragmatic-analytic policymaking can accomplish.

If a contemporary separation of powers approach based on a standard of avoidance of excessive power concentrations is candidly accepted, Congress, in considering particular delegations, and the courts, in reviewing them, might directly focus on power concentration as the critical legitimacy issue. Furthermore, the findings of comparative institutional analysis could be directly utilized in making, and shaping, delegation decisions. Thus, in considering whether a statute should be framed to delegate specific policymaking roles to the courts or to an administrative agency, Congress might consider the relative importance of such functions as interest group participation or extensive fact-finding processes in the particular context, and the comparative capabilities of each agency to perform such functions. Congress might even go further and direct the court or the agency to implement a procedure that specifically provides particular types or degrees of interest group representation or fact-finding processes.

Comparative institutional analysis also suggests some limitations on the delegation process. Officials engaged in pragmatic-analytic policymaking, as exemplified by OCR's New York City Review, appear to require extensive resources to obtain necessary data and oversee a protracted negotiating process. Therefore, administrative policymaking may not be justified in situations in which such resources are not available—or in which the issues lack the continuing congressional oversight attention generated by equality controversies. Without the availability of sufficient resources and the restraint of ongoing accountability, effective administrative policymaking can degenerate into insidious "regulatory unreasonableness."[69]

Precisely where the "formal" legitimacy boundaries for a contemporary separation of powers model should be drawn, it is too early to tell. Clearly there is a need, as Alexander

Bickel has put it, for a continuing "colloquy among the branches"[70] on these issues. We think it clear, however, that the evidence obtained through comparative institutional analysis can provide a critical, and indeed necessary, data base for this endeavor.

# CHAPTER TEN
# CONCLUSIONS

Shortly before this book was completed, more than five years after the two OCR agreements had been negotiated in New York City, the United States Supreme Court decided a case which directly raised the critical legal issue that has been a leitmotif of this study: do policies that have an adverse impact on minorities violate Title VI, even if there is no proof of discriminatory intent? In *Guardians Association v. Civil Service Commission of the City of New York*,[1] an employment discrimination case involving layoffs of minority police officers, a majority of the justices held that Title VI does require a showing of discriminatory intent. But that, surprisingly, did not lay the issue to rest. Rather, in "one of the most fragmented decisions of the [1982–1983] term,"[2] a different majority indicated that, nevertheless, the defendants in the case should be held to an impact standard.[3]

This unusual outcome stemmed from the fact that three of the justices who thought the Title VI statute imposed an intent standard held, nevertheless, that the HEW regulations incorporating an impact standard should still be considered valid. Justice Stevens, articulating the rationale for this point of view, stated that "regulations have the force of law so long as they are 'reasonably related to the purposes of the enabling legislation.' "[4] Justice O'Connor, however, objected strongly to this leap of doctrine, arguing that regulations which are inconsistent with the intent of Title VI, as founded by a majority of the Court, cannot be considered to further the statute's purpose.[5]

Under traditional doctrines of administrative law, Justice O'Connor had the better of the argument. But the traditional doctrines overlook the fact that, as we have shown in the previous chapters, Congress really had no clear intent on this issue and the Court itself could not come to a decision on the meaning of Title VI until nineteen years after its passage; even then, its analysis was based on technical considerations irrelevant to the core intent/impact issues.[6] During these nineteen years, pragmatic-analytic policymaking on these issues by the administrative agencies had resulted in the issuance of numerous administrative regulations, the negotiation of many agreements, and the adoption of impact standards by state and local entities throughout the nation as a part of their basic operating procedures.

Seen in this light, the position of Justice Stevens and at least three of his colleagues is consistent with our findings that important contributions to policymaking on controversial egalitarian issues at times can be accomplished through the pragmatic-analytic decision-making mode of the administrative/regulatory process. Although in the *Guardians* case the current pressures and trends of administrative policymaking were not explicitly linked to the result, or articulated as a new legal doctrine,[7] we think the connection is real and is indicative of the growing significance of the issues raised in this book concerning administrative implementation of egalitarian policies.

The empirical findings reported in this book have yielded a number of hypotheses and conclusions which, if validated by further empirical research and analysis, can be of direct utility in formulating public policy on these issues. In that light, we will offer some concluding comments on the "success" of OCR's policymaking intervention in the affairs of New York City's schools.

Any attempt to assess the "success" of a political enterprise is, of course, fraught with difficulty. By what standard does one measure "success"? For some, only the complete accomplishment of thoroughgoing reforms will receive enthusiastic plaudits. For others, any movement toward reform will be criticized. Moreover, since the implementation process, by its very nature, inevitably tends to result in some sort of compromise position, far from the purity of the original policies proposed by any of the advocates or opponents, evaluation of the "success" of any particular outcome becomes almost insuperably problematic.

Critical appraisals of OCR's massive New York City Review illustrate these points: it has been dismissed by some critics for attempting to do too little and by others for attempting to do too much. Staunch civil rights advocates tend to be in the first camp; they minimized the significance of OCR's effort from the outset because they viewed it as being merely a tactic in the Nixon administration's anti-busing campaign and a retreat from historical student desegregation initiatives.[8] Academic analysts of the administrative process tend to be in the second camp; they criticized OCR for attempting to impose broad and moralistic civil rights standards, without paying sufficient heed to local administrative and political realities.[9]

Our case study findings provide evidence that can refute both of these positions. First, in response to the civil rights advocates, it can be argued that, given the political strictures within which OCR had to operate (that is, no busing and no metropolitan area desegregation), Martin Gerry devised a highly innovative approach to the broadest array of discrimination issues that ever had been tackled in a school system investigation. Although many of these issues got dropped along the way, the 1977 and 1978 compliance agreements contained significant commitments to anti-discrimination standards which led to positive changes in teacher assignment and student tracking practices. Second, in reply to the academic critics, our findings reflect substantial sensitivity to local administrative and political realities. Gerry tended to avoid a confrontation with the White House over busing and with the teachers' union over employment issues; Tatel tried to reach a moderate agreement that the board of education could realistically be expected to implement. Thus, it was not administrative fiat, but rather a process of persuasion and bargaining, that produced two balanced agreements reflecting local program and political realities.

But citing evidence to parry the specific comments of particular critics does not resolve our problem. Beyond all these

particulars, is there not a way to make an overall assessment
of the impact of OCR's intervention? The three-pronged methodological approach used in this book to analyze case study
evidence does, we think, provide such added breadth and
objectivity. Multifaceted analyses of a complex institutional
reform process clearly provide a more accurate portrayal of
the underlying realities; furthermore, approaching the issues
through three different lenses tends to provide a built-in corrective to any analyst's tendency to overstate the significance
of particular conclusions.

In the present study, the ideological analysis showed that
the equality of opportunity and equality of result positions
are indeed complementary strands of an overall fundamental
American egalitarian ideology, since they proved reconcilable
in the two New York City agreements. The absence of the
intense political confrontation that usually accompanies political or judicial discussions of these issues allowed for a
balanced negotiating process, permitting the synthesis of the
ideological positions in two practical documents. Both agreements combined substantial result-oriented institutional reforms with a sensitive maintenance of opportunity-oriented
emphases on individual options and meritocratic standards.

The implementation analysis cautioned us, however, against
exaggerating the implications of this ideological reconciliation. Not only were the conditions for balanced negotiations
rare, but also the inherent problems of goal ambiguity and
the weight of organizational processes limited the issues which
were covered in the agreements to only a handful of those
that had originally been raised. Moreover, even in areas where
agreement was reached, compliance lagged far behind the
agreed standards, and delays and political intervention eventually led to renegotiation of the faculty assignment agreement. Hence, the record on implementation ultimately poses
the issue of whether the results of OCR's intervention in New
York City was commensurate with the millions of dollars and
thousands of work hours devoted by all sides to the project.

The comparative institutional analysis permitted a further

understanding of the significance of OCR's ideological reconciliation, seen as an example of pragmatic-analytic policymaking, in contrast to the rational-analytic policymaking of the judicial process and the mutual adjustment policymaking of the legislative process. And it also shed light on the implementation difficulties by highlighting OCR's institutional lack of "staying power," as compared to that of the courts.[10]

Taken together, these findings point to an overall conclusion that the administrative process can—and should—play an important policymaking role in egalitarian issues, a role, however, that may be inconsistent with the traditional separation of powers perspective. As we argued in chapter 9, in formulating the explicit terms of a delegation of such policymaking to administrative agencies like OCR, Congress should be cognizant of both the institutional strengths (like fact-finding) and institutional weaknesses (like interest group input) of the administrative process.[11] On a broader plane, because of the administrative/regulatory agencies' comparative shortcomings in overseeing long-term implementation, consideration also should be given, in the ongoing "dialogue among the branches," to enhancing the role of the courts in monitoring the implementation of agreements emerging from the administrative process.[12]

Finally, the enhanced administrative policymaking role also can be justified by reference to a more ultimate concept of "success." From a broad societal perspective, institutional reform can be justified and considered "successful" to the extent that it advances overall moral consensus and the enhanced social cohesion that results from such consensus.[13] Positions based on conflicting concepts of equality of opportunity and equality of result currently generate some of the most bitter political confrontations on the American political scene. Nevertheless, the history of the New York City Review has demonstrated that, where suitable conditions prevail, ideological reconciliations that enhance social consensus can be achieved.[14] To the extent that carefully structured policymak-

# 202 CONCLUSIONS

ing delegations can further create conditions favorable for the replication of such ideological reconciliation, without risking the creation of unaccountable power centers that are the concern of separation of powers doctrine, we believe that path should be taken.*

*These conclusions also need to be seen in a broader historical perspective. In the 1960s and 1970s, two American institutions were looked to for accomplishing major social reforms—the public schools and the legal system (particularly the federal courts). In fact, a great deal of progress was made by the activist litigation and vigorous administrative enforcement of that period, and further gains can still be made. However, that model of social reform owed its success to an underlying political commitment to civil rights and egalitarianism, which now is embattled. This change is reflected in the slackening of federal civil rights enforcement, the increasing judicial obstacles to effective civil rights litigation, and the sustained financial pressures and political attacks on the public interest/legal services bar.

In response to these developments I, and a number of my colleagues, have been asking ourselves what we need to be doing as practitioners, scholars, and, perhaps, political activists to renew the fight for social justice, civil rights, and civil liberties. Insofar as scholarship is concerned, one answer to this question is that new avenues need to be opened up in research methodology. Academic law has to be infused with a greater understanding of the relationship between historical changes and the legal system. In similar fashion, social science has to replace its bias toward minimizing the politics of law with a strong focus on the relationship between politics and the use of the legal system for social reform. To accomplish these tasks, I believe that lawyers and social scientists need to be part of a broader effort, shared by all manner of professionals and academics, to build independent organizations in which they can explore the often elusive and frequently controversial questions about the relationship between social activism and scholarship (A. Block).

(Mr. Rebell does not join in this footnote; he does not believe it necessary or appropriate to relate the book's research findings and recommendations, which stand on their own, to political developments occurring at any particular time.)

APPENDIX A

# LIST OF MAJOR INTERVIEWS

(New York, Chicago, Los Angeles, and Philadelphia Case Studies)

NEW YORK

| Name | Date | Identifying Information (Positions or affiliations related to the events being studied) |
|---|---|---|
| Hon. Irving Anker | 6/22/81 | Chancellor, City School District of New York, 1973–1978 |
| Frank C. Arricale II | 10/2/81 | Executive Director, Office of Personnel, City School District of New York, 1974–1978 |
| Felix Baxter, Esq. | 4/24/81 | Policy Analyst and Staff Attorney, City School District of New York, 1976–1978 |
| Cynthia Brown | 9/28/81 | Children's Defense Fund of the Washington Research Project, 1970–1975; Lawyers' Committee for Civil Rights under Law, 1975–1977; Deputy Director, OCR, 1977–1979; Director, Civil Rights Transition Team of the Department of Education, 1979–1980; Assistant Secretary for Civil Rights, 1980–1981 |
| Carol Campbell | 4/23/81 | Equal Educational Opportunity Specialist, OCR, 1973–1980 |
| Richard Caro, Esq. | 6/1/81 | Assistant United States Attorney, 1975–1981, responsible for *Caulfield* and related cases and ESAA cases |
| Frederick Cioffi | 4/23/81 | Acting Assistant Secretary for Civil Rights, Department of Education, 1981; Director, Elementary and Secondary Education Division, OCR |

| Name | Date | Identifying Information (Positions or affiliations related to the events being studied) |
| --- | --- | --- |
| Dr. Perry Davis | 10/26/81 | Assistant to Board of Education Member Steven Aiello, 1974–1978; Director and Acting Director of Office for Funded Programs, City School District of New York |
| Susanna Doyle | 12/81 | Staff, Advocates for Children |
| Arthur Eisenberg, Esq. | 6/3/81, 6/4/81 | Staff Attorney, New York Civil Liberties Union |
| Sandra Feldman | 11/12/81 | Director, United Federation of Teachers |
| David Filvaroff, Esq. | 4/2/82 | Staff Attorney, United States Justice Department, during deliberations on 1964 Civil Rights Act |
| J. Harold Flannery, Esq. | 6/23/81, 12/1/81 | Consultant to and Chief Negotiator for OCR, 1977–1978, while in private law practice as a member of Foley, Hoag & Elliot, Boston, Mass. |
| Martin H. Gerry, Esq. | 9/14/81 | Executive Assistant to the OCR director and OCR investigator, 1969–1974; OCR Deputy Director, 1974–1976; OCR Director, 1976–1977 |
| Dr. Bernard Gifford | 3/19/81 | Deputy Chancellor, City School District of New York, 1973–1977 |
| George Gingerelli | 9/28/81 | President, Delta Research Corporation, automatic data services contractor for OCR |
| Dr. Patricia Alberjerg Graham | 11/24/81 | Director, National Institute of Education, 1977–1979, and consultant to OCR during 1978 EES negotiations |
| Albert T. Hamlin, Esq. | 4/23/81 | Various legal positions in the Justice Department and Department of |

| Name | Date | Identifying Information (Positions or affiliations related to the events being studied) |
|---|---|---|
| | | HEW; responsible for civil rights enforcement, 1966–1977; Acting Director, OCR, 1977 |
| Dawn Hyland | 11/18/81 | Staff, OCR, Region II |
| Leroy Jones, Esq. | 4/23/81 | Civil Rights Specialist; Investigator and Branch Chief, OCR, national office |
| James Meyerson, Esq. | 2/3/81 | Staff Attorney, NAACP |
| Michael Rosen | 3/19/81, 3/20/81 | Counsel to Chancellor |
| Dr. Charles Schonhaut | 10/27/81, 11/13/81 | Senior Assistant to the Chancellor and Chief Negotiator for the Board of Education |
| Harold Siegel, Esq. | 6/10/81 | Counsel and Secretary to the Board of Education, City School District of New York |
| Paul Smith | 4/16/82[a] | Children's Defense Fund of the Washington Research Project |
| David Tatel, Esq. | 4/24/81 | Director, OCR, 1977–1979 |
| Charles Tejada, Esq. | 11/18/81 | Director, OCR, Region II |
| Helen Whitney | 11/18/81, 12/81 | Equal Opportunity Specialist, OCR, Region II, 1973–1980; Branch Chief, OCR, Region II |

## CHICAGO

| Mary Jane Cross | 12/17/81[a] | Equal Opportunity Specialist, OCR, Region V |
| Conrad Harper, Esq. | 10/22/81 | Consultant to and Chief Negotiator for OCR while in private law practice as a member of Simpson, |

| Name | Date | Identifying Information (Positions or affiliations related to the events being studied) |
|------|------|------|
| | | Thatcher & Bartlett, New York, New York |
| Robert M. Healey | 1/7/81[a] | President, Chicago Teachers Union |
| Dr. Joan Raymond | 12/17/81 | Assistant Superintendent for Administration, Chicago School District |

### LOS ANGELES

| Name | Date | Identifying Information |
|------|------|------|
| Henry E. Boas | 1/27/82 | Program Planning Coordinator, Los Angeles Unified School District |
| George Dalton, Esq. | 1/28/82 | Attorney for Plaintiffs—*Zaslowsky et al. v. Board of Education* |
| Sam Kresner | 1/28/82 | Director of Staff, United Teachers of Los Angeles |
| John E. Palomino | 1/29/82 | Chief, Education Branch, OCR, Region IX |
| Dr. Robert Searle | 1/27/82 | Administrator, Personnel Division, Los Angeles Unified School District |
| Dr. James B. Taylor | 1/27/81 | Associate Superintendent, Planning, Los Angeles Unified School District |

### PHILADELPHIA

| Name | Date | Identifying Information |
|------|------|------|
| Michael R. Aaronson | 4/14/82 | Assistant to the Executive Director, Office of Personnel and Labor Relations, Board of Education, School District of Philadelphia |
| Murray Bookbinder | 4/14/82 | Executive Director, Office of Personnel and Labor Relations, Board of Education, School District of Philadelphia |
| Martin Horowitz, Esq. | 4/14/82 | Attorney, Office of Legal Counsel, Board of Education, School District of Philadelphia |

| Name | Date | Identifying Information (Positions or affiliations related to the events being studied) |
|------|------|------------------------------------------------------|
| Barry Keen | 4/14/82 | ESAA Specialist, OCR, Region III |
| Theodore Nixon | 4/14/82 | Chief, Elementary and Secondary Education Division, OCR, Region III |
| Edward B. Penry | 4/14/82 | Director of Research, Board of Education, School District of Philadelphia |
| John Ryan | 4/15/82[a] | President, Philadelphia Federation of Teachers |
| Harry O. Wilson | 4/14/82 | Project Director, Equal Education Services Review, OCR, Region III |

[a] Telephone interview.

# SURVEY QUESTIONNAIRE

In conducting our case study, we obtained most of our information from documents and from free-flowing, in-depth interviews with key participants in the New York City Review. To supplement these in-depth interviews, we also asked all of our interviewees—as well as a number of interest group representatives who did not directly participate in the process—to respond to the standardized questions in our structured opinion survey.

As "opinion survey" implies, our aim was not to obtain hard, "objective" facts or statistically significant responses, but rather to add an additional dimension to our research by obtaining in a standardized format the opinions and perceptions of persons who viewed the administrative enforcement process from different perspectives. In addition, by asking our interview subjects, as well as interest group "outsiders," to respond to the survey, we were able to look for indications of any major differences between the perceptions of the persons closely involved with the process and those of the more peripheral participants. (Through this comparison, we found, for example, that the "outsiders" generally believed that the Title VI fund termination sanction was a powerful threat, whereas a consensus of the "insiders" was that this sanction simply was not credible.)

The choice of respondents for this survey was not intended to be a scientific sampling process. Rather, a survey was sent to any person or organization who our documentary files or interviews indicated might have had some significant interest in the review. As might be expected, especially many years after the fact, several individuals could not be reached and others said that either they had not been significantly involved or their recollections were not keen enough to enable them to respond confidently. In the end, we received twenty-two completed surveys.

The survey responses provided valuable background information. In addition, some of the patterns in the responses were sufficiently clear that they could be cited as further support for particular findings in our report. Again, however, the validity of these inferences from the survey data was not based on any technical or scientific presumptions, but rather on a common-sense use of the information.

A copy of the survey form is reproduced in the following pages.

_____

Person or Agency

OPINION SURVEY
_____

OCR-NYC SPECIAL COMPLIANCE REVIEW STUDY

1. OCR alleged that 10 educational practices and conditions— listed below—occurred in New York City and denied children equal educational opportunity as guaranteed by Title VI of the Civil Rights Act of 1964, Title IX of the Education Amendments of 1972, and the Rehabilitation Act of 1973.

   Please indicate those allegations which you believe were accurate in 1976 by checking the appropriate space under "Accurate in 1976" (column 1). Then, for each allegation checked:
   —if you think the practice or condition was a major problem in 1976 for which remedial action should have been undertaken, check column 2;
   —if you think OCR's intervention improved the situation, check column 3;
   —if you think the practice or condition is a major problem today, check column 4.

APPENDIX B

| ALLEGATION | (1) Accurate 1976 | (2) Problem 1976 | (3) OCR Improved | (4) Problem Today |
|---|---|---|---|---|
| a) Board of Examiners licensing procedures disproportionately disqualified prospective minority teachers. | | | | |
| b) Teacher assignment practices caused minority teachers to be placed disproportionately in schools having predominantly minority student bodies. | | | | |
| c) Predominantly minority schools received fewer resources per pupil than non-minority schools. | | | | |
| d) Ability grouping and other practices led to racially identifiable instruction settings within schools. | | | | |
| e) Minority students were disproportionately represented in the Special Admissions High Schools. | | | | |
| f) Different discipline standards were applied to minority students. | | | | |
| g) Proportionately fewer women than men were appointed to supervisory positions. | | | | |
| h) Fewer resources per pupil were allocated to girls' athletic programs. | | | | |

| ALLEGATION | (1)<br>Accurate<br>1976 | (2)<br>Problem<br>1976 | (3)<br>OCR<br>Improved | (4)<br>Problem<br>Today |
|---|---|---|---|---|
| i) Vocational programs were largely sex-segregated, and girls' programs received fewer resources per capita. | | | | |
| j) Handicapped students were kept waiting for evaluation services and appropriate placements for excessively long time periods. | | | | |

2. How would you characterize OCR's overall performance in gathering and analyzing factual data during the compliance review process? Do you feel that OCR's performance was ... (Check below)

|  | Yes | No | Mixed |
|---|---|---|---|
| Complete? | _____ | _____ | _____ |
| Objective? | _____ | _____ | _____ |
| Methodologically sound? | _____ | _____ | _____ |

3. Which organization(s) do you feel were significantly involved in the compliance review and/or negotiations?

_____

_____

4. Do you think that any organization(s) should have been more involved in the review and/or negotiations? (Please check) Yes_____ No_____. (If yes) which one(s)? (Please explain)

_____

_____

5. To the best of your knowledge, did any organization(s) *attempt* to become more involved in the review and/or negotiations, but

fail to do so? (Please check) Yes____ No____. (If yes) which one(s)? (Please explain)

_____

_____

6. Do you think that the OCR compliance review process significantly increased the influence or power of any local organizations or agencies in educational affairs? (Please check) Yes____ No____. (If yes) which organizations or agencies?

_____

_____

7. Do you think that OCR's compliance review process caused either an increase or decrease in confrontation among local groups (e.g. advocacy groups, public agencies, unions)? (Please check) Increase____ Decrease____ No Change____ Mixed____

8. Do you think that OCR exceeded its proper role or legal authority in the course of the compliance review process? (Please check) Yes____ No____. (If yes) please explain how.

_____

_____

9. If you are affiliated with a group *other than* OCR or the Board of Education, please indicate whether or not you feel your organization's point of view was considered during the negotiations . . . (Please check)

|  | Yes | No |
|---|---|---|
| by OCR? | ____ | ____ |
| by the Board of Education? | ____ | ____ |

10. Some people think that the following four sanctions gave OCR significant leverage to obtain concessions from the Board of Education during the negotiation of the first agreement (employment issues). For each sanction, please indicate whether or not you feel it gave OCR significant leverage.

SURVEY QUESTIONNAIRE                                    213

|                                                                                     | Yes | No |
|-------------------------------------------------------------------------------------|-----|----|
| 1. Negative publicity against the Board of Education                                | ___ | ___ |
| 2. OCR could move for termination of all federal education funds (Title VI)         | ___ | ___ |
| 3. OCR could declare the schools ineligible for grants under the Emergency School Assistance Act (ESAA) | ___ | ___ |
| 4. OCR could declare the schools ineligible for Comprehensive Employment Training Act (CETA) funds | ___ | ___ |

b. Which sanction, if any, do you feel gave OCR the greatest amount of leverage over the Board of Education during the negotiations? (Please circle number of that sanction above.)

11. We are interested in the extent to which you feel certain philosophical views about social justice were reflected in the actions of OCR and the Board of Education during the compliance review process.

For purposes of this survey, we have identified two basic concepts of equality. They are:

*Equality of Opportunity*: removing existing discriminatory barriers so that individuals can advance in accordance with their present abilities.

*Equality of Result*: eliminating the effects of past discrimination by facilitating immediate access to social or economic benefits for the formerly disadvantaged.

a. Do you feel that OCR's positions or actions in the compliance review process consistently reflected one of these philosophies? (Please check the appropriate item below)

Yes, Equality of Opportunity                    ___

Yes, Equality of Result                         ___

Yes, but different philosophies
at different times                              ___

No, OCR's actions did not consistently
reflect either philosophy                                        _____

b. Do you feel that the *Board of Education*'s positions or actions
in the compliance review process consistently reflected one
of these philosophies? (Please check the appropriate item
below)

Yes, Equality of Opportunity                              _____

Yes, Equality of Result                                      _____

Yes, but different philosophies
at different times                                              _____

No, the Board of Education's
actions did not consistently
reflect either philosophy                              _____

12. In recent years, federal court involvement in cases against the
New York City Board of Education, e.g. *ASPIRA, Chance, Lora*
and *Jose P.* have had substantial impact on the school system.
We are interested in how you feel about OCR's compliance
review process as compared to that of the federal courts. Please
read the statements below and indicate for each how much you
agree or disagree with that statement.

| | Strongly agree | Moderately agree | Moderately disagree | Strongly disagree |
|---|---|---|---|---|
| 1. In general, the courts seemed to interfere with day to day school operations more than did OCR. | | | | |
| 2. In general, the judges seemed to understand NYC educational policy better than did OCR officials. | | | | |

| | Strongly agree | Moderately agree | Moderately disagree | Strongly disagree |
|---|---|---|---|---|
| 3. In general, the court decrees seemed to be implemented more effectively than the OCR agreements. | | | | |

13. Is there anything else you would like to tell us concerning the OCR compliance review process?

_____

_____

_____

14. And now just a few last questions about you and your role in the OCR-NYC compliance review.

   a. What is your name? _____

   b. What is your profession or occupation? _____

   c. What positions and/or organizational affiliations did you hold from 1972 to 1981 which are relevant to OCR's New York City Review?

   _____

   _____

   _____

   d. How would you describe the nature of your personal involvement or sources of information regarding the Review?

   _____

   _____

   _____

   Would you like a copy of our survey results?
   Yes_____ No_____

Thank you very much.

# NOTES

## NOTES TO INTRODUCTION

1. Press release statement of Martin H. Gerry, Director of OCR, January 18, 1977.
2. 347 U.S. 483 (1954).
3. Pursuant to its authority under Title IX of the Education Amendments of 1972, which prohibit sex discrimination in federally assisted programs, OCR also looked for indications of denial of equal opportunities to female students in areas such as vocational training and career counseling. It also investigated patterns of apparent underrepresentation of women in supervisory and administrative positions. After the issuance of Department of Health, Education and Welfare (HEW) regulations pursuant to sec. 504 of the Rehabilitation Act of 1973, the review added issues pertaining to equal educational opportunities for handicapped students.
4. An additional agreement on bilingual education issues was concluded in September 1977, without major negotiations. This agreement largely was overshadowed by a pending lawsuit on bilingual education issues that already had produced a major consent agreement.
5. G. Allison, Essence of Decision (1971). Allison undertook to explain the Cuban missile crisis in terms of three separate models: "rational actor," "organizational process," and "governmental politics."
6. P. Peterson, School Politics Chicago Style (1976). Applying Allison's approach to an educational context, Peterson analyzed decision making by the Chicago Board of Education, on the issues of desegregation, collective bargaining, and decentralization, in terms of "rational decision making" "organizational process," and "bargaining" (both "pluralist" and "ideological").
7. These "perspectives" are analogous to social science "models," but we prefer to utilize the former term to make clear that we do not purport to be constructing methodologically rigorous models; instead, we seek to present three coherent and interrelated frame-

works for understanding the nature and causes of the events in the New York City Review.

8. Peterson, *supra* note 6, at 137.
9. D. Bell, The End of Ideology 400 (rev. ed. 1962).
10. MacIver, "Introduction," in European Ideologies 5 (F. Gross ed. 1948).
11. We use the phrase *fundamental ideology* to describe a core set of values and understandings about social equality. This fundamental ideology is less comprehensive in scope than that which German sociologist Karl Mannheim called a *total ideology* (referring to an all-inclusive world view, or a total mind-set of an epoch or a group) in his classic work, Ideology and Utopia (1929). However, it shares with Mannheim's concept the notion of a broad, umbrella perspective of values and concepts that encompasses specific ideological subcategories. All of the significant individuals and organizations involved in the New York City Review shared this fundamental American egalitarian ideology. However, as will be discussed, sharp differences arose under this umbrella perspective.
12. We prefer to use the term *ideological strands* in preference to Mannheim's *particular ideologies*. The latter term has negative connotations of ties to narrow interests. *Strands* implies a complementary relationship, which accurately describes the connection between equality of opportunity and equality of result, as we will define these terms.
13. For example, from the result perspective one will more readily find discriminatory bias in institutional arrangements (e.g., organizing classrooms by ability groups) and social processes (e.g., teacher judgments of student "ability") that are ostensibly neutral but have disparate results.
14. For this reason, *equality of result*, as defined here, should not be confused with *equality of condition*, an egalitarian perspective which builds on Marxist notions of distributing wealth "from each according to his ability, to each according to his needs," and which, as will be discussed in more detail in chapter 1, is foreign to America's egalitarian traditions.
15. "Title VI of the 1964 Civil Rights Act emerged from Congress without a definitive legislative history to serve as an explicit directive for administration" (B. Radin, Implementation, Change and the Federal Bureaucracy: School Desegregation Policy in HEW, 1964-1968 92 [1977]).
16. *See*, e.g., W. Muir, Prayer in the Schools (1967). *See also* T. Becker

and M. Feeley, The Impact of Supreme Court Decisions (2d ed. 1973); Hollingsworth, "The Impact of Student Rights and Discipline Cases on Schools," in ERIC, II Schools and the Courts 45 (1979); Miller, "On the Need for 'Impact Analysis' of Supreme Court Decisions," 53 Geo. L.J. 365 (1965).

17. "During the first 7 years of Title I alone, over $50 million was spent on impact evaluations (M. McLaughlin, Evaluation and Reform: The Case of ESEA, Title I 180 [1975]). See also Kirst and Jung, "The Utility of a Longitudinal Approach in Assessing Implementation: A Thirteen Year View of Title I, ESEA," Program Report No. 80-B18, Institute for Research on Educational Finance and Governance, Stanford University 34 (1980).

18. E. Hargrove, The Missing Link (1975).

19. Kirst and Jung, *supra* note 17, at 3. Examples of "factually dense" implementation studies are E. Mosher and S. Bailey, ESEA: The Office of Education Administers a Law (1968), and Federal Aid to Education (J. Berke and M. Kirst eds. 1972). Also, although not denominated an "implementation study," G. Orfield's The Reconstruction of Southern Education (1969) can nonetheless be seen as one. *See* Sabatier and Mazmanian, "The Implementation of Regulatory Process: A Framework of Analysis," nn.2-7, Research Reports of the Institute for Government Affairs, No. 39 Davis, California, University of California Press (1979); March, "Footnotes to Organizational Change," nn.2-5, Institute for Research on Educational Finance and Governance, Project Report No. 80-A6 (1980).

20. For a discussion of borrowings from various disciplines, see Hargrove, *supra* note 18. For an attempt to use a specific political/ economic theory—utilitarianism—to explain the history of the desegregation of southern schools, see H. Rodgers, Jr. and C. Bullock III, Coercion to Compliance (1976). *Cf.* Social Program Implementation (W. Williams and R. Elmore eds. 1976).

21. *See*, e.g., Van Meter and Von Horn, "The Policy Implementation Process," 6 Ad. & Soc'y 445 (1975); Berman, "The Study of Macro- and Micro-Implementation," 26 Pub. Pol'y 157 (1978).

22. E. Bardach, The Implementation Game 57 (1977).

23. Majone and Wildavsky, "Implementation as Evolution," in J. Pressman and A. Wildavsky, Implementation (2d ed. 1979).

24. This approach is the core of Allison's "rational actor" model. Applying this perspective to the behavior of a corporate entity

220 NOTES TO INTRODUCTION

with divergent internal goals is referred to as the "anthropo-morphic fallacy" (Allison, *supra* note 5, at 265).

25. The implementation perspective also protects against the tendency to attribute failures immediately to particular institutional shortcomings; instead, it promotes a comparative institutional consideration of inherent implementation problems.

26. These key concepts, described under somewhat different headings, are set forth as the key factors in the implementation of reform statutes or policies in Sabatier and Mazmanian, "The Conditions of Effective Implementation: A Guide to Accomplishing Policy Objectives," 5 Pol'y Analysis 481 (1979), and Clune, "A Political Model of Implementation and Implications of the Model for Public Policy, Research and the Changing Roles of Law and Lawyers," 69 Iowa L. Rev. 47, 49 (1983).

27. *See,* e.g., Berman, *supra* note 21, at 157, 166. The implementation problems caused by "policy ambiguity" are well illustrated by Clune's comparison of the relatively clear fiscal equalization policy enunciated by the California Supreme Court in Serrano v. Priest with the amorphous goals of "thorough and efficient" education articulated by the New Jersey Supreme Court in Robinson v. Cahill, both in response to similar legal challenges to the state system of educational finance (Clune, "Serrano and Robinson," in ERIC, II Schools and the Courts 67-120 [1979]).

28. Organizational process is related to Allison's second model (*see* Allison, *supra* note 5). *See also* Elmore, "Organizational Models of Social Program Implementation," 26 Pub. Pol'y 185 (1978); M. Lipsky, Street-Level Bureaucracy (1980); C. Perrow, Complex Organizations (1972).

29. This variable is related to Allison's third model. *See also* Bardach, *supra* note 22.

30. *See generally* Sharp, "The Classical American Doctrine of 'The Separation of Powers,' " 2 U. Chi. L. Rev. 385; G. Shubert, Judicial Policy-Making (1974).

31. *See,* e.g., J. Landis, The Administrative Process (1938); L. Jaffee, Judicial Control of Administrative Action (abridged. 1965); K. C. Davis, Discretionary Justice (1969); Wright's review of Davis, Discretionary Justice (1969), 81 Yale L.J. 575 (1972); Stewart, "The Reformation of American Administrative Law," 88 Harv. L. Rev. 1669 (1975); D. Yates, Bureaucratic Democracy (1982).

32. See Buckley v. Valeo, 424 U.S. 1, 280-81 (1976) (White, J., concurring and dissenting).

33. J. Freedman, Crisis and Legitimacy; The Administrative Process and American Government (1978). In addition to fundamental separation of powers problems, Freedman attributes this "crisis" to departures from judicial norms, public ambivalence about economic regulation in general, and public concern with bureaucratization and administrative expertise.

34. The Supreme Court has invalidated legislation for reasons of improper delegation on only two occasions (Panama Refining Co. v. Ryan, 293 U.S. 388 [1935]; Schechter Poultry Corp. v. United States, 295 U.S. 495 [1935]), leading many to conclude that the doctrine of constitutional limitations on legislative delegation is dead. As may be expected, there are some who argue for its revival (*e.g.*, T. J. Lowi, The End of Liberalism: Ideology, Policy and the Crisis of Public Authority 298 [1969]). *See also* McGowan, "Congress, Courts and Control of Delegated Powers," 77 Colum. L. Rev. 119 (1972), and others who call for other methods of ensuring administrative accountability (*e.g.*, Davis, *supra* note 31; Stewart, *supra* note 31, at 1695-96). One member of the Supreme Court appears to be interested in reviving the delegation doctrine (*see* American Textile Manufacturers v. Donovan, 452 U.S. 490 [1981] [Rehnquist, J., dissenting]; Industrial Union Department AFL-CIO v. American Petroleum Institute, 448 U.S. 607, 809 [1980] [Rehnquist, J., concurring]), but it is not yet clear whether this is the beginning of a serious new trend or a "doctrinally extraordinary approach" which is not likely to be further developed (Diver, "Policy Making Paradigms in Administrative Law," 95 Harv. L. Rev. 393, 427 [1981]). *See also* Aranson, Gellhorn, and Robinson, "A Theory of Legislative Delegation," 68 Corn. L. Rev. 1 (1982). State courts have invoked the delegation doctrine more often. *See*, e.g., City of Saginaw v. Budd, 381 Mich. 173, 160 N.W.2d 906 (1968); State Compensation Fund v. De La Fuente, 18 Ariz. App. 246, 501 P.2d 422 (1972); Sarasota County v. Barg, 302 So.2d 737 (Fla. 1974); People v. Tibbits, 56 Ill.2d 56, 305 N.E.2d 152 (1973).

35. Critics of broad delegation argue for clearer statutory standards, improved agency rule making procedures, new accountability mechanisms, or clearer standards for judicial review. *See* Wright, *supra* note 31; Jaffee, *supra* note 31. The widely held view (*see* Davis, *supra* note 31, at 219) that a substantial amount of delegation of policymaking responsibilities to administrative agencies can be tolerated, consistent with separation of powers ideals, so

long as there is meaningful scrutiny and participation by the public in agency rule making and extensive judicial review, has come under increasing criticism in recent years. *See*, e.g., Stewart, *supra* note 31; J. Mashaw, Bureaucratic Justice (1983).

36. OCR is, of course, a "dependent" administrative agency subject to direct political control by the secretary of education, and its civil rights enforcement responsibilities differ from the economic regulatory responsibilities of the traditional "independent" regulatory agencies, such as the Interstate Commerce Commission and the Federal Trade Commission. But, given the extent of responsibility routinely delegated to all government regulatory or social service agencies and the increasing similarity in the nature of political influence on both types of agencies today, the dependent/independent distinction, for present purposes, has little significance. *See*, e.g., U.S. Senate Committee on Governmental Operations, Study on Federal Regulation, 95th Cong., 1st Sess., vol. I, v (1977); Strauss, "The Place of Agencies in Government: Separation of Powers and the Fourth Branch," 84 Colum. L. Rev. 573, 584 (1984). And although the differences between OCR's civil rights enforcement activities and the economic and social regulatory responsibilities of other agencies must be kept in mind, the major problems of delegation, public participation, fact-finding, and analytical capabilities are highly similar. *See*, e.g., L. Lave, The Strategy of Social Regulation: Decision Frameworks for Policy 135 (1981). *See also* Schuck, "Book Review: The Politics of Regulation," 90 Yale L.J. 702 (1980).

37. M. Rebell and A. Block, Educational Policy Making and the Courts: An Empirical Study of Judicial Activism (1982).

38. Full in-depth case studies were not undertaken in these cities, but the main participants were interviewed and the agreements and other major documents obtained and analyzed. For a list of individuals interviewed in these cities, see appendix A.

NOTES TO CHAPTER ONE

1. J. R. Pole, The Pursuit of Equality in American History ix (1978).
2. "The people of Britain's North American colonies were the first subjects of any of Europe's colonial empire to claim their independence of the Old World. They justified that claim by an appeal to the principle of human equality, to which they accorded the status of a 'self-evident truth.' The concept of equality, thus pro-

claimed in the rhetoric of American independence, entered into the principles of government, where it linked forces with demands arising from newly released sources of popular power (*Ibid.* at 1). *See also* Beck, "Forward," in M. Lewis, The Culture of Inequality (1978).

3. As Herman Melville put it: "Escaped from the house of bondage, Israel of old did not follow often the ways of the Egyptians. To her was given an express dispensation; to her were given new things under the sun. And we Americans are the peculiar, chosen people—the Israel of our time; we bear the ark of the liberties of the world" (R. Bellah, The Broken Covenant 38 [1975]).

4. This thesis is most extensively developed in L. Hartz, The Liberal Tradition in America (1955). Hartz's emphasis on the overriding influence of Lockean liberal ideas on the pre-revolutionary American political consciousness has been challenged by scholars claiming that Locke's books were not widely read in colonial times. *See*, e.g., Dunn, "The Politics of Locke in England and America in the Eighteenth Century," in John Locke: Problems and Perspectives (J. Yolton ed. 1969); G. Wills, Inventing America, Jefferson's Declaration of Independence, chap. 11 (1978). Others have emphasized the "republican," as contrasted with "liberal," orientation of colonial thought. *See*, e.g., G. Wood, The Creation of the American Republic 1776-1787 (1969); J. Pocock, The Machiavellian Moment (1975). Even if Hartz's thesis was somewhat overstated, most scholars would still seem to agree that Locke's influence on political thought in American colonial times, and since, has been of major significance. *See* Puritan Political Ideas 1558-1794 (E. Morgan ed. 1965); B. Bailyn, The Origins of American Politics (1967); C. Becker, The Declaration of Independence (1942); Grey, "Origins of the Unwritten Constitution: Fundamental Law in American Revolutionary Thought," 30 Stan. L. Rev. 843 (1978).

5. America's sharp rejection of aristocratic trappings was definitively articulated by provisions appearing both in the original Articles of Confederation and in the final version of the Constitution that declared, "No Title of Nobility shall be granted by the United States: And no Person holding any Office of Profit or Trust under them, shall, without the Consent of the Congress, accept of any present, Emolument, Office or Title, of any kind whatsoever, from any King, Prince or foreign State" (U.S. Const. art. I, § 9; *cf.* Articles of Confederation, art. VI). For a discussion of the founding fathers' understanding of this clause, see Note, "Eugenic Artificial

Insemination: A Cure for Mediocrity?" 94 Harv. L. Rev. 1350, 1359-61 (1981). For a perceptive discussion of the conflicted, simultaneous hunger for, and hatred of, social pretension in eighteenth-century America, see Wood, *supra* note 4, at 70ff.

6. Pole, *supra* note 1, at 42. Writing of his travels to America in the 1840s, Alexis de Tocqueville summarized this phenomenon. "America, then, exhibits in her social state an extraordinary phenomenon. Men are there seen on a greater equality in point of fortune and intellect, or, in other words, more equal in their strength than in any other country of the world, or in any age of which history has preserved the remembrance" (A. de Tocqueville, Democracy in America 55 [vintage ed. 1945]).

Although plantation owners in the South had some pretensions toward aristocratic mores, they were never able to transplant a viable feudal-type order to the American environment. *See* Hartz, *supra* note 4, pt. 4. Ironically, the enslavement of blacks in the South brought together the poor whites and wealthy landowners and tended to promote equality and democracy within white society as a whole. *See* Pole, *supra* note 1, at 33; J. Blum, The Burden of American Equality 3-4 (1978).

7. G. Myrdal, An American Dilemma 4 (1942).

8. Cox, "Forward: Constitutional Adjudication and the Promotion of Human Rights; The Supreme Court, 1965 Term," 80 Harv. L. Rev. 91 (1966).

9. Tocqueville, *supra* note 6 at 55. *See also* Black, "Forward; 'State Action'; Equal Protection, and California's Proposition 14; The Supreme Court, 1966 Term," 81 Harv. L. Rev. 69 (1967). R. H. Tawney described the phenomenon in terms of the inevitable movement of majoritarian democracy toward increasing egalitarianism. "As the mass of the population becomes conscious of the powers which democracy confers, they naturally use them to press their demands" (Tawney, Equality 30 [1921]). Similarly, J. Roland Pennock has described an inherent thrust toward equality in a legal system. "By a process of association or suggestion, legal equality tends, especially through the operation of the courts, to extend beyond the logical limits of the original ideal. The ideal of law thus exerts a certain 'push' toward the idea of equality" (Pennock, "Law's Natural Bent," 79 Ethics 222, 225 [April 1969]).

10. Note in this regard the fears expressed by the conservative John Adams in 1776 concerning the extension of the franchise. Adams declared that, if the franchise were tampered with, "new claims

will arise; women will demand the vote; lads from twelve to twenty-one will think their rights not closely enough attended to; and every man who has not a farthing will demand an equal voice with any other, in all acts of state" (John Adams to James Sullivan, May 26, 1776, Works IX, 375-78, *quoted in* Pole, *supra* note 1, at 43). Two hundred years later, virtually all of Adams's predictions, incredible as they may have seemed to him at the time, have come true. Women, those who have "not a farthing," and even some of the "lads from twelve to twenty-one" (i.e., those over eighteen) now have been afforded the right to vote.

11. For example, since 1936, the percentage of American families below the official poverty level established by the Office of Economic Opportunity (OEO) has been reduced from 56 percent to less than 10 percent (S. Lebergott, Wealth and Want 3 [1975]). Lebergott goes on to demonstrate this point further: "In 1900, 15 percent of U.S. families had flush toilets; today 86 percent of our poor families do. In 1900, 3 percent had electricity; today 99 percent of our poor do. In 1900, 1 percent had central heating; today 62 percent of the poor do. In 1900, 18 percent of our families had refrigeration, ice refrigeration; today 99 percent of our poor have refrigerators, virtually all mechanical" (*Ibid.* at 7).

12. For example, the share of wealth held by the richest 1 percent of the American population remained basically the same between the years 1810 and 1969 (J. Turner and C. Starnes, Inequality: Privilege and Poverty in America 19 [1976]). In terms of the relative income of all strata of American society, similar substantial disparities have persisted, with the lowest fifth of society receiving 4 to 5 percent of total money income and the top fifth, 40 to 50 percent (H. Miller, Rich Man, Poor Man 49-50 [1971]; L. Thurow, The Zero Sum Society 156 [1980]).

Although there was some narrowing of the differentials in the 1960s and early 1970s, the most recent census figures reveal that income inequalities at the ends of the income ladder increased in the decade from 1970 to 1980. During that time span, the percentage of families with incomes of $35,000 or more rose from 14.8 to 19.5, while the percentage of those with incomes below $10,000 rose from 17.8 to 18.9 ("Inflation Wiped Out Gains in Earnings in 1970's," N.Y. Times, April 25, 1982, at A1). In terms of income disparities between racial groups, from 1960 to 1970 the median family income of black families rose from 55 percent to 61 percent that of whites. However, in the next decade, most of that gain was lost: in 1981, median black family income was 56 percent that of white families. Most of this backsliding trend apparently can be traced to the substantial increase in the proportion of black families headed by women—from one-fifth in 1960 to nearly one-half in 1981 ("Income Gap Between Races Wide as in 1960, Study Finds," N.Y. Times, July 18, 1983, at A1). For further discussion of the statistics on income distribution, see J. Hochschild, What's Fair? chap. 1 (1981); B. Page, Who Gets What From Government (1983); R. de Lone, Small Futures: Children, Inequality and the Limits of Liberal Reform (1979); Thurow, *supra*; and Lucas, "The American Distribution of Income: A Structural Problem," in L. Rainwater, Inequality and Justice 77 (1974).

13. Recent research indicates that, in the United States, West Germany, the United Kingdom, and Sweden, there is an approximate eight to one ratio between the average income of the wealthiest quartile and the poorest quartile. Interestingly, Japan has only a five to one ratio. (A. Shostak, J. Van Til, and S. B. Van Til, Privilege in America: An End to Inequality 28 [1973]). The Gini coefficient, a measure of inequality across all levels of income, is higher for the United States than for all 10 nations, except France, surveyed in a 1976 study by the Organization for Economic Cooperation and Development (OECD) (*see* Hochschild, *supra* note 12 at 11-12). *See also* Thurow, *supra* note 12, at 7-8; F. Parkin, Class Inequality and Political Order 118 (1971).

Parkin also discusses economic differentials in the communist countries of Eastern Europe. He indicates that substantial differentials exist between the professional managerial class and other segments of those societies, although there is greater mobility to the upper classes than in Western society (*Ibid.* at 149-55). Inequalities in the distribution of power and prestige, however, may be greater than those which obtain currently in capitalist societies. *See*, e.g., H. Smith, The Russians chap. 1 (1976); H. Matthews, Class and Society in Soviet Russia (1972); M. Yankowitch, Social and Economic Inequality in the Soviet Union (1977); M. Djilas, The New Class (1957).

Other indicators of egalitarian distribution, such as proportions of national budgets spent on income transfer programs like social security, reveal lesser egalitarianism in the United States. For example, in recent years the United States has spent approximately 7.9 percent of its gross national product on social welfare programs, as compared to 17.5 percent for Sweden, 19.6 percent for

Germany, 18.3 percent for France, 14.4 percent for the United
Kingdom, and 10.1 percent for the USSR (H. Wilensky, The Welfare State and Equality 122 [1975]). Wilensky asserts that the key
variables explaining these figures for countries of similar economic
levels relate to the length of time since social welfare programs
were first implemented and the percentage of elderly people in the
society. Distinctions between capitalist and socialist ideologies, he
believes, provide relatively little explanation for these patterns.
14. For discussion of these issues, see S. Miller and P. Roby, The
Future of Inequality (1970); R. Titmuss, Income Distribution and
Social Change (1962); Miller, *supra* note 12; Rainwater, Poverty
in the United States, in Rainwater, *supra* note 12, at 70; A. Okun,
Equality and Efficiency chap. 3 (1975); M. Weber, "Class, Status,
Party," in From Max Weber (H. Gerth and C. W. Mills eds. 1958).
15. *See* D. Bell, The Cultural Contradictions of Capitalism (1976).
Bell notes that economic imperatives, especially those of an in-
dustrial-technological economy, are marked by an emphasis on
functional rationality, bureaucratization, and hierarchy, factors
that are inconsistent with egalitarian ideals. Thus, although the
status orderings of traditional aristocratic societies were relatively
unknown in America, new status orderings based on bureaucratic
norms and wealth emerged in America. (*See also* R. Heilbroner,
The Limits of American Capitalism [1965].) For an interesting
contrary argument, based on admittedly "utopian premises," that
market-oriented economic efficiency is compatible with thoroughgoing equality, see J. Carens, Equality, Moral Incentives and the
Market: An Essay in Utopian Politico-Economic Theory (1981).
16. *See* M. Weber, The Protestant Ethic and the Spirit of Capitalism
(1905).
17. Some critics have held that Locke's theories were, in fact, intended
to provide a justification for bourgeois status differentiations, and
that Locke assumed that "equality" would apply only to a privileged elite. See McPherson, "The Social Bearing of Locke's Political Theory," in G. Schochet, Life, Liberty and Property (1971).
18. Pole, *supra* note 1, at 144. *See also* E. Baltzell, Puritan Boston
and Quaker Philadelphia chap. 2 (1979).
19. *See* M. Horowitz, The Transformation of American Law 1780-
1860 (1977), for a discussion of how economic development imperatives caused major changes in basic common law standards.
20. *See* Hartz, *supra* note 4; Hochschild, *supra* note 12, at 17-20
and sources cited therein. For an insightful discussion of the "non-

socialist" development of American egalitarianism since the New
Deal, see Beer, "In Search of A New Public Philosophy," in The
New American Political System 10, 29 (A. King ed. 1978).

21. Although notions of egalitarianism, once loosed, may contain
an inherent thrust toward further development (see notes 8 and
9), it has also been noted that "[e]quality is the ideal which aims
at the least natural of all political forms; we might say that it is
the ideal which calls for the extreme denaturalization of the political order. To achieve inequality all we have to do is let things
take their course. Not action but inaction is required. But if we
are to achieve equality we can never afford to relax" (G. Sartori,
Democratic Theory 326 [1962]). *Cf.* R. Nozick, Anarchy, State
and Utopia (1974).

22. *See,* e.g., L. Friedman, A History of American Law, Epilogue
(1973); R. Unger, Law in Modern Society (1976).

23. *See generally* G. Fredrickson, White Supremacy: A Comparative
Study in American and South African History (1981). For a discussion of anti-egalitarian pressures of the "post-industrial" era
of the 1980s, see P. Blumberg, Inequality in an Age of Decline
(1980). Note also that, in the American context, the massive waves
of uneducated, impoverished immigrants also created additional
pressures toward a resuscitation of hierarchical status differentials.

24. Myrdal, *supra* note 7.

25. The explosive dynamic inherent in the American liberal credo
has been described by Louis Hartz through a comparison with
South America. "Since the inclusion of the non-Westerner into the
human group at all requires full equality, during the era of slavery
he is totally excluded by theories of either property or race which
make 'liberal slavery,' if we can use the term, harsher in practice
than feudal. But by the same logic, once humanity is conceded,
the liberal ethic is more compulsively generous, since it demands
completely equal treatment" (L. Hartz, The Founding of New
Societies 17 [1964]).

For a detailed discussion of abolitionist concepts of natural right,
see J. tenBroek, Equal Under Law (1965). Note that, although the
ideology of English abolitionism in the early nineteenth century
emphasized humanitarian and religious ideals, American aboli-
tionists built their theories on notions of inequality (Pole, *supra*
note 1, at 157-58). Thus, Abraham Lincoln repeatedly harked back
to the Declaration of Independence and its egalitarian ideals in
justifying the emancipation of the slaves. (*See* Wills, *supra* note 4,

at xiv ff.) Compare in this regard the South African experience, which lacked both a deep-rooted commitment to liberal natural law ideals and a thoroughgoing, repressive slave economy (Fredrickson, *supra* note 23).

26. Note in this regard that the original "self-evident" propositions concerning the equality of all men which were forcefully pronounced in the American Declaration of Independence were not included in the provisions of the Constitution written two decades later. (*See* Wills, *supra* note 4.) It was only with the adoption of the Fourteenth Amendment, following the Civil War and in response to abolitionist pressures to secure the rights of the newly freed slaves, that the doctrine of "equal protection of the laws" became an explicit part of American higher law.

27. *See* Beer, *supra* note 20. The rapid expansion of judicial activism and the development of equal protection doctrines initiated by the Supreme Court during the Warren era centered, of course, on racial inequality. *See*, e.g., Perry, "Modern Equal Protection: A Conceptualization and Appraisal," 79 Colum. L. Rev. 1023 (1979); Brest, "The Supreme Court, 1975 Term; Forward: In Defense of the Anti-Discrimination Principle," 90 Harv. L. Rev. 1 (1976); Karst, "The Supreme Court, 1976 Term; Forward: Equal Citizenship under the Fourteenth Amendment," 91 Harv. L. Rev. 1 (1977). *See also* Trimble v. Gordon, 430 U.S. 762, 777 (1977) (Rehnquist, J., dissenting—[e]qual protection outside the race context is "endless tinkering"). Once egalitarian concepts were established in this context, however, the inherent thrust of the egalitarian ideal thus "uncabined" has led in recent times to extension of egalitarian rights to other groups, such as women and the handicapped. Serious doctrinal problems arise in some of these areas because legal concepts generated in the racial context may not be directly applicable. Consider, for example, the problems of applying affirmative action concepts to the rights of the handicapped at issue in Southeastern Community College v. Davis, 442 U.S. 397 (1979).

28. D. Rae et al. argue in Equalities (1981) that abstract notions of equality are virtually meaningless. Egalitarian concepts take on meaning only in specific political-implementation contexts. *See also* Westen, "The Empty Idea of Equality," 95 Harv. L. Rev. 537 (1982); Burton, "Comment on Empty Ideas: Logical Positivist Analyses of Equality and Rules," 91 Yale L.J. 1136 (1982); K. Greenawalt, "How Empty is the Idea of Equality?" 83 Colum. L. Rev. 1167 (1983).

29. Both American egalitarian strands are rooted in the American liberal tradition. Therefore, as noted in the Introduction, they are distinct from the socialist-oriented egalitarianism of Europe. They also are distinguishable from what might be termed a "conservative" concept of equality based on a notion of "equality of form." Aristotle discussed such a concept in terms of a notion of equality of distribution. In his view, justice was "a species of the proportionate" (Aristotle, The Nicomachean Ethics bk. 5, chaps. 1-7, 10; The Politics bk. 3, chaps. 12, 13). Equality would be realized when "equals" obtained equal shares and "unequals" obtained "unequal" shares. From this perspective, the dictates of fairness and equality would be satisfied if those who were entitled to a greater share of money, prestige, and power within the hierarchical ordering received precisely that proportion to which they were entitled and no more. Thus stated, the conservative notion of equality, emphasizing fairness and formal proportionality, was consistent with the established order, including slavery.

A more modern understanding of this concept of formal equality is implied in the classical concept of the "rule of law." See A. V. Dicey, Introduction to the Study of the Law of the Constitution (1908). For interesting analyses of the implications of rule of law theories for equality, see Marshal, "Notes on the Rule of Equal Law," and Freedman, "Equality in the Administration of Justice," in R. Pennock and J. Chapman, Equality (1967). See also S. Lakoff, Equality in Political Philosophy (1964).

30. J. Locke, Of Civil Government, chap. 5, para. 31.

31. Ibid. at para. 49.

32. See J. S. Mill, On Liberty (1859). Similarly, although (consistent with liberal egalitarian doctrines) he advocated a general expansion of the suffrage, Mill would limit those of lesser educational accomplishments to partial voting participation (J. S. Mill, Representative Government [1861]). For a detailed analysis of the relationship between classical liberals (including Mill, Jeremy Bentham, Thomas Hobbes, and Immanuel Kant, in addition to Locke) and equality, see A. Gutmann, Liberal Equality (1981), especially chaps. 1 and 2. Gutmann argues that the classical liberals failed to understand the importance of participatory democracy and redistribution for turning liberal ideals into practical political concepts.

33. Inherent in the Lockean notion of equality of opportunity was the invitation to those who were the "most industrious" to amass

whatever degree of wealth their capabilities would allow. This concept provided the nexus between liberal ideology and the capitalistic ethic previously discussed in this chapter. Adam Smith's economic theories taught that the pursuit of economic opportunity by a large number of individuals would, through the beneficent workings of a mythical "invisible hand," harmonize personal gain with overall economic progress for the common welfare. In this way, difficult problems of conscience, especially for descendants of the ascetic Puritans, were overcome. Since commercial prosperity sought through personal enterprise made a contribution to the public interest, "[f]eelings of guilt . . . could be assuaged by resort of ideas of equality. . . . Men of wealth, rank and advantage could rest content with the unequal effects of their efforts" Pole, *supra* note 1, at 37-38.

34. *Quoted in* N. Glazer, Affirmative Discrimination: Ethnic Inequality and Public Policy 18 (1975).

35. The concept of equality of opportunity is also plagued by an additional, inherent problem, as John H. Schaar has forcefully pointed out. "[V]irtually all of the demand for the kind of equality expressed in the equal-opportunity principle, is really a demand for an equal right and opportunity to become unequal" (Schaar, "Equality of Opportunity and Beyond," in Pennock and Chapman, *supra* note 29, at 238). This demand creates a new form of elitism which presents serious difficulties for equality and democracy, however well-earned the achievements of the successful may be. Henry Fairlie explains why. "There could be no more certain prescription for inciting people to Envy [than equality of opportunity], for it leaves the majority of them, who do not succeed, with no alternative but to see themselves as losers. In an equal race, as they have been told it is, they were defeated. If it is merit alone that is rewarded, as they have again been told, then they have been proved to have little or none. But one cannot ask people to accept so sweeping and blindfold a dismissal of their own abilities, and this is one reason why what is so pretentiously described as a meritocracy is popularly described as a rat race" (H. Fairlie, The Seven Deadly Sins Today 75 [1979]). *See also* J. Gardner, Excellence 5-6 (1961); M. Lewis, The Culture of Inequality 15 (1978). In Britain, despite a greater degree of actual inequality, resentment of their "betters" by those in the lower strata seems to be markedly less than might be anticipated because of the British people's acceptance of a natural stratification pattern and their tendency to

compare themselves only with closely related "reference groups."
*See*, e.g., Goldthorpe, "Social Inequality and Social Integration,"
in Rainwater, *supra* note 12, at 32, 34-35.

36. One example of the difficulties involved in attempting to eliminate discriminatory barriers is provided by Owen Fiss's arguments
concerning the ineffectiveness of the profit motive, which is assumed by many (*see*, e.g., A. Goldman, Justice and Reverse Discrimination 53 [1979]) to be an effective incentive for eliminating
discrimination in hiring decisions. He points out that the profit
incentive to hire the most qualified does not hold because, among
other factors, (1) for many simple jobs, persons with different
qualifications nevertheless can be expected to achieve approximately equal productivity; (2) many regulated industries are not
affected by a profit motive; and (3) the bureaucracies of large
business enterprises, quite simply, often make mistakes which are
inconsistent with their own profit motives. (Fiss, "A Theory of
Fair Employment Laws," 38 U. Chi. L. Rev. 235, 249ff. [1971]).

37. L. Johnson, The Vantage Point: Perspectives of the Presidency
1963-1969 166 (1971).

38. *See*, e.g., W. Ryan, Equality 27 (1981). Bruce Ackerman, in Social
Justice in the Liberal State (1980), provides an intriguing, analyt-
ically rigorous liberal theory which would assure scrupulously fair
equal opportunities for all citizens. However, as Ackerman himself
notes, his model is based on ideal theory, which, when one is
grappling with real world problems, must be replaced by "second
best" or "third best" theory.

39. *See* C. Jencks et al., Inequality: A Reassessment of the Effect of
Family and Schooling in America (1972). *See also* The "Inequality"
Controversy (D. Levine and M. Bane eds. 1975); On Equality of
Educational Opportunity (F. Mosteller and D. Moynihan eds.
1972); Miller, *supra* note 12, at chap. 10; J. Coleman et al., Equality of Educational Opportunity (1966). Coleman states that varia-
tions in school facilities and curriculums have little impact on pupil
achievement, but that the backgrounds of other students in that
school strongly influence pupil achievement. He also argues elsewhere that, if one concentrates on certain specific inputs (such as
teacher verbal skills), it can be shown that education can substantially raise attainment levels, although, realistically, equal educational opportunity can never be expected to compensate fully
for all family and background deficiencies (Coleman, "Inequality,
Sociology and Moral Philosophy," 80 Am. J. Soc. 739 [1974]).

*Cf.* S. Bowles and H. Gintis, Schooling in Capitalist America (1976). They argue that if schools were not controlled by a capitalist ruling class they could make a difference.

40. *See,* e.g., de Lone, *supra* note 12, at 3-4; Shostak, Van Til, and Van Til, *supra* note 13, at 21 ("[T]he son of an elite father . . . has sixteen times the chance of the semi-skilled worker's son [to become elite himself]").

Of course, compensating one individual may require a shifting of benefits or resources away from another, and the equities involved in such a process are often far from clear. For an interesting discussion of this point, carried to far-reaching conclusions, see Nozick, *supra* note 21, at 235.

41. See Jencks et al., *supra* note 39; de Lone, *supra* note 12; K. Keniston, All Our Children (1977).

42. "One might speculate about how far this movement of thought might go. The most conservative user of the notion of inequality of opportunity is, if sincere, prepared to abstract the individual from some effects of his environment. . . . Where should this stop? Should it even stop at the boundaries of heredity? Suppose it were discovered that when all curable environmental disadvantages had been dealt with, there was a residual genetic difference in brain constitution, for instance, which was correlated with differences in desired types of ability; but that the brain constitution could in fact be changed by an operation. Suppose further that the wealthier classes could afford such an operation for their children. . . . [W]ould we then think that poorer children did not have equality of opportunity because they had no opportunity to get rid of their genetic disadvantages?" (Williams, "The Idea of Equality," in H. Bedau, Justice and Equality 135 (1971). *See also* Bane, "Economic Justice: Controversies and Policies," in The "Inequality" Controversy, *supra* note 39, at 277, 296; J. Rawls, A Theory of Justice 74 (1971); O'Neill, "How Do We Know When Opportunities Are Equal?" in M. Vetterling-Braggin et al., Feminism and Philosophy 177, 185 (1977).

43. "The issue of equality of opportunity separates liberals and democrats not because they do not share the same ideal, but because they often disagree on how to achieve it" (Sartori, *supra* note 21, at 336).

44. They would, however, probably maintain with Jean Jacques Rousseau that civil society creates social inequalities that aggravate

the natural inequalities. *See* J. J. Rousseau, The Discourse on the Origin of Inequality 209 (L. Crocker ed. 1967).
45. "[R]edistribution would spur creativity among those now poor. There are, we may be sure, as many creative people in that population as in many others, and if they no longer had to worry continually about surviving, they too would be able to act on their need to create" (Gans, "How Equal, Equal How?" Colum. F. 36, 38 [Spring 1975]). *See also*, e.g., Chomsky, "Language Development, Human Intelligence and Social Organization," in Equality and Social Policy 163, 171-75 (W. Feinberg ed. 1978).
46. tenBroek, *supra* note 25, at 19.
47. Rawls, *supra* note 42.
48. *Ibid.* at 100-101. Critics of Rawls have questioned his assumptions concerning the choices rational men would make under the "veil of ignorance." Much of this criticism is discussed in terms of the "max-min" concept. It is not clear, argue the critics, that in the original position a rational man would necessarily seek to maximize his ability to avoid a life of total misery once the veil was removed; he might well be willing to take some prudent risks (such as assuming that he will not be among the most wretched in actual life) and therefore advocate a society that allows modest levels of differentials to maximize individual potential. On these points, see, e.g., Gauthier, "Justice and Natural Endowment: Toward a Critique of Rawls' Ideological Framework," 3 Soc. Theory & Prac. 3 (1974); Sterba, "Justice as Desert," 3 Soc. Theory & Prac. 101 (1974); B. Barry, The Liberal Theory of Justice (1973); J. Fishkin, Tyranny and Legitimacy chap. 13 (1979).

Rawls's max-min concept, of course, gains much of its strength from the utilitarian concept of diminishing marginal utility: taking a good from one who has much and giving it to one who has very little would markedly increase overall social utility. *See* Hare, "Justice and Equality," in Justice and Economic Distribution 116, 124-25 (J. Arthur and W. Shaw eds. 1978). However, Professor Michelman notes in this regard that "[s]atisfying a highly disadvantaged person's basic needs will sometimes be possible only at exceedingly large cost, and a commitment to pay such costs whenever required will apparently force an unacceptable lowering of the minimum assurances which can be extended to the disadvantaged generally. The moral intuition at work here evokes a hybrid of maximin and average utility: it calls for something like the highest attainable level of average provisions for the group of the disadvantaged."

NOTES TO CHAPTER ONE

(Michelman, "Constitutional Welfare Rights and 'A Theory of Justice,' " in N. Daniels, Reading Rawls 319, 333 [1974]).

49. Rawls's concepts also lead back to the "equality of esteem" notions at the core of the original American egalitarian ideal. "Rawls has strengthened philosophical bases of that passion for equality which Tocqueville saw as the deepest desire of the modern age" (Schaar, "Reflections on Rawls' Theory of Justice," 3 Soc. Theory & Prac. 75 [1974]). *See also* Pole, *supra* note 1, at 335; Glazer, *supra* note 34, at 4, 204.

50. For an alternative result-oriented theory that accepts individual differences of wealth and power, but within bounds that prohibit inequitable "domination," see M. Walzer, Spheres of Justice (1983).

51. The phrase is taken from H. Gans, More Equality (1968).

52. *See*, e.g., Bell, "On Meritocracy and Equality," Pub. Int. 29 (1972). Although such views may have been accepted by some of the countercultural writers of the 1960s (*see* note 56), they are not integral to the position of Rawls or other major, contemporary, result-oriented egalitarian writers.

Recent sociological theory has substantially undermined assumptions that hierarchical orderings can ever be eliminated from human society. *See*, e.g., Davis and Moore, "Some Principles of Stratification," 10 Am. Soc. Rev. 242 (1945); Tumin, "Some Principles of Stratification: A Critical Analysis," 18 Am. Soc. Rev. 387 (1953). *See also* Patterson, Inequality, Freedom, and the Equal Opportunity Doctrine, in Equality and Social Policy 17 (W. Feinberg ed. 1978); Davis, "Reply to Tumin," 18 Am. Soc. Rev. 394 (1953). Most important in this regard is the concept of authority. No organization can be administered without some degree of authoritative direction and control. Even Friedrich Engels, who spoke of the withering away of the state, "nevertheless declared that it would be impossible to think of any great, modern industrial enterprise or of the organization of the future communist society without authority—or superiority-subordination relationships" (Westowski, "Some Notes on the Functional Theory of Stratification," in R. Bendix and S. M. Lipset, Class, Status and Power 64, 69 [1966]). *See also* A. Lindbeck, The Political Economy of the New Left 32ff. (1977); R. Dahl, After the Revolution 40-56 (1970).

Even if one assumes that all (or more) men and women are equally capable of assuming leadership roles, some differential rewards, whether in the form of money, power, or prestige, would appear to be necessary to induce some of them to accept the stress, burdens, and responsibility that accompany leadership positions. Moreover, governing norms in any legal system must inherently be closer to the values of some citizens than to those of others (Dahrendorf, "On the Origin of Social Equality," in P. Laslett and W. G. Runciman, Philosophy, Politics and Sociology 88, 102 [1962]). See also R. Dahrendorf, Life Chances chap. 6 (1979); R. Tucker, The Inequality of Nations (1977). For an ambitious effort to provide an empirically based synthesis of functionalist and radical egalitarian perspectives on these issues, see G. Lenski, Power and Privilege (1966).

53. For example, Robert Nisbet postulates that the achievement of an egalitarian political order inevitably is associated with the rise of militaristic political systems and the demise of intermediate associations which are the bedrocks of any meaningful concepts of liberty (R. Nisbet, Twilight of Authority [1975]). See also Isaiah Berlin's discussion of the dangers of "positive liberty" in "Two Concepts of Liberty," in I. Berlin, Four Essays on Liberty 118 (1969); F. A. Hayek, Law, Legislation and Liberty 83 (1976); H. Arendt, The Human Condition (1958). For a counter argument claiming that centralization (at least within the context of the American federal system) promotes both equality and liberty, see Patterson, supra note 52, at 15, 32.

54. Rawls, supra note 42, at 244.

55. Indeed, it is for such reasons that Rawls's theory itself has been called "collectivist." See Coleman, Inequality, Sociology and Moral Philosophy," supra note 39, at 739, 755. Moreover, as some leftist commentators have noted, if Rawls seriously intends for the liberty values of his first principle to be enjoyed by the mass of the population, priority, in fact, will have to be given to the second principle, i.e., to ensuring a basic degree of economic equality and equality of esteem, because these are essential prerequisites for the meaningful pursuit of political and civil liberties. See Nielsen, "Radical Egalitarian Justice: Justice as Equality," 5 Soc. Theory & Prac. 209 (1979); Held, "Men, Women and Equal Liberty," in Equality and Social Policy, supra note 52, at 66.

Gutmann states that, for liberty to be meaningfully assured, certain minimal needs, such as medical services, must be guaranteed to all. Combining rights to provision of minimum services with rights of political participation, she believes, would provide a workable reconciliation of liberty and equality (Guttman, *supra* note 32, at 126). This tenuous balance is appealing in theory; the critics cited *supra* note 53, however, would claim that, in practice, the scale would be weighted toward overbearing governmental interference with individual liberties.

56. *See* R. Wolff, Understanding Rawls (1977). *See also* Fried, "The Artificial Reason of the Lawyer: What Lawyers Know," 60 Tex. L. Rev. 35, 50 (1981). John Schaar has stated that, in this sense, Rawls is more radical than Marx, since he emphasizes each person's needs, but not that each person must contribute to society according to his ability (Schaar, *supra* note 49, at 75, 89).

Much of the radical egalitarian literature which emerged during the counterculture movement in the 1960s was based upon assumptions of widespread economic affluence to be achieved by technology and advanced industrial enterprise. *See*, e.g., M. Bookchin, Post-Scarcity Anarchism (1971); All We Are Saying . . . : The Philosophy of the New Left (A. Lothstein ed. 1970); H. Marcuse, Eros and Civilization (1955); C. Reich, The Greening of America (1970). *See also* J. K. Galbraith, The Affluent Society (1958). In recent years, the realization that there may be ecological limits to growth (*see*, e.g., D. Meadows et al., The Limits to Growth [1972]; W. Ophuls, Ecology and the Politics of Scarcity [1977]; G. Myrdal, Against the Stream [1972]; *cf.* P. Passell and L. Ross, The Retreat from Riches [1971]; W. Beckerman, Two Cheers for the Affluent Society [1974]; R. Barnet, The Lean Years [1980]), as well as seemingly inevitable "positional scarcities" (*see* F. Hirsch, Social Limits to Growth [1976]), have undermined these assumptions.

57. "American Society [tends to reduce] its most troubling controversies to . . . a lawsuit" (R. Kluger, Simple Justice: The History of Brown v. Board of Education and Black America's Struggle for Equality x [1976]). For an overview of the manner in which the courts, rather than political theorists, have molded the substantive content of egalitarian ideals in America, see Karst, "Why Equality Matters," 17 Ga. L. Rev. 245 (1983). *See also* Baker, "Outcome Equality or Equality of Respect: The Substantive Content of Equal Protection," 131 U. Pa. L. Rev. 933 (1983). The role of the courts in giving content to egalitarian ideals undoubtedly has significantly influenced the development of the unique activist institutional role of the courts in America. See Rebell, "Judicial Activism and the Courts' New Role," 12 Soc. Pol'y 24 (1982). For an overview of

the literature on judicial activism, see M. Rebell and A. Block, Educational Policy Making and the Courts: An Empirical Study of Judicial Activism chap. 1 (1982).

NOTES TO CHAPTER TWO

1. 347 U.S. 483 (1954).
2. 438 U.S. 265 (1978).
3. Note, for example, the lengthy discussion of Rawls's Theory of Justice at the beginning of the brief submitted by the American Civil Liberties Union.
4. Although there is of course, much controversy on the extent to which courts should engage in social policymaking activities, the courts are generally acknowledged to be the institution best constituted for *principled* decision making (*see*, e.g., Wechsler, "Toward Neutral Principles of Constitutional Law," 73 Harv. L. Rev. 1 (1959); R. Dworkin, Taking Rights Seriously chap. 4 (1977); A. Bickel, The Least Dangerous Branch (1962). The "rational-analytic" mode of judicial decision making is considered at length in M. Rebell and A. Block, Educational Policy Making and the Courts: An Empirical Study of Judicial Activism (1982).
5. 163 U.S. 537 (1896).
6. 347 U.S. at 493.
7. *See*, e.g., Missouri ex. rel. Gaines v. Canada, 305 U.S. 337 (1938) (payment of tuition at out-of-state law school did not provide equal opportunity); Sweatt v. Painter, 339 U.S. 629 (1950) (separate in-state black law school did not provide adequate faculty, variety of courses, and opportunity for specialization); McLaurin v. Oklahoma State Regents, 339 U.S. 637 (1950) (separate "ghetto" bench in graduate school facility impaired black plaintiff's ability to learn).
8. 347 U.S. at 495.
9. The specific phrase "equal educational opportunity" was repeated at least half a dozen times in the course of the Court's opinion.
10. 347 U.S. at 492 (emphasis added). James Coleman discussed the Brown decision in somewhat similar terms. "In a decision of the Supreme Court, this unarticulated feeling began to take more precise form. The essence of it was that the *effects* of such separate schools were, or were likely to be, different. Thus, a concept of equality of opportunity which focused on *effects* of schooling began to take form. The actual decision of the court was in fact a

confusion of two unrelated premises: this new concept, which looked at results of schooling, and the legal premise that the use of race as a basis for school assignment violates fundamental freedoms. But what is important for the evolution of the concept of equality of opportunity is that a new and different assumption was introduced, the assumption that equality of opportunity depends in some fashion on effects of schooling" (Coleman, "The Concept of Equality of Educational Opportunity," 38 Harv. Educ. Rev. 7, 14 [1968]). *See also* D. Kirp, Just Schools: The Idea of Racial Equality in American Education 41 (1982).

11. Briggs v. Elliott, 132 F. Supp. 776, 777 (E.D.S.C. 1955). Indeed, early decisions of the Supreme Court also hinted that open admissions was the full extent of the constitutional mandate. *See,* e.g., Cooper v. Aaron, 358 U.S. 1, 7 (1958); Goss v. Board of Education, 373 U.S. 683 (1963); Griffin v. County School Board, 377 U.S. 218 (1964).

12. In the 11 southern states during the 1963-1964 school year, only 1.17 percent of black children attended school with white children. By the 1965-1966 school year, this figure had risen to 6.01 percent, largely as a result of the passage of the 1964 Civil Rights Act. However, Alabama, Louisiana, and Mississippi each had less than 1 percent of their black children in school with whites. In the same year, for the 17 southern and border states, 10.9 percent of black children attended school with white children (United States v. Jefferson County Board of Education, 372 F.2d 836, 854 [5th Cir. 1966]).

State legislatures enacted a variety of statutory schemes designed to obstruct the desegregation process. Among these were tuition grants to enable children to attend private schools (*see* Griffin v. County School Board, 377 U.S. 218 [1964]); closing of the public schools (*see* James v. Almond, 170 F. Supp. 331 [E.D. Va.], *appeal dismissed*, 359 U.S. 1006 [1959]); and freedom of choice plans (*see* Green v. County School Board, 391 U.S. 430 [1968]). A significant device utilized in connection with the early freedom of choice plans was state pupil placement boards, which automatically reassigned children to the school they had been attending, unless the student requested a transfer. Blacks seeking to transfer had to satisfy strict criteria, including achievement levels well above the median of the class into which they sought to transfer. *See* Green v. School Board, 304 F.2d 118 (4th Cir. 1962); Shuttlesworth v. Birmingham Board of Education, 358 U.S. 101 (1958);

Johnson, "School Desegregation Problems in the South: An Historical Perspective," 54 Minn. L. Rev. 1157 (1970).

13. 391 U.S. 430 (1968).

14. 391 U.S. at 439. *See also* Alexander v. Holmes Country Board of Education, 396 U.S. 19 (1969) (southern school districts ordered to "begin immediately to operate as unitary school systems").

15. 402 U.S. 1 (1971). See also Fiss, "The Charlotte-Mecklenberg Case—Its Significance for Northern School Desegregation," 38 U. Chi. L. Rev. 697, 704 (1971) ("The net effect of Charlotte-Mecklenberg is to move school desegregation doctrine further along the continuum toward a result-oriented approach").

16. 402 U.S. at 30.

17. *See*, e.g., Dimond, "School Segregation in the North: There is But One Constitution," 7 Harv. C.R.-C.L. L. Rev. 1 (1972). Justices Powell and Douglas advocated abandonment of the *de jure-de facto* distinction in their concurring opinions in *Keyes*, n.19, at 214, 217.

18. *See*, e.g., Oliver v. School District of Kalamazoo, 346 F. Supp. 766 (W.D. Mich. 1972), *aff'd*, 448 F.2d 635 (6th Cir. 1972); Jackson v. Pasadena City School District, 382 P.2d 878, 882 (Sup. Ct. Cal. 1963); Johnson v. San Francisco Unified School District, 339 F. Supp. 1315 (N.D. Cal. 1971); Spangler v. Pasadena City Board of Education, 311 F. Supp. 501 (C.D. Cal. 1970).

19. 413 U.S. 189 (1973). From the perspective of egalitarian theory, acceptance of a strict *de facto* position might be tantamount to acceptance of an equality of condition approach. The Court's insistence in *Keyes* and later cases on at least a scintilla of discriminatory purpose or discriminatory intent illustrates the point made in the preceding chapter that even strong assertions of the equality of result position in America ultimately are tied to a concept of opening opportunities, rather than of redistributing benefits.

20. 418 U.S. 717 (1974).

21. In 1970, the Detroit public school system's student body was 64 percent black, while the metropolitan area as a whole was 81 percent white. The district court had noted that if the scope of the remedy was limited to the Detroit city limits, the best result that could be achieved would "leave many of its schools 75 to 90 percent black" (418 U.S. at 765). For a discussion of *Milliken's* severe, detrimental impact on possibilities for effective desegregation in major urban areas, see Gewirtz, "Remedies and Resistance, 92 Yale L.J. 585, 628-665 (1983). The Court has indicated,

however, that in certain instances (not yet found to occur in major metropolitan settings) where indicia of inter-district segregatory intent are present, metropolitan desegregation remedies will be approved. *See* Hills v. Gatreaux, 425 U.S. 284 (1976): Evans v. Buchanan, 393 F. Supp. 428 (D. Del. 1975), *aff'd*, 423 U.S. 963 (1975). *See also* Berry v. School District of Benton Harbor, 698 F.2d 813 (6th Cir. 1983), *on remand*, 564 F. Supp. 617 (W.D. Mich. 1983); Liddell v. Board of Education of the City of St. Louis, 567 F. Supp. 1037 (D. Mo. 1983) (voluntary inter-district desegregation plan between city school district and 21 suburban districts).

22. *See* Washington v. Davis, 426 U.S. 229 (1976); Arlington Heights v. Metropolitan Housing Development Corporation, 429 U.S. 252 (1977); Personnel Administration of Massachusetts v. Feeney 442 U.S. 256 (1979); Memphis v. Greene, 451 U.S. 100, 129 (1981) (White, J., concurring). *See also* Note, "Reading The Mind of the School Board: Segregative Intent and the *De Facto/De Jure* Distinction," 86 Yale L.J. 317 (1976).

23. *See*, e.g., Griggs v. Duke Power Co., 401 U.S. 424 (1971); Lau v. Nichols, 414 U.S. 563 (1974); Board of Education of the City School District of New York v. Harris, 444 U.S. 130 (1979); Guardians Association v. Civil Service Commission of the City of New York, 103 S. Ct. 3221 (1983). Note also the continued result orientation (limited, of course, to an intra-district basis) in decisions upholding strong remedial action, such as the extensive compensatory education ordered in Milliken v. Bradley, 433 U.S. 267 (1977) (*Milliken II*).

24. 443 U.S. 526 (1979).

25. 443 U.S. 449 (1979).

26. One might well argue that the Court has maintained a consistent, result-oriented posture in its desegation rulings, with the single but highly significant exception of *Milliken I*. From this perspective, the Court has insisted continually, from 1954 to the present, on effective dismantling of dual school systems, and it took a different tack in *Milliken* only because of the weight it gave to countervailing values of local control. (Of course, one may wonder whether local control is a valid description of educational governance in Michigan or most other states, or, in any event, whether it is a value weighty enough to justify the severe impediment to urban education wrought by *Milliken*.) *See* Cover, "The Origins

242          NOTES TO CHAPTER TWO

of Judicial Activism in the Protection of Minorities," 91 Yale L.J. 1287, 1309 (1982).

27. 443 U.S. at 538. Justice Rehnquist, in a strong dissent, stated that this approach of basing present liability on actions in the "remote past" effectively eliminates the *de jure-de facto* distinction (443 U.S. at 542). *See also* Washington v. Seattle School District No. 1, 458 U.S. 157 (1982) (intent standard not applied to state-wide initiative to prohibit mandatory busing; initiative invalidated for placing "special burdens on minorities"). *But cf.* Crawford v. Board of Education of the City of Los Angeles, 458 U.S. 527 (1982) (proposition precluding state courts from ordering busing except in accordance with federal fourteenth amendment standards upheld).

28. The concepts of discriminatory intent and discriminatory impact are, of course, highly interrelated, as are the concepts of equality of opportunity and equality of result, to which they may be an-alogized. Thus, the Court has specifically held that a clear indication of detrimental impact upon a minority population consti-tutes one important factor to be considered in assessing whether discriminatory intent was at play (*see* Arlington Heights, 429 U.S. at 266), a factor which, standing alone, at times can be fully determinative (Castaneda v. Partida, 430 U.S. 482 [1977]). *But cf.* Feeney, *supra* note 22, with Mobile v. Bolden, 446 U.S. 55 (1980). *See also* Note, "Discriminatory Purpose and Proportionate Impact: An Assessment After Feeney," 79 Colum. L. Rev. 1376 (1979); Note, "Making the Violation Fit the Remedy: The Intent Standard and Equal Protection Law," 92 Yale L. J. 328 (1982).

Similar doctrinal oscillations between equality of opportunity and equality of result perspectives have occurred in other areas of equal protection law during the Burger Court era, as, for example, in voting rights (*compare* Mobile v. Bolden, *supra*, with Rogers v. Lake, 102 S. Ct. 3272 [1982]); welfare rights (*compare* Goldberg v. Kelly, 397 U.S. 254 [1970] with Dandridge v. Williams, 397 U.S. 471 [1970] and with United States Department of Agriculture v. Moreno, 413 U.S. 528 [1973]); and access to the courts (*compare* Griffin v. Illinois, 351 U.S. 12 [1956] with Boddie v. Con-necticut, 401 U.S. 371 [1971] and with Ross v. Moffitt, 417 U.S. 600 [1974]).

29. For general overviews of the development of desegregation law, see G. Orfield, Must We Bus? (1978); J. Wilkinson, From Brown to Bakke (1979); Kirp, *supra* note 10; D. Days, "Radical Justice"

in Our Endangered Rights (N. Dorsey ed. 1984). *See also* Yudof, "School Desegregation: Legal Realism, Reasoned Elaboration, and Social Science Research in the Supreme Court," 42 Law & Contemp. Probs. 57, 58 (Autumn 1978).

30. "For *Bakke* posed the arch conflict between equality and meritocracy. . . . *Brown* had not involved any such conflict. Segregated schools were not only separate and unequal; they were also unmeritocratic. . . . In *Brown*, for a fleeting moment, equality and meritocracy seemed one . . . [but] soon this uneasy truce began to fray" (Wilkinson, *supra* note 29, at 264).

31. For example, for black applicants accepted into medical schools in the mid-1970s, the average score on the science section of the Medical College Admissions Test (MCAT) was 127 points lower than that of accepted white applicants and 80 points lower than that of white applicants in general (A. Sindler, Bakke, DeFunis and Minority Admissions: The Quest for Equal Opportunity 111 [1978]).

32. Adherents of equality of opportunity argue that only the credentials of each individual applicant, based on objective test scores, should be considered. They emphasize "our most basic ideal that individual merit and individual need should be the only relevant considerations for societally distributed rewards and benefits." (Graglia, "Special Admission of the Culturally Deprived to Law School," 119 U. Pa. L. Rev. 351, 352 [1970]). *See also* A. Goldman, Justice and Reverse Discrimination (1979); N. Glazer, Affirmative Discrimination: Ethnic Inequality and Public Policy (1975); B. Gross, Reverse Discrimination (1977); Lavinsky, "DeFunis v. Odegaard, The 'Non-Decision' With a Message," 75 Colum. L. Rev. 520 (1975); Sowell, "The Plight of Black Students in the United States," Daedalus 179 (Spring 1974).

Goldman points out that preferential hiring practices often compensate for discrimination suffered by older generations of women or blacks by giving preferential status to younger members of these groups who, in fact, have had full opportunities, in a nondiscriminatory environment, to develop their potential. Glazer emphasizes that even benign racial classifications lead to a host of complex difficulties in classifying individuals according to their racial characteristics. (*Cf.* Nickel, "Preferential Policies in Hiring and Admissions: A Jurisprudential Approach," 75 Colum. L. Rev. 534, 558 [1975], which advocates a program permitting blacks, Chicanos, and "anyone else who thinks he is entitled" to apply for

preference in admissions.) Sowell contends that much of the problem in this area results from the phenomenon of "mismatching,"
in that minority students who are objectively qualified to be admitted to programs at a certain level enter programs at a higher
level, creating unnecessary problems for all concerned.

33. Proponents of preferential admissions argue that subtle patterns
of discrimination have not been effectively eliminated by anti-
discrimination laws and regulations. Therefore, race-conscious admissions policies not only are justifiable, but also are the only
means of providing meaningful equal opportunity. See, e.g.,
B. Bittker, The Case for Black Reparations (1973); Fiss, "Groups
and the Equal Protection Clause," 5 Phil. Pub. Aff. 107 (1976).
Furthermore, it is claimed, preferential policies need not open the
door for a reimposition of quotas and racial stereotyping, because
non-stigmatizing "benign" discriminatory policies adopted by a
legislative majority "against itself" are not comparable to the in-
vidiousness of discriminatory policies imposed on powerless minority groups (Ely, "The Constitutionality of Reverse Racial Discrimination," 41 U. Chi. L. Rev. 723 [1974]). For critiques of Ely's
position, see Sandalow, "Racial Preferences in Higher Education:
Political Responsibility and the Judicial Role," 42 U. Chi. L. Rev.
653 (1975); Greenawalt, "Judicial Scrutiny of 'Benign' Racial Preference in Law School Admissions," 75 Colum. L. Rev. 559, 573
(1975).

Ronald Dworkin argues that the basic tenets of fair individualized treatment are met when there is "treatment as an equal,"
meaning that if the potential loss of a white applicant is seriously
considered, his interests may ultimately be outweighed for broader
policy reasons which will benefit the community as a whole
(R. Dworkin, Taking Rights Seriously 223-239 [1977]). See also
S. Benn, "Egalitarianism and the Equal Consideration of Interests," in R. Pennock and J. Chapman, Equality 61 (1967) (concept
of "equal consideration of interests").

34. Opponents of preferential admissions argue that, because opportunities such as higher education are limited, available places
should be reserved for those who can make the most of them.
They also believe that the objective tests used to measure "merit"
for university admissions purposes, though not perfect, are probably more effective than any alternatives ever utilized. See, e.g.,
J. Gardner, Exellence: Can We Be Equal and Excellent Too? 48
(1961). Virtually all commentators on this subject tend to agree

that scores on scholastic aptitude tests, law school admissions tests, and medical college aptitude tests, for example, correlate substantially with performance in basic college and graduate school courses. *See*, e.g., Sindler, *supra* note 31, at 115; O'Neil, "Preferential Admissions: Equalizing the Access of Minority Groups to Higher Education," 80 Yale L.J. 699, 733 (1971); Greenawalt, *supra* note 33, at 586; Goldman, *supra* note 32, at 59. Similarly, although modern I.Q. tests are not infallible, because of the interplay of additional factors such as motivation and perserverence, they have been shown to be a necessary indicator of success in schooling at all levels. *See* R. Herrnstein, I.Q. in the Meritocracy 113 (1973).

Advocates of preferential admissions retort that although standardized tests measure reasonably well those attributes they measure, they do not even purport to deal with the wide range of creative aspects of human thought. *See*, e.g., A. Gartner et al., The New Assault on Equality: I.Q. and Social Stratification 4 (1974); Hudson, "The Limits of Human Intelligence," in J. Benthall, The Limits of Human Nature 176 (1974). For a fascinating exploration of the disquieting implications of a pure "meritocratic" social policy, see M. Young, The Rise of the Meritocracy: 1870-2033 (1958). Furthermore, there has not been adequate demonstration that academic performance, as presently defined, is a fair indicator of ability to perform well in actual job situations. McClelland, "Testing for Competence Rather than for Intelligence," in Gartner, *supra*, at 168; Karst and Horowitz, "Affirmative Action and Equal Protection," 60 Va. L. Rev. 955, 969 (1974); Bell, "In Defense of Minority Admissions Programs: A Response to Professor Graglia," 119 U. Pa. L. Rev. 364, 367 (1970).

35. Under present admissions criteria, only a relatively few individuals at the top of the admissions pool are outstandingly qualified and a relatively few at the bottom clearly unqualified. The broad middle range of candidates is usually acknowledged to be capable of competent performance at the institution. Proponents of preferential admissions argue, therefore, that until such time as truly validated selection standards are devised, selection decisions among this broad middle range of applicants should be on a random basis, for reasons of basic fairness. Alternatively, if social policy is to be a consideration, preferential admissions would be justified on the basis of broad notions of social utility which include, in addition to consideration of economic productivity, goals

such as the promotion of racial integration (or, stated another way, the elimination of racial tensions and confrontation). These are legitimate "macroproductivity" needs of society. *See* Daniels, "Merit and Meritocracy," 7 Phil. Pub. Aff. 206 (1978); Karst and Horowitz, *supra* note 34, at 963. Of course, pure academic "merit" has never been the sole criterion for university admissions, since "social utility factors," such as promotion of alumni relations, geographic diversity, and likely future career directions, have always been considered. See Wasserstrom, "Racism, Sexism and Preferential Admissions: An Approach to the Topics," 24 U.C.L.A. L. Rev. 581, 617 (1977).

36. 438 U.S. 265 (1978). Similar issues had been involved in the controversy concerning preferential admissions practices at the University of Washington Law School, in DeFunis v. Odegaard, 416 U.S. 312 (1974). The Supreme Court managed to avoid squarely facing these highly charged issues in that case, however, by declaring the controversy moot in light of the fact that the plaintiff, who had been temporarily admitted pending his appeal, was about to graduate by the time the Supreme Court was called upon to issue a final decision.

37. Interestingly, Bakke had both a higher grade point average and higher MCAT scores than the average of those students admitted to the 84 regular places in the class; apparently, he was denied admission originally because of his comparatively low rating on the interview aspects of the admissions process (438 U.S. at 277 n.7). Bakke's age—he was thirty-two when he first applied—also may have been an unstated factor. *See* Sindler, *supra* note 31, at 65-66.

38. We will set aside for present purposes the complex, legal disputes concerning the applicable constitutional equal protection standards and the legislative intent behind Title VI (which will be considered in the next chapter).

39. 438 U.S. at 370.

40. *See*, e.g., the discussion at 438 U.S. 360-61.

41. 438 U.S. at 369. Justice Marshall, in a moving separate opinion, analyzed in detail the history of discrimination against blacks in the United States, emphasizing that, because of this unique history, all blacks were entitled to an immediate result-oriented preferential policy. His emphasis on the unique history of blacks in America was intended to answer the "no stopping point argument" and

the claim that individual middle-class blacks had not suffered discrimination (*see* 438 U.S. at 400-401).

42. 438 U.S. at 295.

43. The record in the case indicated that the University of California had adopted the preferential admissions policy voluntarily, and that there was no finding that the university had discriminated in admissions in the past. Some commentators have indicated, however, that because of the unique setting of the *Bakke* case, which was argued by a white plaintiff and a white-controlled university, minority group interests who may have been able to show that patterns of racial discrimination did exist at the University of California were not afforded a real opportunity to do so. *See* Bell, "Bakke, Minority Admissions and the usual Price of Racial Remedies," 67 Cal. L. Rev. 3 (1979).

44. Blasi, "Bakke as Precedent: Does Mr. Justice Powell Have a Theory?" 67 Cal. L. Rev. 21 (1979). *See also* "The Supreme Court, 1977 Term," 92 Harv. L. Rev. 57, 135-37 (1978); Tribe, "Perspectives on Bakke: Equal Protection, Procedural Fairness or Structural Justice," 92 Harv. L. Rev. 864-65 (1978).

45. This argument generally had been viewed (from a social policy point of view) as the weakest of the university's justifications. *See* Greenawalt, "Unresolved Problems of Reverse Discrimination," 67 Cal. L. Rev. 87, 122 (1979).

46. 438 U.S. at 323.

47. *See* "The Supreme Court, 1977 Term," *supra* note 44, at 57, 146; Blasi, *supra* note 44, at 65. For a detailed analysis of how an admissions program can be structured to meet the Bakke standards, see Lesnick, "What Does Bakke Require of Law Schools?" 128 U. Pa. L. Rev. 141 (1979). *See also* Doherty v. Rutgers School of Law-Newark, 651 F.2d 893 (3d Cir. 1981) (unsuccessful white applicant denied standing to challenge law school admissions policies).

48. Note also that nowhere in the 156 pages of the lengthy *Bakke* decision is direct consideration given to the significant issue of whether the standardized admissions procedures used at Davis were "validated" or reasonably related to the purposes for which they were being used. There was substantial evidence, submitted in *amicus* briefs and noted in prior lower court decisions, that, although there was a correlation between scores on the MCAT and course grades in the first two years of medical school, the test was not validated either to grades in clinical courses during the

latter years of medical school or to actual performances on the job after graduation. *See*, e.g., Sindler, *supra* note 31, at 119; Alevy v. Downstate Medical Center, 39 N.Y.2d 326, 330 (1976). *Cf.* Justice Douglas's dissenting opinion in *DeFunis*, 416 U.S. at 327-30. Thus, the Court totally ignored the major questions concerning fairness of current testing procedures and the application of standards, discussed in note 34.

49. The lower courts have had difficulty in applying the complex *Bakke* holding to other cases. *See*, e.g., Uzzell v. Friday, 591 F.2d 997 (4th Cir. 1979), 625 F.2d 1117 (4th Cir. 1980), *cert. denied*, 446 U.S. 951 (1980) (application of *Bakke* to race-conscious student election cases); Association Against Discrimination in Employment v. City of Bridgeport, 594 F.2d 306 (2d Cir. 1979), 647 F.2d 224 (2d Cir. 1981) (issues concerning preferential hiring system for firefighters reconsidered in light of *Bakke* and other authorities). However, there appears to be a tendency to read *Bakke* as generally permitting racially conscious affirmative action plans in a variety of circumstances. *See*, e.g., Detroit Police Officers Association v. Young, 608 F.2d 671 (6th Cir. 1979), *cert. denied*, 452 U.S. 938 (1981) (reversal of invalidation by lower court of race-conscious hiring system for police officers on the basis of *Bakke*); Firefighters Institute v. City of St. Louis, 588 F.2d 235 (8th Cir. 1978), *cert. denied*, 443 U.S. 904 (1979) (immediate promotion of all black firefighters ordered on basis of *Bakke* precedent); Setser v. Novack Investment Co., 657 F.2d 962 (8th Cir. 1981) (race-conscious affirmative action hiring plan upheld under 42 U.S.C. § 1981).

50. 443 U.S. 193 (1979). See also Firefighters Local Union No. 1784 v. Stutts. 104 S. Ct. 2576 (1984) (Title VII consent decree does not justify preliminary injunction calling for affirmative action layoff plan).

51. 448 U.S. 448 (1980).

52. Justice Powell's separate concurring opinion emphasized the need to justify the Court's actions in traditional equal protection terms; in this situtation, he would find a "compelling governmental interest" in eradicating the continuing effects of past discrimination identified by Congress (448 U.S. at 496-97); in other words, given proper congressional imprimatur, Justice Powell would accept an equality of result approach as being constitutionally compelling. Justices Marshall, Brennan, and Blackmun, in their concurring opinions, argued for the middle-ground "substantial relationship"

approach to equal protection issues, which they had articulated in *Bakke* (448 U.S. at 517-19). Under this less rigorous constitutional standard, they had little difficulty in upholding the result-oriented minority set-aside program. Justice Stevens's dissent applied traditional equality of opportunity arguments to the facts of the case; he stated that any discrimination that may exist in the contracting area might justify legislation to improve bidding procedures or to provide access to financing sources for minority contractors, but it would not justify a preferential approach which gives benefits to a broad range of "minority" contractors, including wealthy black businessmen and Eskimos and Orientals who may never have suffered any discrimination and may need no such assistance (448 U.S. at 543-44).

53. The opinion of the Court, written by Chief Justice Burger and joined by Justices White and Powell, discussed in detail the history of Congress's acknowledgement of discrimination in the construction industry (although no direct hearings were held in connection with this bill), and it analogized Congress's approach in this area to that of the federal courts in fashioning remedies in desegregation cases. Thus, it might almost be said that the Court, which has in the past been criticized for "usurping" the policymaking prerogatives of the legislative branch, is now inviting Congress to "upsurp" its traditional role of finding constitutional violations and fashioning equitable remedies. *Cf.* dissenting opinion of Stewart, J., 448 U.S. at 527.

In recent cases that had been expected to clarify the meaning of *Bakke* and *Fullilove*, the Supreme Court instead found technical grounds for disposing of the cases and thereby avoided deciding the substantial legal issues. *See* Johnson v. Chicago Board of Education, 457 U.S. 52 (1982); Minnick v. Department of Corrections, 452 U.S. 105 (1981).

## NOTES TO CHAPTER THREE

1. G. Orfield, The Reconstruction of Southern Education 23 (1969).
2. The pivotal figures, the administration calculated, would be William McCulloch, the senior Republican on the Judiciary Committee in the House, and Everett Dirksen, the Senate Minority Leader. If these respected moderate-to-conservative Republicans would support a civil rights bill, they would pull with them the necessary swing votes.

The account in this chapter of the administration's legislative strategy is based largely on interviews with Professor David Filvaroff of the University of Texas Law School. As an assistant to Deputy Attorney General Nicholas Katzenbach, Professor Filvaroff was substantially involved in administration strategy and in the negotiations with legislators and their staffs. See also Abernathy, "Title VI and the Constitution: A Regulatory Model for Defining 'Discrimination,' " 70 Geo. L.J. 1, 4-10 (1981).

3. Subcommittee No. 5 held 22 days of hearings between May 8, 1963, and August 2, 1963. The hearing's involved 101 witnesses and 2,649 pages of transcripts and exhibits (*Civil Rights: Miscellaneous Proposals Regarding the Civil Rights of Persons Within the Jurisdiction of the United States: Hearings Before Subcomm. No. 5 of the House Comm. on the Judiciary,* 88th Cong., 1st Sess. [1963]). Also, Attorney General Robert Kennedy testified at length before the full committee on October 15 and 16, 1963 (*Civil Rights: Hearings on H.R. 7152 as amended by Subcomm. No. 5 of the House Common the Judiciary,* 88th Cong., 1st Sess. 2651-2780 [1963]).

4. Filvaroff interview. (All interviews referenced in the text were conducted by one or both of the authors. Affiliations of the interviewees and dates of the interviews are set forth in appendix A.)

5. However, the full committee did tone down the subcommittee bill in other respects. Most notably, it added a proviso excluding from Title VI's coverage federal assistance in the form of any "contract of insurance or guarantee." What the legislators had in mind was home mortgage assistance. This exclusion was added to ensure that Title VI could not be used as an open housing law.

6. The unusual procedures involved in the passage of the Act have deprived legal researchers of some of the prime materials normally used to determine legislative intent. Since the House immediately accepted all of the Senate amendments, rather than negotiating a compromise, there was no House-Senate conference committee report. Furthermore, because the Senate amendments were worked out on the floor and in an unofficial negotiating group, there was no authoritative Senate committee report. (The original report of the House Judiciary Committee, of course, does not address the substance of later amendments in the Senate.) However, the unusually careful management of Senate floor debate by Senator Humphrey and other sponsors of the bill provides a well-developed

record which justifies assigning relatively more importance to the
floor debates when analyzing the legislative history of this bill.
7. An important dimension of this "moderation" was addressed to
constituencies in the North. An amendment to Title VI pertaining
to "racial balance" was intended as assurance that federal officials
would not be trying to remedy northern style *de facto* segregation.
And in Title VI itself, the exclusion of "contract of insurance or
guarantee" would prevent federal funding leverage from being
used against housing discrimination. (*See* note 5.)
8. The full bill in its final form, Pub. L. No. 88-352, 78 Stat. 241
(1964), contained the following components: Title I (voting
rights); Title II (public accommodations); Title III (public facilities);
Title IV (public school desegregation); Title V (United States Commission on Civil Rights); Title VI (federally assisted programs);
Title VII (equal employment opportunities); Title VIII (registration
and voting statistics); Title IX (intervention on behalf of plaintiffs
by the attorney general); Title X (community relations service);
Title XI (miscellaneous provisions). Title VI was codified at 42
U.S.C. §§ 2000d-2000d-4; § 2000d-5 was added in 1966, and §
2000d-6 was added in 1970.
9. "No person in the United States shall, on the ground of race,
color, or national origin, be excluded from participation in, be
denied the benefits of, or be subjected to discrimination under any
program or activity receiving Federal financial assistance" (42
U.S.C. § 2000d).
10. 42 U.S.C. § 2000d-1.
11. 42 U.S.C. § 2000d-2.
12. 42 U.S.C. § 2000d-3. Federal agencies were precluded from
taking action in connection with employment practices "except
where a primary objective of the federal financial assistance is to
provide employment."
13. 42 U.S.C. § 2000d-4.
14. Emphasis added. Sec. 602, 42 U.S.C. § 2000d-1.
15. These rules "shall be consistent with achievement of the objectives of the statute authorizing the financial assistance" (42 U.S.C.
§ 2000d-1).
16. *Ibid.*
17. Judicial review would be pursuant to the Administrative Procedure Act 5 U.S.C. §§ 701-706, with the statutory stipulation
that agency actions pursuant to sec. 601 "shall not be deemed

committed to unreviewable agency discretion" (42 U.S.C. § 2000d-2).

18. In the debates, Senator Humphrey observed: "The unhappy experience in Prince Edward County, Va., shows that, while everyone suffers when public schools are closed, Negroes are the hardest hit. The same is true when the level of school services is reduced. What is needed, therefore, is a balance between the goal of eliminating discrimination and the goal of providing education, food, and so forth, to those most in need of it, including Negroes and members of other minority groups. Title VI in its present form seeks to preserve enough flexibility in method [sic] of achieving compliance to make such a balance possible," *quoted in* 2 Statutory History of the United Stated Civil Rights 1222 (B. Schwartz ed. 1970) [hereinafter cited as Schwartz].

19. After 1964, Congress enacted certain amendments to Title VI that affected the enforcement procedures. In 1966, following an abortive effort by the Office of Education (OE) to defer $32 million in federal funds from the Chicago School District (see chapter 4), Congress added a provision limiting to 60 days the duration of deferral of action by the Commissioner of Education on funding applications, unless the applicant is afforded a prompt administrative hearing culminating in "an express finding on the record" that the applicant has engaged in discrimination (Pub. L. No. 89-750, Title I, § 182, 80 Stat. 1209 [1966] [codified as amended at 42 U.S.C. § 2000d-5]).

In 1970, a provision was added requiring that Title VI be applied "uniformly" in all regions of the country. This amendment originated as the "Stennis Amendment," and its purpose was to apply the same legal standards to *de facto* and *de jure* segregation. But this intention was diffused by a provision, added over the senator's objection, which defined "uniformly" to mean a single policy for *de jure* segregation "wherever found" and a single policy for *de facto* segregation "wherever found" (Pub. L. No. 91-230, § 2, 84 Stat. 121 [1970] [codified as amended at 42 U.S.C. § 2000d-6]).

In addition, Congress passed a confusing array of provisions, not all of them codified with Title VI, that substantially affected Title VI enforcement. The most important of these were antibusing provisions, prohibiting HEW from requesting "voluntary" desegregation remedies that included mandatory reassignment of pupils to schools outside their neighborhoods. *See,* e.g., Pub. L. No. 94-206, § 209, 90 Stat. 22 (1976) (Byrd Amendment); Pub.

L. No. 93-380, § 215(a), 88 Stat. 517 (1976) (codified at 20 U.S.C. § 1714(a)) (Esch Amendment); Pub. L. No. 93-380, § 203(b), 88 Stat. 514 (1976) (codified at 20 U.S.C. § 1702(b)) (Scott-Mansfield Amendment—weakening effect of Esch Amendment); Pub. L. No. 94-206, § 208(b), 90 Stat. 22 (1976) (Eagleton-Biden Amendment). *See generally* Brown v. Califano, 627 F.2d 1221, 1226-27, nn.26-27 (D.C. Cir. 1980).

20. Regents of the University of California v. Bakke, 438 U.S. 265 (1978), and the other major affirmative action cases discussed in the previous chapter have caused lawyers and courts to focus in detail on the legislative intent behind Title VI. Methodologically, the analysis of legislative intent set forth in this chapter is more strictly historical than the approach taken in these judicial decisions. For example, consistent with the Court's responsibility to decide the issues posed by the *Bakke* case at the time it reached the Court, Justice Brennan's detailed analysis of legislative intent draws upon "[t]he legislative history of Title VI, administrative regulations interpreting the stature, subsequent congressional and executive action, and the prior decisions of [the Supreme] Court" (438 U.S. at 328). Our interpretation relies almost exclusively on the contemporaneous legislative materials, because our concern is to compare and contrast those materials with later "administrative regulations, . . . [and] subsequent congressional and executive action."

21. At first glance, it might appear that, while the operative term "discrimination" is ambiguous, the other operative terms, "excluded" and "denied . . . benefits," are fairly precise. But without reference to a concept of equality, even the latter terms lack substantial meaning. For example, in Lau v. Nichols, 414 U.S. 563 (1974), the Supreme Court had to decide whether non-English-speaking children who were admitted to a school system on the same basis as those who were proficient in English were nevertheless "excluded" from or "denied the benefits" of "educational services." Clearly, the concepts of "fair opportunity" and "results" were inherent in the consideration of whether these students were improperly "excluded."

22. Representative Oren Harris stated: "Nowhere in the bill is this word defined so it can only be drawn from inference from the language of the bill or defined by courts at such later times as it becomes necessary and in such a manner as may at the time prove convenient" (110 Cong. Rec. 1923 [1964]).

One stated reason why *discrimination* had been left undefined is that Attorney General Kennedy and other administration officials had told Congress that federal funding programs were too numerous and too diverse to fit neatly within a single definition (Filvaroff interview). *See Civil Rights: Hearings on H.R. 7152 Before the House Comm. on the Judiciary*, 88th Cong., 1st sess. 2652-2771 (1963) (testimony of Attorney General Kennedy). *See also* letter from Deputy Attorney General Nicholas Katzenbach to Chairman Emanuel Celler (*Ibid.* at 2772-79); Abernathy, *supra* note 2.

Congress's failure to define clearly the operative egalitarian concepts, discussed here in regard to the 1964 Civil Rights Act (*see* Bryner, "Congress, Courts and Agencies: Equal Employment and the Limits of Policy Implementation," 96 Pol. Sci. Quart. 411 [1981], for a discussion of ambiguity in the bill's equal employment provisions), also appears to have extended to other areas of anti-discrimination legislation. *See*, e.g., Schuck, "The Graying of Civil Rights Law: The Age Discrimination Act of 1975," 89 Yale L.J. 27 (1979); Wegner "The Antidiscrimination Model Reconsidered: Ensuring Equal Opportunity without Respect to Handicap Under Section 504 of the Rehabilitation Act of 1973," 69 Corn. L. Rev. 401 (1984).

23. Some opponents of the Act indicated that they might accept a bill based on the type of "conservative" or "formal" equality discussed in chapter 1, note 29. The formal equality position was that if a law or policy was, in its face, colorblind, then it was *ipso facto* nondiscriminatory. For example, a freedom of choice enrollment plan in a formerly *de jure* segregated school district was said to afford equal treatment, even though it was well known that blacks who sought to enroll their children in white schools were subjected to threatened (and actual) retaliation by employers, landlords, and officials. From this point of view, sufficient "egalitarian" rights existed and if blacks did not take advantage of them, it was because of their own failings. Thus, Representative Thomas Gerstle Abernethy warned that the stronger egalitarian approach of the bill "would rob all Americans of precious freedom on the theory that this can give economic, cultural, and social equality to a minority of Americans who, let us face it, have failed to achieve such equality on their own initiative" (Schwartz, *supra* note 18, at 1133).

24. 110 Cong. Rec. 1519 (1964) (remarks of Representative Celler).

25. *See* remarks of Senator Humphrey at 110 Cong. Rec. 5022 (1964). *See also* Schwartz, *supra* note 18, at 1234.
26. 110 Cong. Rec. 4746 (1964). Similarly, Senator Russell warned: "Any effort to legislate social equality can have only one effect, and that is to bring down our people to the lowest common denominator. I do not believe that there can be any such thing as compulsory equality" (110 Cong. Rec. 4753 [1964]).
27. 110 Cong. Rec. 5423 (1964).
28. 110 Cong. Rec. 1600 (1964).
29. 42 U.S.C. § 2000e-2(j). This provision became the central focus of the Supreme Court's consideration of the Kaiser Aluminum Company's 50 percent quota for its apprenticeship training program, in United Steelworkers of America v. Weber, 443 U.S. 193 (1979). Although the company had clearly instituted the program in response to pressures from the Equal Employment Opportunity Commission (EEOC), it was held to be "voluntary" because it had not been mandated by a court order. The Supreme Court's majority opinion, written by Justice Brennan, held that Congress intended to "permit" such affirmative action programs, because otherwise the provision quoted above would have clearly spelled out that Title VII was not intended either to "require" or to "permit" preferential treatment. Since Title VII was designed to maximize voluntary efforts by private employers to promote minority employment, Congress could not have meant to preclude voluntary plans that would achieve this result. However, this interpretation of the legislative history had to distinguish numerous remarks by supporters of the Act indicating that Title VII would not allow establishment of systems "to maintain racial balance in employment." Justice Rehnquist and Chief Justice Burger, in dissent, strongly pressed these references and argued that the language of the statute clearly prohibited racial preferences. The majority was accused of convoluted semantics and a biased reading of the legislative history.
30. Schwartz, *supra* note 18, at 1104.
31. "Nothing contained in this subchapter shall be construed to authorize action under this subchapter by any department or agency with respect to any employment practice of any employer, employment agency, or labor organization except where a primary objective of the Federal financial assistance is to provide employment" (sec. 604, 42 U.S.C. § 2000d-3). It is important to note, however, that Senator Humphrey interpreted this employment

amendment as not precluding use of the fund cutoff sanction in cases in which "racial discrimination in employment or assignment of teachers . . . affected the educational opportunities of students" (Schwartz, *supra* note 18, at 1218).

32. 42 U.S.C. § 2000c-6. This proviso actually was contained in Title IV (dealing with desegregation suits by the attorney general). Senator Humphrey explicitly assured the sponsors of the bill that the administration intended this provision to apply also to Title VI (Schwartz, *supra* note 18, at 1345). Interpretive problems still remained, however, since under Title VI federal officials do not "issue orders," but instead make findings of noncompliance and withhold funds.

33. Indeed, Title VII, as originally enacted in 1964, specifically incorporated an "impact" standard (*see* pp. 31-32) in its operative definition of unlawful employment practices. Thus, 42 U.S.C. § 2000e-2 prohibits the use of employment selection devices which are "designed, intended *or used* to discriminate because of race, color, religion, sex or national origin" (emphasis added). *See* Griggs v. Duke Power Co., 401 U.S. 424 (1971). Although racial imbalance in itself would not trigger liability, a heavy burden would be placed on employers to justify the job-relatedness of employment selection devices which resulted in racial imbalance. In practice, this impact test has tended to promote implementation of result-oriented, affirmative action approaches. *See* Rebell and Block, "Competency Assessment and the Courts: An Overview of the State of the Law," in The Assessment of Occupational Competence, ERIC Document No. ED 192-169 (1980); Ability Testing: Uses, Consequences and Controversies, Part I: Report of the Committee on Ability Testing, Assembly of Behavioral and Social Sciences, National Research Council 101-105 (1982). *Cf.* Bartholet, "Application of Title VII to Jobs in High Places," 95 Harv. L. Rev. 947 (1982).

34. "[Title VI] was necessary to rescue school desegregation from the bog in which it had been trapped for ten years" (United States v. Jefferson County Board of Education, 372 F.2d 836, 856 [5th Cir. 1966]).

35. "The problem confronting Congress was discrimination against Negro citizens at the hands of recipients of Federal moneys. . . . Over and over again, proponents of the bill detailed the plight of the Negroes seeking equal treatment in such programs. There simply was no reason for Congress to consider the validity of hypo-

thetical preferences that might be accorded minority citizens; the legislators were dealing with the real and pressing problem of how to guarantee those citizens equal treatment" (*Bakke*, 438 U.S. at 285) (Powell, J.).

36. In *Bakke*, five of the justices (four joining in Justice Brennan's opinion and Justice Powell) concluded that Congress had intended to incorporate developing constitutional standards (although Justice Powell differed from the others on how these standards had developed). Although the four justices who joined in Justice Stevens's opinion disagreed and argued that Congress meant to codify a "colorblind" equality of opportunity perspective, regardless of later constitutional developments, two of them (Justices Stewart and Rehnquist) later joined in a dissenting opinion in Board of Education v. Harris, 444 U.S. 130, 152 (1979), that intimated an acceptance of the majority view on this point.

37. There was one significant exception to this conclusion. The Fourteenth Amendment only regulated "state action," and Congress realized that some federal fund recipients might be considered purely private entities. Title VI provided that "private" fund recipients would still have to meet constitutional discrimination standards. See 110 Cong. Rec. 12677 (1964) (Senator Gordon Allott).

38. The drafters and legislative leaders also were aware that Title VI's coverage would be broader than the constitution because some federally assisted programs might remain sufficiently non-governmental as to fail the "state action" requirement. But the discrimination standard that would be applied to any person subject to Title VI was perceived to be the "constitutional" one.

39. 110 Cong. Rec. 5253 (1964).

40. 110 Cong. Rec. 7057 (1976).

41. 110 Cong. Rec. 6562 (1964).

42. Bell v. School Board, City of Gary, Indiana, 324 F.2d 209 (7th Cir. 1963), *cert. denied*, 377 U.S. 924 (1964).

43. Schwartz, *supra* note 18, at 1344. He went on to say; "[i]f the bill were to compel [integration], it would be a violation [of the constitution] because it would be handling the matter on the basis of race and we would be transporting children because of race" (*Ibid.* at 1345).

44. 110 Cong. Rec. 6050 (March 24, 1964). In discussing the *de facto-de jure* distinction as it was raised in the Title IV context, Senator Humphrey noted: "The key purpose of the pending Dirk-

sen-Mansfield/Humphrey-Kuchel substitute is to make clear that the resolution of these problems is to be left where it is now, namely, in the hands of local school officials and the courts. . . . Obviously, this provision could not affect a court's determination concerning racial imbalance and possible corrective measures; this is dependent upon the court's interpretation of the 14th amendment" (110 Cong. Rec. 13820 [1964]).

45. *See* G. Orfield, The Reconstruction of Southern Education (1969); Note, "The Courts, HEW, and Southern School Desegregation," 77 Yale L.J. 321 (1967). *See also* the discussion in chapter 4.

46. Federal departments can, however, defer funding for new programs. In 1965, the first year of The Elementary and Secondary Education Act (ESEA), HEW (without express statutory authority) deferred funds for many school districts because of alleged Title VI violations. Following the political uproar caused by HEW's deferral of funds for Chicago (*see* p. 59), Congress amended Title VI in 1966 to provide that this interim sanction could be used for an extended period only if HEW conducted hearings and made findings of violations on the record. *See* 42 U.S.C. § 2000d-5; Board of Public Instruction v. Cohen, 413 F.2d 1201 (5th Cir. 1969).

47. *See* e.g., Mandel v. HEW, 411 F. Supp. 542 (D. Md. 1976) (injunction issued against Title VI enforcement by OCR pending clearer specification of steps necessary for compliance); Board of Public Instruction v. Finch, 414 F.2d 1068 (5th Cir. 1969) (Title VI fund cutoff reversed, because lower court findings were not "programmatically oriented").

48. Pub. L. No. 92-318, Title VII, 86 Stat. 354 (1972) (*codified* as amended at 20 U.S.C. §§ 1601-1619), amended, Pub. L. No. 95-561, Title VI, 92 Stat. 2252 (1978) (recodified at 20 U.S.C. §§ 3191-3207), amended, Pub. L. No. 97-35, Title V, § 577(3), (7), 95 Stat. 474 (1981) (recodified at 20 U.S.C. § 3832(3), (7) (Elementary and Secondary Education Block Grant). References to ESAA will be to the first codification at 20 U.S.C. §§ 1601-1619. Title VIII of the Education Amendments of 1972 contained provisions restricting the use of busing to achieve desegregation.

49. As we shall see, OCR in later years tended to combine these carrot and stick approaches to gain maximum leverage in its compliance negotiations with local school districts.

50. Note also that unless the school district obtained a federal court injunction reserving its claimed funds, the money for the current fiscal year would be spent elsewhere. Furthermore, because ESAA grant applications were considered on one-year cycles, school districts were subject to frequent OCR reviews of their continuing compliance.

51. Senator Javits, the Republican senator from New York with a liberal record on civil rights, was the Senate sponsor in 1970 of the original administration bill, and, as a facilitator and mediator, he played a principal role throughout the two years of deliberations. His involvement in the passage of this bill (and of Title V of the 1964 Civil Rights Act) must have been a factor in his measured responses to complaints by New York City education officials and union officials about OCR's enforcement activities under these two statutes. *See* chapter 5, note 87.

52. 116 Cong. Rec. 18109 (1970).

53. Under President Nixon's funding formula, districts desegregating under court orders or HEW agreements would receive twice as much aid as districts trying to achieve racial balancing voluntarily. Thus, districts that were found to be in violation of the Constitution 16 years after Brown v. Board of Education would be receiving in essence, "a bonus."

54. One commentator summarized this skeptical view in these words: "The South's remaining segregated schools had to desegregate, the Supreme Court and the lower federal courts had made further delay impossible, and the Administration had no practicable choice but to make the process as acceptable and rewarding as it could. Most of the requested $1.5 billion in special funds . . . is earmarked, Congress willing, for Southern school districts that are integrating now or have integrated in the past two years. . . . The chief and declared objective is to reward while helping the white South in its enforced surrender to integration" (J. Osborne, The First Two Years of the Nixon Watch 85-86 [1971], *quoted in* G. Orfield, Congressional Power: Congress and Social Change 174 [1975]).

55. For example, Senator Mondale's Quality Integrated Education Act of 1971 (S. 683) reserved "40 to 45% of the funds for creating and maintaining stable, quality, integrated schools"; "10 to 15% of the funds for promising pilot programs in racially or ethnically isolated schools in districts with over 50% minority students or 15,000 minority students"; "10% of the funds for education

parks"; "10% of the funds for the Commissioner to allocate as
he sees fit among the various activities authorized in the Act";
"6% of the funds for funding private nonprofit groups to promote
equal educational opportunity by encouraging the participation of
parents, students and teachers in the education process"; "5% of
the funds for integrated children's educational television programs"; "3% of the funds . . . for reimbursement of attorneys'
fees"; and "1% of the funds . . . for evaluation" (117 Cong. Rec.
2183 [1971]). The proponents of a liberal ESAA, then, were not
consciously promoting a new or radical equality principle. They
wanted to make the old one work. The "real issue," said Mondale,
is how to "recapture" the federal government's concern for the
educational needs and equal educational opportunity of "all of
our children" (117 Cong. Rec. 2177 [1971]).

56. One report was done by the General Accounting Office ("Need
to Improve Policies and Procedures for Approving Grants Under
the Emergency School Assistance Program"), excerpts of which
are reprinted at 117 Cong. Rec. 6658-59 (1971), and the other
by a joint project supported by six civil rights groups: American
Friends Service Committee; Delta Ministry of the National Council
of Churches; Lawyers Committee for Civil Rights Under Law;
Lawyers Constitutional Defense Committee; The National Association for the Advancement of Colored People, (NAACP) Legal
Defence and Education Fund, Inc.; and Washington Research Project ("The Emergency School Assistance Program: An Evaluation"),
excerpts of which are reprinted at 116 Cong. Rec. 43956 (1970).

57. 116 Cong. Rec. 43963 (1970), quoting the civil rights group
report, "The Emergency School Assistance Program: An Evaluation." The report was based on nearly 300 on-site visits and a
review of over 350 funding applications. In less than 10 percent
of districts visited was there no evidence of illegal practices (116
Cong. Rec. 43956 [1970]).

58. 116 Cong. Rec. 43958 (1970). One application was approved
by HEW before being received (116 Cong. Rec. 43955 [1970]
[remarks of Senator Mondale]).

59. 20 U.S.C. § 1605(d) (1) (A)-(D). The language of these provisions
actually originated in the "assurances" required of the ESAP program under the HEW regulations. Senator Mondale's Quality Integrated Education Act incorporated the language as statutory
eligibility requirements; these requirements were adopted almost
verbatim from Mondale's bill into the Act.

60. 20 U.S.C. § 1605(d)(1)(B) (emphasis added). In Board of Education v. Harris, 444 U.S. 130 (1979), the Supreme Court held that the second clause—"or otherwise engaged in discrimination"—was also intended by Congress to constitute an "impact" test.
61. 20 U.S.c. § 1605(d)(1)(C) (emphasis added).
62. *Ibid.*
63. The Nixon administration expanded this narrow waiver provision by issuing a regulation permitting a waiver upon a showing that the school district was "making progress" toward desegregation (38 Fed. Reg. 18899 [1973] [to be codified at 45 C.F.R. § 185.44(d)(3)]). The United States Court of Appeals for the District of Columbia Court held that this regulation was inconsistent with the statute (Kelsey v. Weinberger, 498 F.2d 701 [1974]). Several years later, however, when OCR under the Carter administration tried to enforce strictly the "cease to exist" language in New York City, the Second Circuit Court of Appeals reached the opposite conclusion and held that a phase-in plan was sufficient (Board of Education v. Harris, 622 F.2d 599 [2d Cir. 1979], *cert. denied sub nom.* Hufstedler v. Board of Education, 449 U.S. 1124 [1981]).
64. ESAA prohibited federal funding for busing and encouraged experimentation with a number of other integration techniques which were not as politically sensitive, such as interracial programs, minority language programs, mobile units, and teacher education. For a detailed discussion of the politics and legislation of busing, see G. Orfield, Must We Bus? (1978).
65. At the present time, the Department of Education's grant compliance enforcement activities under ESAA are being substantially terminated through the Reagan administration's "block grants" legislation. Under the Education Consolidation and Improvement Act of 1981, federal desegregation aid was made part of multipurpose education block grants to be allocated and administered by the states, effective October 1, 1982 (Pub. L. No. 97-35, Title V, § 577(3), (7), 95 Stat. 474 [1981] [codified at 20 U.S.C. § 3832(3), (7).

## NOTES TO CHAPTER FOUR

1. G. Orfield, The Reconstruction of Southern Education 23 (1969) [hereinafter cited as Reconstruction].
2. 42 U.S.C. § 2000d-1. For a summary of current Title VI enforce-

ment procedures, see Block, "Enforcement of Title VI Compliance Agreements by Third Party Beneficiaries," 18 Harv. C.R.-C.L. L. Rev. 1, 8-16 (1983).
3. Reconstruction, *supra* note 1, at 52.
4. *See* 29 Fed. Reg. 16298, 16300 (1964) (codified at 45 C.F.R. pt. 80).
5. *See* the discussion in chapter 3, p. 39.
6. *See* H. R. Rodgers and C. R. Bullock, Coercion to Compliance (1976).
7. Assistant Secretary James M. Quigley opposed the development of formal standards. He preferred to maximize pressures for desegregation through negotiations on a case-by-case basis. Any "minimum" standards issued by OCR, he feared, would quickly become "maximum" standards as well. David Seeley, newly appointed chief of OE's Office of Equal Educational Opportunity (OEEO), and OE Commissioner Francis Keppel, however, believed that effective administrative enforcement of school desegregation had to be "regularized, formalized and made predictable" (B. Radin, Implementation, Change and the Federal Bureaucracy, School Desegregation Policy in HEW, 1964-1968 104-105 [1977]).
8. 30 Fed. Reg. 9981 (1965) (codified at 45 C.F.R. § 181.5(b)(1)).
9. Maintenance of segregated faculties had been one of the major techniques for impeding successful operation of freedom of choice plans. In the absence of meaningful faculty integration, certain schools remained identified as "black schools," while others were known as "white schools." Although parents theoretically could choose to cross these implicit color lines, few were likely to do so; the absence of black faculty as both role models and support figures made it even more unlikely that black parents would choose to send their children to white schools.
10. Reconstruction, *supra* note 1, at 106.
11. *See* Reconstruction, *supra* note 1, at 151-207; Center for National Policy Review, Justice Delayed and Denied 7-9 (1974). The account of these events by Joseph Califano, secretary of HEW in the Carter administration, includes a statement by President Johnson to Pope Paul VI, with whom he was meeting on the day these developments broke, that "[o]ne of my own Cabinet members wants to stop funds for poor children in one of our largest cities, run by a fine Catholic mayor. But, we'll help those children" (J. Califano, Governing America: An Insider's Report from the White House and the Cabinet 222 [1981]).

After the Chicago episode, Illinois Senator Dirksen sponsored an amendment to Title VI prohibiting deferral of new program funds unless a timely administrative hearing was held and findings made on the record. *See* 42 U.S.C. § 2000d-5; *cf.* chapter 3, note 19.

12. Until Martin Gerry turned OCR's attention to the Big City Reviews, no sustained efforts were made by HEW to develop test cases and precedents for challenging northern patterns of discrimination under Title VI. OCR responded to reiterated congressional pressures for "uniform" enforcement by targeting small suburban school districts like Ferndale, Michigan and Union Township, New Jersey, which did not have the resources to play political trump cards. Even after Congress had passed the Green amendment to ESEA, requiring uniform application of HEW guidelines and regulations throughout the country (Pub. L. No. 90-247, § 2, 81 Stat. 783 [1968], repealed, Pub. L. No. 91-230, Title IV, § 401(e)(1), 84 Stat. 173 [1970] [current version at 20 U.S.C. 1232(c)]), OCR looked only to moderate-size districts. Just before the 1968 elections, in response to a further amendment to an appropriation bill (Pub. L. No. 90-557, § 410, 82 Stat. 995 [1968]) requiring HEW to equalize its investigation staffs in the North and South, regional offices of OCR were opened in New York, Chicago, Boston, and San Francisco.

13. By January 1966, OCR had a professional staff of 50, which oversaw a docket including 65 enforcement proceedings, 1,900 voluntary desegregation plans, 27,000 assurances of compliance, and 164 court orders (E. Mosher and S. Bailey, E.S.E.A.: The Office of Education Administers a Law 154 [1968]).

14. "Statement of Policies for School Desegregation Plans under Title VI of the Civil Rights Act of 1964," 45 C.F.R. pt. 181 (1966).

15. 45 C.F.R. § 181.13(d) (1966).

16. For example, § 181.54 provided that "[i]f a significant percentage of the students, such as 8 percent of 9 percent, transferred from segregated schools for the 1965-66 school year, total transfers in the order of at least twice that percentage would normally be expected [for the 1966-1967 school year]."

17. 372 F.2d 836, 852 (5th Cir. 1966), *aff'd en banc*, 380 F.2d 385 (5th Cir. 1967), *cert. denied sub nom.* Caddo Parish School Board v. United States, 389 U.S. 840 (1967). The *Jefferson County* decision was a landmark case for Title VI enforcement in the South. Because the original HEW regulations had specified that compli-

ance with Title VI could be met either by filing a desegregation plan acceptable to OCR or by complying with a plan approved by a court, a number of southern districts had adopted the strategy of trying to play off the courts against OCR. As the HEW standards became tighter, these districts rushed to court to obtain judicial approval for desegregation plans which clearly would not meet the more stringent HEW guidelines. But in *Jefferson County*, the Fifth Circuit held that the courts should defer to the HEW guidelines precisely because "the standards of court-supervised desegregation should not be lower than the standards of HEW-supervised desegregation (*Ibid.* at 848).

The interplay between OCR and the Fifth Circuit in the development of Title VI compliance standards in the mid-1960s is itself worthy of note. The Fourth Circuit (covering the states of Maryland, North Carolina, South Carolina, Virginia, and West Virginia) and the Fifth Circuit (covering Alabama, Florida, Georgia, Louisiana, Mississippi, Texas, and the Canal Zone) were the main federal appellate courts on the desegregation firing line in the post-*Brown* era. The decisions of the Fifth Circuit tended to be more liberal than those of the Fourth. OCR relied on these Fifth Circuit precedents in formulating the board standards in its various guidelines. Validation of the guidelines by the Fifth Circuit in *Jefferson County*, therefore, could be seen as a final step completing the circle of interrelated Title VI policymaking by the Fifth Circuit and OCR. *See* Radin, *supra* note 7, at 117-18.

18. Pub. L. No. 90-247, § 2, 81 Stat. 783 (1968). *See* chapter 3, note 19.

19. "Policies on Elementary and Secondary School Compliance with Title VI of the Civil Rights Acts of 1964," 33 Fed. Reg. 4955 (1968). For example, the regulations prohibited inequities in resource allocation, in the provision of student services such as guidance and counseling, and in the assignment of staff to minority schools.

20. *Ibid.* § 10.

21. *Ibid.* § 11.

22. Radin, *supra* note 7, at 14.

23. Rabkin, "Office for Civil Rights," in The Politics of Regulation 338 (J. Wilson ed. 1980) (footnote omitted).

24. 396 U.S. 19 (1969).

25. 402 U.S. 1 (1971).

26. N.Y. Times, August 4, 1971, at 15, col. 1, *quoted in* D. Kirp and M. Yudof, Educational Policy and the Law 394 (1974).
27. *Ibid.* President Nixon's announcement came on the very day that OCR Director J. Stanley Pottinger published an article indicating that OCR expected to act more aggressively in light of *Swann* and *Alexander.* Pottinger described OCR's systematic efforts to define, identify, and eliminate racially identifiable schools in the South. *Swann,* he said, had made clear that "non-contiguous zoning or the additional transportation typically resulting from it . . . are legitimate tools, and . . . must be used if necessary to disestablish the dual system" (Pottinger, "HEW Enforcement of *Swann,*" 9 Inequality in Educ. 6, 9 [1971]). Although Pottinger advocated a balanced and practical assessment of desegregation plans so as to avoid "excess" busing, he concluded that transportation should not be regarded as illegitimate "simply as a method of avoiding the constitutional duty to eliminate racially-identifiable schools" (*Ibid.* at 10).
28. Findings of the court in Adams v. Richardson, 351 F. Supp. 636, 640 (D.D.C. 1973).
29. For example, in 1970-1971, 113 school districts had reneged on prior approved desegregation plans, and 74 of these were still out of compliance by 1973. OCR had commenced administrative proceedings against only 7, had referred 8 cases to the Justice Department, and had filed lawsuits only in 3. In the area of higher education, 5 out of 10 states that had been requested to file desegregation plans totally ignored the request, and the other 5 had filed unacceptable plans; nevertheless, 18 to 36 months later, no formal comments and no enforcement proceedings had been initiated by OCR (*Ibid.* at 637-38).
30. 351 F. Supp. at 642.
31. Adams v. Richardson, 356 F. Supp. 92, 95-96 (D.D.C.), *aff'd and modified en banc,* 480 F.2d 1159 (D.C. Cir. 1973). In upholding the general findings of the court below (but modifying the order in regard to the higher education issues), the Appeals Court emphatically rejected OCR's purported reliance on voluntary compliance in light of the admitted effectiveness of fund termination proceedings in the past (480 F.2d at 1163 n.4).
32. 35 Fed. Reg. 11595 (1970). The standards were set forth in a memorandum dated May 1970, but they were not published in the Federal Register until the following July.
33. 414 U.S. 563 (1974). The court found that San Francisco had

violated Title VI by failing to provide language services for large numbers of non-English-speaking children of Chinese descent.

34. Barber, "Swann Song from the Delta," 9 Inequality in Educ. 4, 4-5 (1971).

35. G. Orfield, Must We Bus? 315 (1978).

36. Holmes, "The Role of the U.S. Department of Health, Education and Welfare," 19 HOW. L.J. 51, 61 (1975).

37. Gerry interview.

38. While it may be possible to achieve substantial compliance in a small district by ordering a specific remedy, Gerry believed that, in a large district, "you can only talk about a process as a remedy, and the major element of that process would have been accountability and fairly close information collection" (Gerry interview).

39. Senator Javits's request most likely was influenced by the Commission's findings, requests from constituents, and his long-standing support of civil rights legislation. His request came in the final phases of the two-year debate over ESAA legislation which, as noted in chapter 3, acquainted him with the problems of second generation discrimination.

40. Orfield, *supra* note 35, at 301.

41. Letter from Martin Gerry to New York City Schools Chancellor Harvey Scribner (August 8, 1972).

42. "Issue Areas to be Reviewed During Initial Phase of the Equal Educational Services Review of New York City Public Schools and Other Federally Assisted Programs: 1971-1974," (U.S. Office for Civil Rights, unpublished looseleaf working paper).

43. The comparability section of the outline was 88 pages long. Besides tracing local and state funds, OCR planned to look in detail at instructional expenditures, the existence and condition of physical facilities, the quantity and quality of equipment and materials (20 categories), allocation of special instructional services (29 categories), and many other items.

44. This category was meant to address the quality of services for and the compatibility of learning environments to the cultural, linguistic, and educational needs of minority children. It attempted to relate broad (and often controversial) theories of learning, such as the Cardenas Theory of Incompatibilities, to numerous specific issues pertaining to how curriculum, textbook use, achievement levels, and testing devices affected minorities. For example, the instruction for data analysis specified: "4. Determine whether a statistically significant difference exists in the relative gain in raw

score, grade equivalent and percentile rank (based on pre-test and post-test comparison) for students on the basis of race, ethnic group and primary language in [selected grades and classes]" (Issues Outline, *supra* note 42, at 117).

45. Assignment and grouping for instruction cut across a number of unsettled educational policy issues, such as the validity of using standardized tests or assessment criteria to group children for instruction.

46. The concern in this area was whether discrimination or vague criteria limited the availability to minority children of noninstructional services (such as social work or psychological counseling) or extracurricular activities (such as athletics, dramatics, or social events). Similarly, the Issues Outline posed a detailed set of questions about the procedures, practices, and statistical patterns regarding exclusion of children from services (i.e., suspension or expulsion).

47. Houston later was dropped from the Big City Reviews.

48. Holmes, *supra* note 36, at 58-61.

49. *Ibid.* at 60.

50. Wilson interview.

51. Many civil rights leaders rejected OCR's rationale for the Big City Reviews. On December 10, 1975, a coalition of 58 civil rights and civic organizations sent HEW Secretary Mathews a letter condemning what it called "the persistent and continuing failure of [HEW] to protect the rights of racial and ethnic minority groups, women, and handicapped persons." One of nine "serious deficiencies" cited in the letter was "[t]he decision to divert a large portion of resources into four massive, computerized, but overly broad investigations of big city school systems whose results, if any, will be years in coming."

Essentially, the civil rights groups saw the Big City Reviews as an excuse to siphon off huge portions of resources from complaint investigation into inconclusive studies. For example, with "[v]irtually the entire New York Regional Office education staff" working on the review for years at a time, other school districts and other subject areas could not be serviced. The signatory organizations advocated instead "carefully targeted reviews in selected areas" and "clear national compliance policies in all areas where discriminatory practices occur, and consistent enforcement in a number of districts regardless of size" (Letter from American Association of University Professors, Committee on Women, et al.

to David Mathews [December 10, 1975]). Attached to the letter was a memorandum entitled "Inadequacies in the HEW Anti-Discrimination Enforcement Program."

NOTES TO CHAPTER FIVE

1. For general overviews of the New York City school system's history and its governance structure, see D. Ravitch, The Great School Wars: New York City 1805-1973 (1974); D. Rogers, 110 Livingston Street: Politics and Bureaucracy in the New York City School System (1969); J. Viteritti, Across the River: Politics and Education in the City (1983). For a description of the school decentralization law, see N.Y. Educ. Law Art. 52-A (McKinney 1981); Rebell, "New York School Decentralization Law: Two and A Half Years Later," 2 J. L. & Ed. 1 (1983).
2. See L. Panetta and P. Gall, Bring us Together: The Nixon Team and the Civil Rights Retreat (1971).
3. Morgan v. Hennigan, 379 F. Supp. 410 (D. Mass.), aff'd sub nom. Morgan v. Kerrigan, 509 F.2d 580 (1st Cir. 1974).
4. Adams v. Richardson, 351 F. Supp. 636, 356 F. Supp. 92 (D.D.C.), aff'd and modified en banc, 480 F.2d 1159 (D.C. Cir. 1973); Brown v. Weinberger, 417 F. Supp. 1215 (D.D.C. 1976).
5. For example, statistical patterns in teacher assignment can establish a strong case against a school district because the district has direct control over employment; when statistical patterns occur in areas like school discipline and tracking, however, it is much more difficult to prove intentional discrimination, the test Tatel believed OCR would have to meet.
6. Anker was deputy chancellor from 1970 to 1972 and chancellor from 1973 to 1978.
7. Parents Association of Andrew Jackson High School v. Ambach, 598 F.2d 705 (2d Cir. 1979).
8. Anker interview.
9. See, e.g., Strayer and Yavner Report (2 Mayor's Committee on Management Survey, Administrative Management of the School System of New York City 755 [1951]); Schinnerer Report (Report by Dr. Mark C. Schinnerer to the New York State Department of Education [1961]); Cresap, McCormick & Paget Report (Management Study for the New York City Board of Education [1962]); Griffiths Report (Teacher Mobility in New York City: A Study of Recruitment, Selection, Appointment, and Promotion of Teachers

in New York City Public Schools, New York University [1963 and 1966]); Theobald Report (in Agenda for a City, Institute for Public Administration [1970]).

10. 330 F. Supp. 203 (S.D.N.Y. 1971), aff'd, 458 F.2d 1167 (2d Cir. 1972). A full case study analysis of *Chance* appears as chapter 6 of M. Rebell and A. Block, Educational Policy Making and the Courts: An Empirical Study of Judicial Activism (1982).

11. Civ. No. 2240/74 (S.D.N.Y.)

12. Gerry interview.

13. *See* the discussion of Gerry's Issues Outline in chapter 4.

14. The 5 percent figure appeared to be based on an analysis in a working paper that had been prepared by Deputy Chancellor Bernard Gifford: Gifford, "Seniority and Layoffs: A Review of Recent Court Decisions and Their Possible Impact on the New York City Public School System" (November 1975). The main exhibits to the complaint contained excerpts from this paper.

15. Administrative Complaint, U.S. Dept. of HEW, Office for Civil Rights (2/17/76). This interrelationship is illustrated by the personal professional history of one of the complainants, Delilah Cheese. She was a black teacher who was laid off in 1975, even though she had taught in the system since 1956. She had accumulated no seniority because throughout this period she was licensed as a "regular substitute," even though she did the work of a regular appointment because she twice failed the applicable Board of Examiners tests. She now alleged that the licensing tests discriminated against her on the basis of race, depriving her of 10 years of seniority and thereby causing her to lose her job.

16. Caulfield v. Board of Education, No. 77 Civ. 2155 (E.D.N.Y. May 15, 1979) (testimony of Martin Gerry, trial transcript, at 617-18).

17. Employment discrimination issues never became part of the Big City Reviews in the other three cities. This was partially because massive layoffs had not become a problem in those settings, and also, more fundamentally, because each of the other cities had a substantially higher percentage of minority teachers. Thus, for 1974-1975, in comparison with New York City's 13.2 percent of minority teachers, Chicago had 43.2 percent, Los Angeles 31.1 percent and Philadelphia 40.2 percent (appendix C to First Letter of Findings).

18. In setting forth the background to the investigation, Gerry compared New York with other large cities in terms of its percentage

of minority teachers, its percentage of minority students, and the inverse relation between these two percentages. After noting that New York had hired minority teachers at a much lower rate than the other cities had, he said that this pattern raised questions for OCR that—together with the specific complaints—led it to conduct the New York employment investigation. Although the *Cheese* complaint had argued that inter-city comparisons actually *proved* an "irrefutable presumption of discrimination" against New York, Gerry neither expressly nor implicitly accepted this position, and he never based any of his findings on a comparison of New York with other cities or on the relative proportions of teachers and pupils. Nevertheless, in the following years, critics of OCR would repeatedly level charges at the agency for allegedly having based its findings on fallacious comparisons of student ethnicity with faculty ethnicity.

19. This requirement that previous lists be exhausted directly contradicted the idea that ranking by test scores purportedly resulted in hiring by merit. If rank truly reflected merit, how could the system justify denying an appointment to a person ranking number one on a test given in 1975 until after the appointment of a person ranking number five hundred on a test given in 1972?

20. It stood to reason that the two-track hiring system that Gerry had discussed under the "access" issue should also contribute substantially to the creation of racially identifiable faculties matching the racial composition of the schools' student populations. Interestingly, Gerry did not make this argument. Instead, his allegations of discriminatory assignments were based solely on broad statistical patterns. Later, there would be lively debate within the board, between the board and OCR, in court hearings, and in the press about how much of the segregatory assignment patterns was caused by the alternative systems created by the New York State legislature and how much might have been caused by intentional discrimination.

21. The letter also contained detailed findings relating to sex discrimination. Gerry said that the school system had, on the basis of sex, "(1) denied females equal access to positions as principals and assistant principals throughout the system; (2) provided a lower level of financial support for female athletic coaching programs; and (3) deprived female teachers of seniority rights and other compensation through failure to eliminate the effects of past discriminatory leave policies."

22. N.Y. Times, November 14, 1976, at 7, col. 5.
23. Shanker's first specific criticism of the letter was that Gerry had based his findings of discrimination on statistical comparisons of the percentages of minority school children with the percentages of minority teachers. In fact, as indicated in note 18, none of Gerry's conclusions were based on such reasoning.
24. 402 U.S. 1 (1971).
25. 426 U.S. 229 (1976).
26. The coalition included the American Civil Liberties Union, ASPIRA of New York, the Coalition of Associations of Black and Puerto Rican Educators and Supervisors, the NAACP, the New York Civil Liberties Union, the New York Urban League, the PEA, and the Puerto Rican Legal Defense and Educational Fund, Inc.
27. Gifford Report at 41.
28. An example of an area in which Gifford tried to do a more penetrating analysis than OCR had done was the relationship between the 1969 Decentralization Law and racially identifiable faculty assignments. As noted earlier, OCR's finding about faculty segregation was based solely on statistical patterns resulting from two-track hiring system. In response to this conclusion, Shanker, the American Jewish Congress, and other opponents pointed out that proponents of community control, largely from minority areas, had pushed for the Decentralization Law and for these particular provisions. The critics pictured OCR as an ignorant Washington bureaucracy that had not bothered to learn the fundamentals of local history and politics. Gifford, however, set out to show that this "conventional wisdom" about the history of the Decentralization Law was actually a myth used to cover up a long history of discrimination. Specifically, Gifford compared racial/ethnic concentrations of teachers as they occurred in the 1969-1970 term with those in the 1974-1975 term. He used the concept of an "even distribution standard" to indicate the number of minority teachers who would be assigned to a particular group of schools if teachers were being assigned randomly. On this basis, he reported that, in 1969-1970, the group of schools that had minority enrollments of 90 percent (or greater) had assigned to them 64.5 percent of all minority teachers in the school system, instead of the even distribution figure of 36.8 percent, thereby creating a disparity ratio of 1.75. At the other end of the racial spectrum, in schools which were 90 percent (or greater) non-minority, the disparity ratio indicated almost 7 times more non-

minority teachers than were called for under an even distribution standard (*Ibid.* at 79). Thus, Gifford's first conclusion was: "Insofar as the schools of New York City are racially identifiable in terms of staff, this condition existed prior to the passage of the 1969 Decentralization Law" (*Ibid.* at 139).

Gifford then asked whether there were any indications that decentralization had changed this pre-existing segregatory pattern. The answer was striking. In the schools with 90 percent or greater minority enrollment, the disparity ratio actually had lessened slightly between 1969-1970 and 1974-1975. In the predominantly white schools, there was some increase in racial concentration. Overall, Gifford concluded that "the situation remained essentially unchanged" (*Ibid.* at 79).

The methodological soundness of Gifford's labor pool study was criticized sharply by experts working for the Justice Department and for the board of education. Economist Stephan Michelson, an independent consultant, advised United States Attorney Richard Caro that the analysis was technically deficient, incomplete, and unconvincing—although Gifford's conclusion, nevertheless, might well be nearly correct (Caro interview). Similarly, a board of education statistician concluded that there were errors in Gifford's econometric model of the labor market that "render it useless" (Memorandum from unidentified expert to Bernard Esrig [October 24, 1977]).

29. Gifford Report at 142-44.

30. *Ibid.* at 58.

31. "Response of the Board of Education of the City of New York to the November 9, 1976 Letter from the Office of Civil Rights, United States Department of Health, Education, and Welfare" (April 22, 1977) [hereinafter cited as Board Response].

32. The Board Response to the Title IX issues, which had not been addressed in the Gifford Report, disputed each of Gerry's three main allegations of sex discrimination and presented counter-analyses. First, the board argued that women were not underrepresented in supervisory positions. Compared to New York State and to the United States, the response noted, New York City had a much higher percentage of female supervisors. (Ironically, this methodology of making comparisons with other cities was inconsistent with the board's criticism of Gerry's inter-city comparisons of the percentages of minority teachers.) The response also challenged Gerry's figures pertaining to the percentage of women

teachers meeting all certification requirements for promotion to supervisor. An "exploratory study" by the board indicated that 25 percent of its male teachers but only 10 percent of its female teachers had earned course credits in the area of administration and supervision. If substantiated, these figures would provide a benign explanation for the disparity in advancement rates between male and female teachers. Despite this counter-analysis, the response also noted the board's "[concern] with the real drop in the number and percentage of female principals and assistant principals in the elementary and junior high schools over the last seven years" (Board Response at 12). Implicitly, this statement was referring to the increased involvement by community school boards in the supervisory selection process, which was created in Chance v. Board of Examiners, as a remedy for racial discrimination in the hiring of supervisors (see note 10). Second, the board argued that both OCR's facts and legal analysis regarding allocation of coaching services were incorrect. Third, in reference to maternity leave practices, the board said that Gerry was asking for remedies that went beyond the congressional intent in either Title VII of the 1964 Civil Rights Act or Title IX of the Educational Amendments of 1972. And, in any event, these legal issues were currently pending in a case before the Supreme Court.

33. New York City's proposed voluntary plan was substantially weaker than those proposed by Chicago and Los Angeles in their initial responses to OCR's findings of discrimination in teacher assignments. In both of these cities, the boards of education proposed specific numerical goals and anticipated time lines for final compliance. Although OCR rejected these plans because the numerical goals were too broad and the time lines too tentative, both plans were more concrete than the New York City proposal. In Philadelphia, because of an urgent need to obtain ESAA funding for the coming school year, the board accepted from the start OCR's mandatory transfer and numerical requirements, and it did not offer a voluntary plan of its own or enter into any negotiations.

34. In Griggs v. Duke Power Co., 401 U.S. 424 (1971), the United States Supreme Court had upheld regulations issued by the EEOC for implementing Title VI's prohibitions against employment discrimination. In addition, specific EEOC validation standards were cited with approval by the Court in Albemarle Paper Co. v. Moody, 422 U.S. 405 (1975). *But cf.* Washington v. Davis, 426 U.S. 229 (1976). For a detailed analysis of the Supreme Court's attitude

toward specific test validation standards in these cases, see Rebell and Block, "Competency Assessment and the Courts: An Overview of the State of the Law," in The Assessment of Occupational Competence, ERIC Document No. ED 192-169 (1980).

35. A fourth issue was employment of women supervisors. Tatel's letter accepted the board's "commitment" to develop criteria and regulations that would be fairer to female candidates, and he said the parties should work together toward this end.

36. An OCR staff memorandum that Tatel attached to his letter responded to the Decentralization Law arguments (which apparently were taken quite seriously) by emphasizing significant racial disparities in the assignment of teachers in the high schools and in the assignment of supervisors generally. In neither of these areas, it noted, did the alternative hiring procedure of the Decentralization Law operate.

On the labor pool issue, Tatel tried to get the discussion back into focus. OCR did not contend "that the ethnicity of race of the teacher population should mirror that of the student population." The real issue was whether there were "many qualified minority teacher applicants who are seeking employment with the New York City school system and who are thwarted by deployment of the nonvalidated Board of Examiner's [sic] test."

37. In Los Angeles the year before, the Gerry regime had obtained a mandatory transfer plan after a relatively uneventful 30-day negotiating process. The Los Angeles Board of Education had consciously decided not to adopt a confrontational mode (in light of the heavy financial sanctions OCR could wield), and the teachers' union joined in that stance. In 1978, similar concessions were made by the Philadelphia Board of Education and the local union, and a mandatory transfer plan was accepted with virtually no negotiations.

38. The less confrontational "negotiations" in Los Angeles and Philadelphia were conducted by local regional staff.

39. In Chicago, OCR also had hired a special consultant, New York attorney Conrad Harper, to be its chief negotiator. (Although several major issues were discussed in Washington, Tatel did not participate directly in the Chicago negotiations.) According to Harper, the idea for hiring an outside negotiator originated with Secretary Califano who, after "12 years of inefficacious" formal procedures for dealing with integration problems in Chicago, wanted results in short order. There was a feeling among some of the

Washington officials that the local OCR people "could not be effective," partially because the new administration was not sure it could trust them and partially because an outsider, starting afresh, could take an "Olympian view" and break through to new ground. (Harper later came to respect greatly the Chicago OCR staff—as did Tatel, who called them into New York to help reinvestigate EES issues.) Califano's account of his reasons for appointing Harper also emphasized the personality clashes "between OCR staffers in HEW's Chicago Regional Office and the city's education hierarchy" (J. Califano, Jr., Governing America: An Insider's Report from the White House and Cabinet 22 [1981]).

40. Tatel interview.

41. *Ibid.*

42. Feldman interview. The UFT's ability finally to gain a place at the bargaining table exemplified its enormous power and influence. The teachers' unions in the other three big cities were rigidly excluded from the negotiating room, although in each case the board did consult extensively with them, going so far in Chicago as to engage at times in "shuttle diplomacy" between the OCR negotiating table and union representatives in an adjoining room (Harper, Raymond interviews).

43. Feldman's strongest impression of OCR's presence at the negotiations was the contrast between Tatel, who was "politically astute," and the OCR staff lawyers, who were "zealots" and did not understand the racial and educational politics of New York City and who did not care in the least about "standards."

44. Letter from James Meyerson to Stuart Baskin (September 14, 1977).

45. Rosen, "Staff Integration and the New York City School System: Origins and History of the 1977 Agreement Between the Board of Education of the City of New York and the United States Department of Health, Education and Welfare 54 (unpublished paper, 1980) [hereinafter cited as Rosen Paper]. The author of this paper, Michael Rosen, was counsel to the chancellor throughout the period of the OCR investigation and negotiations.

46. On the other hand, the threat of a cutoff may have exerted pressure on the board indirectly because of New York City's efforts to improve its standing in the bond markets. The federal threat would have to be reported on disclosure statements for potential investors in city securities, and these investors might not have discounted OCR's threat so easily (Schonhaut interview).

276 NOTES TO CHAPTER FIVE

47. This threat was moderated somewhat by the expectations of Tatel and the board that, by September, waivers could be approved for several of the community school district ESAA applications, even if the central board did not receive a waiver for its own application. Imminent loss of $23 million and $24 million in ESAA funds in Los Angeles and Philadelphia, respectively, sums which represented much larger portions of the district budgets than the threatened ESAA funds represented in New York, had a much stronger influence on the boards' positions in those cases.

48. Rosen Paper *supra* note 45, at 54-55.

49. *Ibid.* at 55.

50. It is clear that the imbalance patterns in teacher assignments in New York City were comparable to those invalidated by the courts in numerous cases. *See*, e.g., Bradley v. Milliken, 338 F. Supp. 582 (E.D. Mich. 1971), *aff'd*, 484 F.2d 215 (6th Cir. 1973), *rev'd on other grounds*, 418 U.S. 717 (1974); Kelly v. Guinn, 456 F.2d 100 (9th Cir. 1972); Morgan v. Hennigan, 379 F. Supp. 410 (D. Mass.), *aff'd sub nom.* Morgan v. Kerrigan, 509 F.2d 580 (1st Cir. 1974). However, all the prior cases, including those like Swann v. Charlotte-Mecklenburg Board of Education, 402 U.S. 1 (1971), which were specifically cited by OCR, involved findings of purposeful discriminatory intent which were absent in New York City (although the issue of whether a violation of Title VI requires finding of discriminatory intent had not been finally decided by the Supreme Court. *See* Guardians Association v. Civil Service Commission of the City of New York, 103 s. Ct. 3221 (1983) and the discussion in chapter 10. Case decisions at the time (especially Washington v. Davis, 426 U.S. 229 [1976]) indicated that the board could mount a very plausible legal defense. However, the contrary legal conclusions in the Gifford Report (written by a non-lawyer), which did not give full credence to significant developments in the law and to the intent/impact distinctions, apparently were never analyzed or reconsidered by the chancellor's legal staff or by the Corporation Counsel's Office.

51. *See supra* note 4.

52. His goals for the agency were to bring the nationwide complaint processing at OCR up to the court-ordered standards and then to focus on his (and Secretary Califano's) priority civil rights goals. He also thought that if major desegregation cases were to be brought against large northern cities, the core issue of student integration, rather than Gerry's secondary items, should be

pressed. Tatel did, in fact, press a major desegregation case in Chicago. *See* U.S. v. Chicago, 554 F. Supp. 912 (D. Ill. 1983).

53. Conrad Harper offered similar comments concerning the backing he got from Chicago and Tatel in Chicago. He mentioned one specific instance when the union "tried to approach Carter through the back door." Despite possible pressures from the White House, however, Califano and Tatel stood firm. After this confrontation, he said "the union took a dive, they just went away" (Harper interview).

54. Letter from Michael Rosen to Michael Rebell, at 3 (February 16, 1981).

55. Feldman interview.

56. Schonhaut interview.

57. Flannery interview.

58. Tatel interview.

59. 419 F.2d 1211 (5th Cir. 1969), *rev'd in part on other grounds sub nom.* Carter v. West Feliciana Parish School Board, 396 U.S. 290 (1970). (*Singleton*, of course, was a classic southern *de jure* segregation case.)

60. OCR had recently obtained agreements in Chicago and Los Angeles mandating specific staff integration ratios, although in both cases a disparity of approximately 10 percent, rather than the 5-percent *Singleton* standard, was accepted. (In Chicago, a deviation slightly in excess of 10 percent was agreed to for teachers, but the assignment of principals was to be in precise proportion to ethnic ratios in the system with no deviation.)

61. Letter from M. Rosen to M. Rebell, *supra* note 54, at 3.

62. Rosen Paper, *supra* note 45, at 58, 64, and 70.

63. While the board agreed to the 5-percent standard as part of the compromise package, its negotiators still emphasized that the *Singleton* precedent, rooted in southern *de jure* segregation, was not legally applicable to New York City.

64. Cioffi interview. Frederick Cioffi, a ranking career official with the Office of Education, served as acting assistant secretary for civil rights in the Department of Education during the beginning of the Reagan administration.

65. After intense negotiations, the obligation in the first two paragraphs of the agreement to meet the *Singleton* standard was qualified by the phrase, "for each educational level and category." This qualification meant that racial integration standards would be calculated separately for elementary/junior high/senior high schools

and for special programs in elementary/junior high schools operated directly by the central board (e.g., special education).

66. Although this phrase was potentially ambiguous, the negotiators understood it to be a "word of art" in the education area, referring to such situations as the disproportionate number of Hispanic teachers that would have to be assigned to bilingual classes (Letter from J. Harold Flannery, Jr. to Arthur Block [August 18, 1982]).

67. Note, however, that because New York had a substantially lower complement of minority teachers than the other cities had, a 10-percent deviation ratio in New York would have permitted all-white faculties in many schools. (A 10-percent deviation from New York's 13-percent average minority teacher population would mean that the permissible number of minority teachers would range between 3 and 23 percent. By way of contrast, in Los Angeles, where the basic minority integration was 30 percent, the 10-percent deviation ratio meant that the number of minority teachers would range between 20 to 40 percent in each school.)

68. Rosen Paper, *supra* note 45, at 66.

69. *See* Caulfield v. Board of Education, No. 77 Civ. 2155 (E.D.N.Y. May 31, 1979) (testimony of J. Harold Flannery, trial transcript, at 1959-63); *Ibid.* (testimony of Charles Schonhaut, trial transcript, June 6, 1979, at 2000-2014). This much is clear: the board put forward statistics and projections which showed that faculty integration could be achieved in three years without forced transfers, and OCR was respectful of the board's desire to meet the *Singleton* standards without resorting to involuntary teacher transfers.

70. Flannery interview.

71. Tatel interview. Flannery also states that, in order to make a "reciprocal gesture of good faith," he deliberately decided to recommend accepting Anker's oral commitment "without formalistic trappings" at the very beginning of the negotiations. Experience had taught him the importance of establishing "mutual reliability" for the overall success of a negotiation of this kind and for the good faith implementation of an agreement after negotiations were over.

72. Anker interview.

73. According to Rosen's written summary of the negotiations, "both the Board and HEW recognized that a certain number of involuntary transfers might be required to achieve the goals" (Rosen Paper *supra*, note 45, at 66). Rosen, like OCR, says that the key

to dealing with the ambiguity of the text is that forced transfers were *not excluded*. OCR's position was simply "that the Board must commit itself to achieving the goals of the agreement through whatever devices were available, and that since transfers were one such device, HEW could not approve an agreement in which the use of an appropriate device was forbidden. The means by which the agreement would be implemented was a matter to be determined by the Board, not HEW. HEW was only concerned with the results" (*Ibid.* at n.191). Rosen does not say that the board anticipated or agreed to "wholesale transfers," as Anker put it, but he does say that some community school boards had already become eligible for ESAA grants, and the UFT had indicated "its willingness to look the other way and give only token opposition"; thus, the board expected that, if necessary, a similar accommodation could probably be worked out with the UFT to complete compliance with the *Singleton* standard in 1980 (*Ibid.* at 65).

74. At the time, it was possible that Title VI violations would have to be based, instead, on proof of intentional discrimination under constitutional standards. *See* Washington v. Davis, 426 U.S. 229 (1976). In 1983, the United States Supreme Court finally ruled directly on these issues in *Guardians, supra* note 50. The complex *Guardians* decision indicated that discriminatory intent is not required to establish a Title VI violation where reasonable administrative regulations adopted pursuant to Title VI prescribe an effects standard. However, the decision limited the scope of the relief available to private plaintiffs in such cases. (*See* the discussion in chapter 10.)

75. Exclusive reliance on the NTE as a teacher hiring device had been invalidated by the federal courts in Walston v. City School Board, 492 F.2d 919 (4th Cir. 1974); Baker v. Columbus Municipal Separate School District, 329 F. Supp. 706 (N.D. Miss. 1971), *aff'd*, 462 F.2d 1112 (5th Cir. 1972); Georgia Association of Educators v. Nix. 407 F. Supp. 1102 (N.D. Ga. 1976). *But cf.* United States v. South Carolina, 445 F. Supp. 1094 (D.S.C. 1977), *aff'd*, 434 U.S. 1026 (1978).

76. Flannery interview.

77. Predictive, or "empirical," validation "requires an analysis of the relationship between performance on a test or other 'predictor' and performance on the job being tested for" (Bartholet, "Application of Title VII to Jobs in High Places," 95 Harv. L. Rev. 945, 1018 [1982]).

78. 1970 EEOC Guidelines on Employment Selection Procedures, 35 Fed. Reg. 12333 (1970) (codified at 29 C.F.R. pt. 1607).
79. 20 C.F.R. § 1607.14(C)(1). The Uniform Guidelines were first published at 43 Fed. Reg. 38, 290 (1978). These guidelines were being negotiated at the time of the agreement, but the trend toward permitting greater use of content validation was already evident in the temporary Executive Agency Guidelines then in effect. *See* 41 Fed. Reg. 51744 (1976).
80. "A test is said to be content-valid with respect to a job when it measures performance of tasks that constitute a relatively complete sample of those called for on the job" (Bartholet, *supra* note 77, at 1016).
81. Feldman interview; Rosen Paper, *supra* note 45, at 192.
82. Feldman interview.
83. Feldman interprets "as exemplified" to mean that the Board of Examiners could "go on doing what they were doing already."
84. The full text of paragraph 6 reads:

> "The Board agrees, as soon as practicable to have performed a study of the relevant qualified labor pool by race, ethnicity, and sex by an independent expert acceptable to the parties and pursuant to methodology and standards agreed to by the parties. Through the adoption and implementation of the affirmative action procedures and legislation provided in paragraph 4 of this Memorandum and other efforts taken or to be taken by the Board, the Board commits that by September of 1980, the levels of minority participation in the teaching and supervisory service will be within a range representative of the racial and ethnic composition of the relevant qualified labor pool.
>
> "It is understood that this commitment shall not require the Board to lay off any teacher currently employed by the Board or to hire any teacher who has not met appropriate requirements for employment, not inconsistent with this agreement. It is further understood that the commitment made herein does not establish quotas. Failure to meet this commitment shall not be considered a violation of this agreement if the Board demonstrates that it had implemented the provisions of this agreement in a good faith effort to meet the commitment made herein.
>
> "The Board has advised the Office for Civil Rights that the

Board expects to consult with the United Federation of Teachers and others regarding the selection of the independent expert and the standards and methodology to be used in the above study. Likewise, the Office for Civil Rights has advised the Board that it expects to consult with other governmental agencies, civil rights organizations, and others regarding the selection of the independent expert and the standards and methodology to be used in this study."

85. Rosen Paper, *supra* note 45, at 69; Flannery interview.
86. Rosen Paper, *supra* note 45, at 69. The acceptability of the agreement also was enhanced by its use of important "buzzwords" about quotas, the merit system, good faith, and incumbent teachers' rights. At the last minute, the board's secretary counsel, Harold Siegel, recommended, as well, that the board's commitment be referenced to the recent decision in Hazelwood School District v. United States, 443 U.S. 299 (1977), a Supreme Court decision which he interpreted as bolstering school board flexibility by permitting labor pools to be based on broader geographical areas.
87. Rosen Paper, *supra* note 45, at 68 and nn.170-71.
88. The final agreement dropped all references to the issues of instructional resources, coaches' pay, and maternity leave. The following paragraph concerning affirmative action for female supervisors was included:

"8. The Board of Education commits itself to pursue a program of affirmative action to increase the number of women in the supervisory service, including a plan to reach a systemwide level of participation by women within a range representative of the pool of individual qualified women by a date to be agreed upon with the Office for Civil Rights. The Board further agrees that it will establish a procedure whereby no person shall be appointed to a supervisory position until an affirmative action officer in the central personnel administration has studied the file of applicants for the particular position and determined that the appointment process demonstrates good faith compliance with the affirmative action plan. The Board agrees to review with the Office for Civil Rights the appropriateness of standards and procedures for selection of supervisory personnel to insure conformity to this paragraph."

89. Senator Javits did not get deeply involved in the political uproar

282 NOTES TO CHAPTER FIVE

surrounding the hiring hall procedures. However, at one point he did make a speech on the Senate floor defending the agreement. Although Anker generally supported Moynihan's remarks, another high board official involved in the negotiations was extremely disappointed in Moynihan's reaction, not only because it hindered implementation of the agreement, but also because Moynihan's staff had implicitly "cleared" the agreement after being kept well-informed about the negotiations.

90. 449 F. Supp. 1203 (E.D.N.Y.), *aff'd in part, rev'd in part and remanded,* 583 F.2d 605 (2d Cir. 1978), *on remand,* 486 F. Supp. 862 (E.D.N.Y. 1979), *aff'd,* 632 F.2d 999 (2d Cir. 1980).

91. The UFT's intervenor complaint did not contest the validity of those provisions in the agreement that the UFT had "co-signed under protest." Nor did the UFT agree with the plaintiffs' claim that ethnic surveys were unconstitutional. The UFT did join, however, in the central challenge to the faculty integration provisions. Still, the UFT probably would not have gone to court independently at that time to contest those provisions; rather, it would have waited to see how they worked out in practice. The *Caulfield* complaint had made it necessary for the UFT to intervene in order to be involved in decisions that would affect its membership (Feldman interview).

92. The American Jewish Congress and the Anti-Defamation League of B'Nai B'Rith participated as *amicus curiae* supporting plaintiffs. The defendants were the board of education, HEW, and the State Commissioner of Education.

93. In January 1977, the central board and 16 community school boards filed a total of 32 applications with HEW for ESAA grants. When the Office of Education reviewed these applications for quality and availability of funds, it tentatively approved 20 grants totaling approximately $17.5 million. These funds were held up, however, by OCR's determination that alleged violations cited in OCR's First Letter of Findings disqualified all of the New York City school districts. On October 25, 1977, the central board received formal notification that, notwithstanding the agreement, it was still ineligible for ESAA funds. However, almost all of the community school districts' applications now were deemed eligible because the districts had agreed to plans which would immediately bring about faculty integration in the schools within their jurisdiction. HEW, therefore, provided them with $13.5 million of the reserved funds.

The board filed a complaint in Board of Education v. Califano on September 27, 1977. On November 18, 1977, Judge Jack Weinstein issued a decision rejecting the board of education's key contention that, because it was not found guilty of intentional discrimination, it was not responsible for racially disparate teaching assignments, but also finding that HEW had unjustifiably refused to consider in its administrative hearing certain evidence offered by the board. He remanded the case to HEW. After further administrative fact-finding, OCR adhered to its original determination. Judge Weinstein then considered the board's challenge on its merits and ruled in favor of HEW on April 18, 1978. This order was affirmed by the Second Circuit (584 F.2d 576 [2d Cir. 1978]), and then by the United States Supreme Court (Harris v. Board of Education, 444 U.S. 130 [1979]) in a major decision which held that Congress intended eligibility for ESAA grants to be based on a discriminatory impact standard.

The board was more successful with the remaining question of the standards for granting waivers of ineligibility. In a separate case, based on the ESAA funding cycle for 1978-1979, the board eventually won a court order declaring that HEW was not legally prohibited from granting (in its discretion) a waiver of ineligibility if an agreement has been reached "terminating all active discrimination and beginning prompt elimination of the results of past discrimination [even] where the effects of past discriminatory teacher assignment have not been fully eliminated" (Board of Education v. Califano, 464 F. Supp. 1114, 1127 [E.D.N.Y. 1979], aff'd, 622 F.2d 599 [2d Cir. 1979], cert. denied, 449 U.S. 1124 [1981]. Accordingly, the matter was remanded to HEW for further consideration. See Board of Education v. Hufstedler, 641 F.2d 68 (2d Cir. 1981). In 1982, HEW approved the waiver and released the escrowed funds to New York City.

94. Even so, the chancellor had to exercise his authority under N.Y. Educ. Law § 2590-1 to suspend Community Board 26 for failing "to comply with any applicable provisions of law," in order to have the racial census actually conducted in that district.

95. Caulfield v. Board of Education, 449 F. Supp. 1206-7.

96. Caulfield v. Board of Education, 583 F.2d 605 (2d Cir. 1978). The court held that Title VI's "statutory scheme requires a hearing with notice only when HEW seeks fund termination" (Ibid. at 615). The Second Circuit also affirmed Judge Weinstein's order denying plaintiffs' motion for an injunction against the ethnic

surveys. The *Caulfield* trial was held April to June 1979. Judge
Weinstein issued a decision finding the agreement lawful on its
merits (486 F. Supp. 862 [E.D.N.Y. 1979], *aff'd*, 632 F.2d 999
[2d Cir. 1980]).

97. Chancellor Anker had not submitted the plan when it was due
in January 1978.

98. New York City Public School System, "A Progress Report and
Plan to Implement the Memorandum of Understanding Between
the New York City Public School System and the Office for Civil
Rights, United States Department of Health, Education and Welfare" (December 15, 1978).

99. Letter from Lloyd Henderson to Frank Macchiarola (April 10,
1979). That OCR took four months to respond to what OCR
itself later called a vague plan is typical of the erratic pattern of
OCR's communications with the board of education during this
period.

100. Letter from Chancellor Macchiarola to Lloyd Henderson
(March 30, 1979).

101. An analysis prepared for OCR by the Delta Research Corporation in June 1980 indicated that 2,250 elementary and 1,050
junior high school teachers would need to be moved to achieve
full compliance. (No figures were presented for high schools.)

102. Opinion and Award, American Arbitration Association Case
No. 1339-0485-80.

103. New York Association of Black Educators II (NYABE) v. United
States Department of Education, No. 77 Civ. 2531 (E.D.N.Y.).

104. Letter from Frank Macchiarola to Clarence Thomas (July 9,
1981).

105. *See* N.Y. Times, June 3, 1982, at 1, col. 1; June 10, 1982, at
1, col. 1.

106. Memorandum of Understanding Between the Board of Education of the City of New York and the Office for Civil Rights,
United States Department of Education (November 1982) [here-
inafter cited as 1982 Agreement]. *See* N.Y. Times, November 24,
1982, at 1, col. 1; November 28, 1982, at 6E, col. 6; December
8, 1982, at A30, col. 1 (editorial).

107. "Each school in the New York City public school system shall
reflect, within a range of 15 percent, the racial/ethnic composition
of the school system's teacher corps as a whole, at both district
and high school levels, to be determined on a *borough-wide* basis"

(emphasis added) (Affirmative Action Plan annexed to 1982 Agreement, at 2). *Cf. supra* note 65.
108. *See supra* note 67.
109. Interestingly, however, the chancellor did initiate a federal lawsuit against the Board of Examiners in August 1981, charging that the tests they had recently administered for supervisory positions were racially discriminatory and not valid (Macchiarola v. Board of Examiners, No. 81 Civ. 4798 [S.D.N.Y.]). This suit was settled, at least tentatively, in July 1982, by an agreement on methods for developing new tests.
110. The board transmitted its expert labor pool study to OCR in December 1979. However, OCR's own expert consultant, Stephan Michelson, was extremely critical of the draft of the labor pool study prepared by the board's consultant, Seymour Wolfbein, and was likely to reject the final work product as well. OCR merely reported that its review of Wolfbein's report still was pending.
111. The *NYABE* plaintiffs have claimed that the board and OCR violated their rights in purporting to supersede the 1977 Agreement with the 1982 Agreement. They have asked the court to invalidate the 1982 Agreement and to enjoin the board and OCR to implement the 1977 provisions. As of January 1984, the case was still in discovery, after Judge Weinstein had denied the plaintiffs' motion for summary judgment. In denying the motion, the judge stated that he wanted to have a full factual picture of current assignment patterns and practices in the school system before he would consider any possible court intervention.

NOTES TO CHAPTER SIX

1. In the other locales of the Big City Reviews, the original student services issues were also de-emphasized early in the process. In Chicago, teacher assignments and bilingual programming were intensely negotiated in 1977; after that, the other areas of student services were dropped as OCR pursued broader issues of segregation in school assignments, culminating in the filing of a suit by the Department of Justice (*see* United States v. Board of Education, City of Chicago, 544 F. Supp. 912 [E.D. Ill. 1983]). In Los Angeles, OCR Region IX consciously made a decision, at the outset, not to pursue any issues beyond faculty assignment and bilingual education (Palomino interview). In Philadelphia, substantial analytical work was done on a variety of student services items. On some

of these (faculty salaries, coaching, and discipline), OCR found no indications of discrimination; in other areas (resource allocation, ability grouping, and handicapped placements), the local office was told to drop the investigation shortly before letters of findings were to be issued because the items had become "low priority." However, in one area (curriculum offerings), successful informal negotiations (prior to the issuance of any letter of findings) solved the problem. As in Chicago and Los Angeles, bilingual education issues were formally pursued (Wilson Interview).

2. Second Letter of Findings from Martin Gerry to Irving Anker (January 18, 1977), at 3-10 [hereinafter cited as second letter].

3. *Ibid.* at 10-18.

4. For example, standardized achievement tests were heavily relied upon for assignment decisions, even though they were "not intended to be used as diagnostic instruments." Furthermore, the use of self-contained classrooms meant that assignments made on the basis of reading test scores—even assuming that these were valid indications of reading ability—would determine a child's placement for instructional areas like math, science, art, and physical education, which supposedly were not even covered by the grouping criterion.

5. Gerry's approach in this letter was to anticipate justifications the board might offer and to refute them in advance. This anticipatory approach was unusual for OCR letters of finding.

6. Other alleged segregatory tracking practices were the overrepresentation of minority children in classes labeled "emotionally handicapped," "mentally handicapped," and "educable mentally retarded," and the underrepresentation of minority children in "special progress" classes at the junior high school level.

   In addition to segregated institutional settings, the denial of educational opportunity through language barriers was alleged in an additional subsection under this heading.

7. Second letter, *supra* note 2, at 18-25.

8. On its face, OCR's evidence was a mixed bag. Some of the investigative survey responses seemed vulnerable to challenge. On the other hand, some simple and verifiable facts were quite striking, for example, the allegation of completely unnecessary sex segregation patterns in vocational schools such as Queens Vocational High School, where "8 of the 12 English courses . . . are single sex (100% male or female) and 4 are sex identifiable" (second letter, *supra* note 2, at 24).

9. Second letter, *supra* note 2, at 25-27.
10. Press statement by Martin H. Gerry (January 18, 1977).
11. N.Y. Times, January 20, 1977, at 41, col. 1.
12. Although Hamlin and Henderson had different opinions on how seriously the letter was flawed, they agreed on one point—OCR had to be prepared to prove the allegations of discrimination with evidence that would hold up in federal court. As Hamlin put it, "New York had a history of litigating" (Hamlin interview).
13. There was some mention at the time of also taking a fresh look at the first letter, but it was decided that that document met agency standards in its formulation and its evidentiary back-up materials.
14. 426 U.S. 229 (1976).
15. Apparently, OCR also sought the approval of Senator Javits's office (Memorandum from Albert Hamlin to David Tatel, [May 17, 1977]).
16. Perhaps because of this atmosphere, perceptions of the competence and work product of the Chicago investigators in New York varied widely among our interviewees. Some offered the highest praise for their abilities, while others claimed that they never sufficiently understood New York City and dealt superficially with many serious allegations in the letter.
17. A good example is found in the section on discipline, where OCR found a *prima facie* violation of Title VI. The section concludes with a request for: "1. an explanation, if any, for the findings of disparate racial impact of the District's present discipline practices; 2. a detailed, formal articulation of the District's present discipline policy together with specific information as to its dissemination; 3. a plan for a detailed nondiscriminatory discipline policy which will be implemented uniformly system-wide forthwith; and 4. a description of the record-keeping system you maintain or, in the event that a satisfactory system has not yet been formulated, a plan for maintaining records which will be effective as soon as practicable" (revised second letter, at 10).
18. The statistics cited in the revised letter are not readily comparable to statistical references in the original letter addressing the same issues. Gerry made greater use of general statistical patterns; Tatel tried to highlight very glaring denials of services. For example, in regard to classroom segregation, Gerry argued in terms of numbers of segregated grades, whereas Tatel's unit of analysis was classrooms and, ultimately, children. Hence, Tatel concluded that there were at least 1,998 segregated classrooms shaping the educational

experience of 41,182 minority students and 35,083 non-minority students (revised second letter, at 4).

Similarly, Gerry's analyses of the racial composition of special progress classes and of the availability of bilingual guidance personnel were expressed in terms of overall ratios of minority underrepresentation, but Tatel focused on figures showing absolute denial of services to identifiable children. Along these lines, the revised letter reports that over 80 percent of minority junior/senior high school students attended schools where there were *no* special progress classes, and that thousands of Hispanic and Asian children with limited English language abilities attended schools where guidance counselors and/or disciplinary personnel who spoke their language were altogether absent.

19. The *Lau* issues, identification of and curriculum for language-minority children, do not appear, but only because Chancellor Anker had already submitted a school system plan for services for language-minority children in September 1977 (Plan to Comply with Title VI CRA also Submitted as Part of Application for Waiver of Ineligibility" [September 15, 1977]).

20. Besides classroom segregation, four other Title VI issues were included in the letter: accessibility of appropriate guidance and disciplinary services to national-origin minority group children; discipline practices; availability of enrichment opportunities; and accessibility of bilingual psychologists and adequate psychological assessment instruments to national-origin minority group children.

21. Five issues were featured: denial of educational services to handicapped children due to excessive waiting lists; shortened school day for handicapped children; inadequate evaluation and placement; failure to "mainstream" children, when appropriate; and inadequate identification procedures.

22. To maximize accuracy, OCR had utilized figures only from schools where there were sufficient numbers of minority and non-minority children to make integration practicable. Furthermore, it did not question the validity of the basic ability grouping structure; that is, racial segregation was considered only within each established ability level.

OCR had data on the student racial/ethnic composition of 31,466 regular classrooms. By utilizing the methodology described above, it narrowed its examination to 32 percent of the broader sample. However, one limitation of OCR's analysis of its subsample was that OCR only controlled for four ability levels per grade when, in fact, many New York City schools divided grades into many more tracks. OCR's methodology was based on the assumption that using more than four ability tracks in a single grade level rarely (if ever) could be justified educationally.

23. *See supra* p. 96.

24. Letter from William Taylor to Peter Libassi (March 24, 1978).

25. In the Matter of the City School District for the City of New York, HEW Administrative Proceeding, No. 78-VI-4 (April 6, 1978). The notice alleged two legal violations—classroom segregation (Title VI) and waiting lists for handicapped children (sec. 504).

26. For example, Chancellor Anker agreed that when statistical anomalies appear in a school's discipline practices, the principal should be required to explain them.

27. "Response to HEW Office for Civil Rights October 4, 1977 Letter of Findings" 6 (November 22, 1977). The largest group covered by the explanation (45 percent) included classes in which segregative patterns were caused unavoidably by the requirements of bilingual education programs (*Ibid.* at 7). The next largest category (29 percent) and the one that was to become the main focus of debates about educational policy at the negotiating table, included the racially identifiable classes that allegedly were organized by "ability grouping of pupils according to reading scores and other educational criteria" (*Ibid.* at 8).

28. ASPIRA of New York, Inc. v. Board of Education, No. 72 Civ. 4002 (S.D.N.Y. August 29, 1974). At first, OCR had taken the position that the decree was being implemented in an unnecessarily segregatory manner. This argument also was made periodically by local advocacy groups.

29. OCR objected to these practices only to the extent that they caused racially identifiable or isolated instructional groupings. OCR clearly had no authority to insist on changes in ability grouping practices that were racially neutral in effect.

30. Emphasis added. Memorandum from David Tatel, director of OCR, to Joseph Califano, secretary of HEW (March 24, 1978) at 1.

31. *Ibid.* at 4.

32. *Ibid.* at 7. The National Institute of Education (NIE), a division of the Department of Education, conducts and funds scholarly research, program evaluation, and related activities in the area of education.

33. Tatel gave three reasons for preferring administrative enforcement over referral to the Justice Department: (1) negotiations could continue during preparation for the hearing, (2) the Justice Department was overloaded with referrals in school desegregation matters prompted by Congress's anti-busing amendments, and (3) "it is important that we revitalize the administrative enforcement remedies that have remained dormant for the past 8 years" (*Ibid.* at 10).

34. Graham is currently dean of the Harvard Graduate School of Education.

35. Graham interview.

36. Aside from the academic literature, Schonhaut reported that there was still a general belief among New York City educators that all children were better off if grouped by ability. This belief would shape teacher behavior regardless of whether it was supported in the scholarly studies.

   Although it was agreed that there were no reliable standardized testing instruments for assessing ability at the kindergarten and first grade levels, the board had argued for intra-class groupings based on nondiscriminatory criteria such as reviewable maturity indicators, reading readiness levels, and ability to recognize symbols ("Suggested New York City Board of Education policy for integrating classes (OCR II)," attached as TAB D to Memorandum from D. Tatel to J. Califano [March 24, 1978]).

37. *See* 45 C.F.R. §§ 185.43(c), 185.44(e) (1973).

38. For example, if a principal has four second grade classrooms and he wants to divide the grade into instructional groupings based on ability, he or she must create a minimum of eight sequential groupings. This ensures that no single classroom can consist merely of one ability group. Furthermore, contiguous groups may not be assigned to the same classroom. Thus, a classroom may consist of ability groups 1 and 4 or 5 and 7, but it may *not* be made up of groups 1 and 2 or 6 and 7. The purpose is to guarantee a minimum amount of integration of children at different levels of functioning within each second grade classroom.

39. A comparison with the agreement reached in Chicago, the only other of the big cities where OCR raised this issue, is instructive. The Chicago Agreement basically instructed principals to "insure that the racial ethnic composition of each regular classroom deviates no more than 20 percentage points from the racial composition" of the grade. If any such deviation does occur, the prin-

cipal must reassign students or provide "an educational justification." The district was required to develop an internal mandatory procedure to evaluate the purported educational justifications, and it was to provide detailed reports annually to OCR (Letter from Patricia Roberts Harris to Joseph P. Hannon [September 15, 1979] appendix, at 5-6).

40. Consistent with OCR's original position, the agreement imposed no restrictions on ability grouping of any kind that did not cause racially identifiable instructional settings. See supra note 29.

41. At least some local advocacy representatives were skeptical of OCR's assessment. Susanna Doyle, of AFC, said that the OCR negotiators were much too gullible about the board's factual claims, including those concerning the feasibility of implementation. The OCR negotiators, she said, "were like pillows, they could absorb anything" (Doyle interview).

42. "A Brief Analysis of the Civil Rights Compliance Agreement between the Board of Education and the U.S. Office for Civil Rights" (unattributed and undated, but identified in the cover letter to "Public Interest Lawyers" from Advocates for Children [July 17, 1978] as a memorandum prepared by Martin Gerry).

43. Gerry also charged that the new procedures for reporting on student discipline did not constitute a meaningful remedy. He noted, as well, that all of the charges relating to sex discrimination under Title IX had been dropped from the revised student services letter "[a]fter nine months of closed discussions between the Board and OCR and other HEW officials."

44. Participants at the meeting had discussed possible strategies for having stronger requirements imposed on the board, including lobbying President Carter, urging the Attorney General's Office to find the agreement in noncompliance with civil rights laws, and pursuing court action to set aside the agreement. Alternatively, based on Gerry's statement that the agreement still left New York City drastically out of compliance with the ESAA requirements on racially isolated instructional settings, it was suggested that a suit be filed to cut off New York City's ESAA funds. The question was also raised about the potential for challenging the agreement in the context of the Brown case. (The Brown court, however, had never previously inquired into the substance of any OCR compliance agreement.)

45. Apparently, the impending deadline under the employment agree-

ment for teacher integration by September 1980 stirred up activity in the student services area as well.

46. Delta Research Corporation Reports NYC 42-15 and NYC 42-16. As mentioned above, no report was generated for 1980-1981.

47. There is obviously no organized constituency pressing for change in this area. In response to a questionnaire distributed in connection with this study (*see* chapter 7, note 17), we found that only one of seven interest group respondents indicated an awareness that the number of racially identified classrooms had been reduced through OCR's intervention. By comparison, five of the eight OCR respondents said that OCR intervention had improved this area, and only two of them considered it still to be a problem today.

48. In assessing the favorable statistics in the instructional grouping area, one must keep in mind that these statistics assume that the board of education has assigned students to ability groups accurately and in good faith compliance with the complex requirements of the agreement. For example, although the 1979-1980 Delta report indicated 142 identifiable classes by controlling for ability grouping, it also noted that, if ability groupings were ignored, there would be 687 racially identifiable classes. Thus, ability grouping is the automatic justification for 545 classes. Detailed analysis, of course, might raise questions about whether all of these classes belong in that category.

49. Board of Education, Addendum to Special Circular No. 103, 1969-1970 (June 13, 1978). A copy of this addendum is an appendix to the Letter of Agreement.

50. The addendum explained that a "disproportionate rate will be defined as being clearly beyond random chance." The technical specifications for this definition are set forth as follows in Delta's Report to OCR, July 31, 1979:

> 1. Junior and senior high schools having 20 or more suspensions during the time period are reported "if the proportion of Minority suspensions to Minority enrollment is greater than 1.25 times the proportion of Non-Minority suspensions to Non-Minority enrollment."
> 2. For all elementary schools and for other schools having fewer than 20 suspensions during the period analyzed, "the probability of arriving at the number of Minority suspensions is calculated based on the ethnic composition of the total school enrollment, using the Binomial probability formula." A school appears in the report "[i]f the probability of Minority

suspensions is less than .2 given the Minority percentage in the school."

51. Form letter from Chancellor Macchiarola (September 24, 1979).
52. "Response to: HEW Office for Civil Rights Suspension Analysis Report, September 1978-January 1979" (November 30, 1979). Examples of the categories of responses are incorrect data, failure to differentiate special education pupils, adjustment problems, and high mobility rate.
53. Some of his criticisms were set forth in his letter to the chancellor of December 12, 1979.
54. Doyle interview and confidential AFC contemporaneous memorandum of the meeting.
55. A statistical disparity in suspensions does not, of course, necessarily indicate discrimination. The fundamental question is whether there are racial disparities in the numbers of students suspended who actually committed offenses punishable by suspension (or who were suspended for no good cause). Thus, a disparity could be explained by demonstrating that minority students committed more such offenses in this category, and that punishments were meted out evenly among students of all races who committed such offenses.
56. In June 1980, OCR transmitted to the board Delta's reports on staff integration and instructional groupings, but it is unclear whether the September 1979-January 1980 semiannual discipline report was transmitted or discussed, or whether a Delta report was generated for the next semester, February 1980-June 1980. As noted in note 46, for the subsequent period, school year 1980-1981, there was no contract with Delta Research Corporation.
57. "Record Keeping on Student Discipline Procedures and Actions in School Districts" (August 1975).
58. AFC pressed its grievances about the board's discipline practices in a federal court case, Boe v. Board of Education, No. 80 Civ. 2829 HFW (S.D.N.Y.), and obtained substantial relief in a quasi-consent judgment signed on December 30, 1982.

OCR has not seriously attempted to follow up the unresolved handicapped education issues (shortened school day, improper identification and evaluation, lack of mainstreaming) or to monitor compliance with commitments made by the board in the agreement to clear an extensive backlog of children who were still waiting for an evaluation or placement many months after their parents requested they be evaluated for special education. Apparently,

OCR regards these issues pertaining to educational services for handicapped children as being preempted by federal court proceedings. Jose P. v. Ambach, 3 E.H.L.R. 551:245 (E.D.N.Y. 1979), *aff'd*, 669 F.2d 865 (2d Cir. 1982), a class action suit, was filed by South Brooklyn Legal Services in February 1979 on behalf of all handicapped children on the waiting lists, charging the board of education with violation of federal and state laws in regard to timely evaluation and placement. Soon afterwards, a parallel lawsuit, UCP v. Board of Education, 3 E.H.L.R. 551:251 (E.D.N.Y. 1979), repeated the claims about the waiting lists but, in addition, raised numerous other issues concerning program quality, architectural accessibility, and lack of mainstreaming. Yet a third related case was then brought based on the rights of language-minority handicapped children (Dyrcia S. v. Board of Education 79 Civ. 2562). For a detailed discussion of the joint-court decree entered in these cases and the follow-up implementation problems and accomplishments, *see* Rebell, "Implementation of Court Mandates Concerning Special Education: The Problems and the Potential," 10 J. L. & Educ. 335 (1981).

NOTES TO CHAPTER SEVEN

1. Similar conclusions have been reached in studies of the implementation of other equality statutes. For example, "[t]he language of Title VII of the Civil Rights Act of 1964 is stated in functional terms that deal with a variety of personnel actions, e.g., hires, discharges, compensation, deprivation of opportunities. Its thrust is to eliminate discrimination by assuring equal treatment in job *mobility*—that is, equal opportunity. . . . The enforcement agencies, on the other hand, interpret Congressional policy as requiring more than mobility, that what should be done is to eliminate the effects of past discrimination *immediately*. In other words, job *parity* or a numerical equivalency in the number of jobs *held* and levels of compensation *received* must be achieved at once rather than awaiting the effects of equal opportunity" (McGuiness, "Foreword," in Comparable Worth: Issues and Alternatives vi [E. Livernash ed. 1980]). Note also that aside from OCR, all of the approximately 40 federal departments and agencies adopting standards interpreting Title VI took a result-oriented/discriminatory impact approach (Guardians Association v. Civil Service

Commission of the City of New York, 103 S. Ct. 3221, 3241 [1983] [Marshall, J., dissenting]).

2. Of course, as illustrated by the Adams v. Richardson case, discussed in chapter 4, OCR also engages in avoidance techniques when it decides to drop or ignore enforcement of certain issues or in certain geographical areas. The point here is that when OCR does act, it tends to press in a consistently result-oriented direction.

3. Rabkin, "The Office For Civil Rights," in The Politics of Regulation 331 (J. Wilson ed. 1980).

4. *See* the discussion in chapter 3 concerning the legislative history of sec. 604, 42 U.S.C. § 2000d-3.

5. *See* United States v. Jefferson County Board of Education, 372 F.2d 836, 883 (5th Cir. 1966); 45 C.F.R. § 80.3(c)(3)(1964). *See also* Rogers v. Paul, 382 U.S. 198, 200 (1965); Swann v. Charlotte-Mecklenberg Board of Education, 402 U.S. 1, 18 (1971). *Cf.* Vaughns v. Board of Education, Prince George's County 574 F. Supp. 1280 (D. Md. 1983) (faculty assignment plan need not be maintained after segregation is eliminated); Kromnick v. School District of Philadelphia, 739 F.2d 894 (3d Cir. 1984) (voluntary faculty assignment plan may be continued after segregation is eliminated).

6. In the context of the "voluntary" agreements negotiated by OCR in New York City, the federal courts have since held that sec. 604 is not a bar to enforcement of Title VI faculty segregation issues in the North. *See* Caulfield v. Board of Education, 486 F. Supp. 862, 876 (E.D.N.Y. 1979). *See also* Zaslawsky v. Board of Education, 610 F.2d 661 (9th Cir. 1979); North Haven Board of Education v. Bell, 102 S. Ct. 1912 (1982) (infection theory upheld in enforcement of Title IX sex discrimination standards).

7. *See*, e.g., Oliver v. Kalamazoo Board of Education, 346 F. Supp. 766 (W.D. Mich. 1972), *aff'd*, 448 F.2d 635 (6th Cir. 1971); Spangler v. Pasadena City Board of Education, 311 F. Supp. 501 (C.D. Cal. 1970), *aff'd*, 427 F.2d 1352 (9th Cir. 1970); Johnson v. San Francisco Unified School District, 339 F. Supp. 1315 (N.D. Cal. 1971). Note, however, that even at this time a majority of the federal courts indicated that discriminatory intent was necessary to establish a constitutional violation. *See*, e.g., United States v. School District 151 of Cook County Illinois, 286 F. Supp. 786 (N.D. Ill. 1968), *aff'd*, 404 F.2d 1125 (7th Cir. 1968), *cert. denied*, 402 U.S. 943 (1971).

8. 413 U.S. 189 (1973). After *Keyes*, most of the prior federal court

decisions which had found constitutional violations in situations
of *de facto* segregation were reversed or reconsidered. *See*, e.g.,
Johnson v. San Francisco Unified School District, 339 F. Supp.
1315 (N.D. Cal. 1971), *rev'd*, 500 F.2d 349 (9th Cir. 1974); United
States v. Texas Education Agency, 467 F.2d 848 (5th Cir. 1972),
*aff'd in part, rev'd in part en banc*, 532 F.2d 380 (1976) (intent
approach adopted and satisfied); Oliver v. Kalamazoo Board of
Education, 368 F. Supp. 143 (W.D. Mich. 1973).
9. 426 U.S. 229 (1976).
10. The Supreme Court held in *Swann* that "[i]ndependent of student
assignment, where it is possible to identify a 'white school' or a
'Negro school' simply by reference to the racial composition of
teachers and staff, the quality of school buildings and equipment,
or the organization of sports activities, a *prima facie* case of violation of substantive constitutional rights under the Equal Protection Clause is shown" (402 U.S. 1, 18 [1971]). Even before
*Swann*, the Supreme Court's strong emphasis on elimination of
faculty desegregation was indicated by its holding in United States
v. Montgomery County Board of Education, 395 U.S. 225 (1969),
in which it reversed the Court of Appeals for the Fifth Circuit and
reinstated a district court's desegregation order that contained
numerical ratio requirements for faculty assignments.
11. In northern cities, the courts looked to a variety of factors as
indicia of discriminatory intent, such as dual attendance zones
(Bradley v. Milliken, 338 F. Supp. 582 [E.D. Mich. 1971], *aff'd*,
484 F.2d 215 [6th Cir. 1973], *rev'd on other grounds*, 418 U.S.
717 [1974]; United States v. Board of School Commissioners, 332
F. Supp. 655 [S.D. Ind. 1971], *aff'd*, 474 F.2d 81 [7th Cir. 1973],
*cert. denied*, 413 U.S. 920 [1973]); transfer policies that accentuated white flight and deterred blacks from attending white
schools (Booker v. Special School District No. 1, 351 F. Supp. 799
[D. Minn. 1972] [busing past the nearest school]; United States v.
School District 151 of Cook County Illinois, 286 F. Supp. 786
[N.D. Ill. 1968], *aff'd*, 404 F.2d 1125 [7th Cir. 1968]); and use
of school construction policies that fostered racial imbalance (*Milliken, supra*; Morgan v. Hennigan, 379 F. Supp. 410 [D. Mass.],
*aff'd sub nom.* Morgan v. Kerrigan, 509 F.2d 580 [1st Cir. 1974]).
In addition, patterns of faculty segregation themselves constituted
an important factor in determining discriminatory intent. *See*, e.g.,
Kelly v. Guinn, 456 F.2d 100, 107 (9th Cir. 1972). Professor
Orfield has indicated that, under these standards, most large north-

ern and western cities tended to be found guilty of intentional discrimination "when integration was seriously pursued" (G. Orfield, Must We Bus? 24 [1978]). However, in one of the two major desegregation cases that have been brought against particular New York City schools, the board of education prevailed (Parents Association of Andrew Jackson High School v. Ambach, 598 F.2d 705 [2d Cir. 1979]. *But cf.* Hart v. Community School Board, 383 F. Supp. 699 [E.D.N.Y. 1974], *aff'd*, 512 F.2d 37 [2d Cir. 1975]).

12. *See*, e.g., Kelly v. Guinn, *supra* note 11 (faculty reassignment order was issued for majority black schools that had 80 percent black teachers); Booker v. Special School District No. 1, *supra* note 11 (61 percent of black elementary school teachers were in 14 elementary schools, each of which had over 15 percent black students); Morgan v. Hennigan, *supra* note 11 (75 percent of black teachers were in schools that had over 50 percent black students).

13. Judge Weinstein later indicated that with the statistics on faculty assignment patterns presented by OCR, "a strong case could be made for intentional discrimination" (Caulfield v. Board of Education, 486 F. Supp. 862, 920 [E.D.N.Y. 1979]).

14. The issue of whether Title VI requires an intent or an impact standard was unsettled throughout this period. The Supreme Court's opinion in Lau v. Nichols, 414 U.S. 563, 568 (1974), upheld an impact standard in the Title VI bilingual regulations, but a majority of the justices in Regents of the University of California v. Bakke, 438 U.S. 265 (1978), seemed to call for an intent standard. The Second Circuit was requiring a showing of intent in its major decisions (Parents Association of Andrew Jackson High School v. Ambach, *supra* note 11; Lora v. Board of Education, 623 F.2d 248 [2d cir. 1980]. *See also* Harris v. White, 479 F. Supp. 996 [D. Mass. 1979]).

In 1983, in a complex decision, five members of the Supreme Court upheld an impact standard in the context of a testing case, with three of the justices basing that view on the Title VI regulations, rather than on the statute itself (Guardians Association v. Civil Service Commission of the City of New York, 103 S. Ct. 3221 [1983]). *Guardians* is discussed in detail in chapter 10.

15. Although Tatel, when interviewed after the fact, did refer to the need to marshal sufficient evidence to establish discriminatory intent in the event that the issues had to be brought to court, it is significant that he rejected the board's equal opportunity plan

precisely because it did not contain commitments to achieve specific results. *See* the discussion in chapter 5.

16. In Los Angeles, the school district's defense against the original letter of findings had emphasized that faculty imbalance patterns resulted largely from the district's attempts "to be responsive to community demands for greater minority representation" ("Position of the District," submitted to OCR on May 9, 1975, cited in a letter from Floyd L. Pierce to William J. Johnston, [March 5, 1976]). OCR's regional director took this to be a blatant admission of discriminatory intent, writing that, whether motivated by community pressures or not, such a policy "reinforces, rather than undercuts the presumption of segregative intent with respect to students, since it would logically suggest herding black students into their own schools where they can be taught by their proper black role models. . . . The defendants are thus hoist by their own petard" (*Ibid.* at 3).

Note that in northern school desegregation cases, after intentional discrimination had been found, the courts rejected the "role model argument" on both policy and legal grounds. *See*, e.g., Morgan v. Hennigan, *supra* note 11; Arthur v. Nyquist, 439 F. Supp. 206 (W.D.N.Y. 1977), *aff'd*, 573 F.2d 134 (2d Cir. 1978).

17. As a quantitative supplement to our in-depth interviews, we sent follow-up questionnaires to all of our interviewees and to a number of additional persons who had some connection to the process. (*See* the Appendix for a discussion of methodology.) When asked to categorize OCR's position in terms of the opportunity/result dichotomy, as defined in chapter 1, six of the seven board of education respondents replied that OCR's position reflected a result orientation (two of these respondents said it also reflected an opportunity perspective). Five of the respondents labeled the board of education's position as fully or partially "opportunity-oriented," and one called the board's position "result-oriented."

Of nine OCR/Justice Department respondents, seven said the board's position reflected no consistent philosophical orientation (one had no opinion). Four of the government respondents thought OCR's position fully or partially represented a result perspective, while seven said it fully or partially represented an opportunity perspective.

Overall, considering the complexity of the opportunity/result definitions and the politically sensitive connotations of a government official's admitting to an equality of result philosophy, we believe that these responses tend to support our view that the board/OCR positions largely reflected a classic opportunity/result contrast.

18. Chancellor Anker felt so strongly about these issues that he attached to the questionnaire he returned to us a letter with the following comments: "You will notice that I found it difficult to respond to many of the choices. There is, to my mind, great danger that any report will assume that disparate effects of policies will be taken to be evidence of discrimination. The result could set back the cause of civil rights and of equal opportunity for all groups. For example ... [c]ertainly there were more minority teachers in schools in so-called minority pupil areas (as principal of Franklin HS, I employed more minority teachers than did principals in middle class areas. This did not necessarily imply discrimination by others. Of course, I do not declare *all* innocent of discrimination). But minority teachers did tend to drift, of their own volition at times, to such schools. School boards in such districts actively recruited teachers of their ethnic background at times. A second examination track (and an easier one) was created by the Decentralization Law to open the way to more easily obtain minority staff, etc."

19. Title VII, and especially the NTE cases, had demonstrated consistently that slight numerical differences in test scores could not be psychometrically defended as valid indicators of differences in actual ability or confidence. *See*, e.g., Bridgeport Guardians v. Members of Bridgeport Civil Service Commission, 482 F.2d 1333 (2d Cir. 1973); Baker v. Columbus Municipal Separate School District, 329 F. Supp. 706 (N.D. Miss. 1971), *aff'd*, 462 F.2d 1112 (5th Cir. 1972); Walston v. County School Board, 492 F.2d 919 (4th Cir. 1974); U.S. v. North Carolina, 400 F. Supp. 343 (E.D.N.C. 1975), *vacated*, 425 F. Supp. 789 (E.D.N.C. 1977); Georgia Association of Educators v. Nix, 407 F. Supp. 1102 (N.D. Ga. 1976).

20. The lack of clarity on this issue, of course, became an important problem in the implementation process, which will be analyzed in the next chapter.

21. Note in this regard the board's defense of the agreement in the *Caulfield* litigation. The fact that later difficulties experienced in the implementation stage and a major change in the political climate in Washington allowed the board to obtain substantial modifications of the agreement in 1982 does not, of course, detract

from the historical significance of the 1977 Agreement, which still
exemplifies how equality of opportunity and equality of result
perspectives can be reconciled in a situation in which both are
being strongly pressed.
22. *See*, e.g., Singleton v. Jackson Municipal Separate School System,
419 F.2d 1211, 1219 (5th Cir. 1969), *rev'd in part on other
grounds*, 396 U.S. 290 (1970); Lemon v. Bossia Parish School
Board, 444 F.2d 1400, 1401 (5th Cir. 1971). *See also* Moses v.
Washington Parish School Board, 330 F. Supp. 1240 (E.D. La.
1971), *aff'd*, 456 F.2d 1285 (5th Cir. 1972); McNeal v. Tate
County School District, 508 F.2d 1017, 1020 (5th Cir. 1975)
(ability grouping may be acceptable if it is a remedy to improve
educational opportunities); Castaneda v. Pickard, 648 F.2d 989
(5th Cir. 1981) (remand on issues of impact of ability grouping
upon Mexican-American students).
23. However, passing reference to these issues has been noted by
other courts. *See* Spangler v. Pasadena City Board of Education,
311 F. Supp. 501, 519 (C.D. Cal. 1970), *aff'd*, 427 F.2d 1352 (9th
Cir. 1970); Hart v. Community School Board, *supra* note 11. In
Larry P. v. Riles, 343 F. Supp. 1306 (N.D. Cal. 1972), *aff'd*, 502
F.2d 963 (9th Cir. 1974), 495 F. Supp. 926 (N.D. Cal. 1979),
methods of classifying and tracking mentally retarded students,
which had racially discriminatory effects, were invalidated. *Compare* Parents in Action on Special Education v. Hannon, 506 F.
Supp. 831 (N.D. Ill. 1980); Vaughns v. Board of Education, Prince
George's County, 574 F. Supp. 1280 (D. Md. 1983). In Berkelman
v. San Francisco Unified School District, 501 F.2d 1264 (9th Cir.
1974), however, the Ninth Circuit refused to invalidate the practices governing admission to an elite high school. For a more
detailed analysis of the student tracking cases, see Rebell and
Block, "Competency Assessment and the Courts: An Overview of
the State of the Law," in The Assessment of Occupational Competence, ERIC Document No. ED 192-169 (1980); Kirp, "Schools
As Sorters: The Constitutional and Policy Implications of Student
Classification," 121 U. Pa. L. Rev. 705 (1973); Sorgen, "Testing
and Tracking in Public Schools," 24 Hastings L.J. 1129 (1973);
Bersoff, "Regarding Psychologists Testily: Legal Regulation of Psychological Assessment in the Public Schools," 39 Md. L. Rev. 27
(1979).
24. 269 F. Supp. 401 (D.D.C. 1967), *aff'd sub nom.* Smuck v. Hobson, 408 F.2d 175 (D.C. Cir. 1969). Although the Washington,

D.C. school system had been operated on a *de jure* segregated basis prior to the Supreme Court's decision in Brown v. Board of Education (and its Fifth Amendment analogue, Bolling v. Sharpe, 347 U.S. 497 [1954]), the *Hobson* decision was not based on findings of intentional discrimination, and, in fact, the Court emphasized that the superintendent in Washington was apparently motivated by valid educational considerations. See *Hobson* at 443.

25. The reasons why other courts did not follow the *Hobson* precedent, at least in the early years before firm requirements for discriminatory intent were established, are not immediately clear. Apparently, civil rights activists in the North considered classic student desegregation suits a higher priority. Martin Gerry turned his attention to ability grouping and the other student services issues largely because Nixon administration policies precluded active pursuit of traditional student desegregation cases that might require busing.

Tracking practices were considered by Congress in the ESAA legislation. Thus, 20 U.S.C. § 3196(c)(1)(C), *repealed by* Pub. L. No. 97-35, Title V, § 587(a)(1), 95 Stat. 480 (1981), denied eligibility to school systems which have in effect a procedure that "results in the separation of minority group from non-minority group children for a substantial portion of the school day." Note that an exception was provided for any "bona fide ability grouping," but what "bona fide" meant in this context was not specified.

26. OCR did not pursue student ability grouping issues in the Los Angeles and Philadelphia reviews.

27. 45 C.F.R. §§ 185.43(c), 185.44(e)(1973). The regulations contained more result-oriented requirements than the ESAA statutory standards did. For example, they defined "bona fide" in terms of objective selection tests and instruction calculated to bring about academic improvement (especially for those in the lower tracks). Also, assignments based on these criteria were limited to the parts of the school day when the relevant instruction was being given. For a discussion of the background and application of these regulations, see Board of Education, Cincinnati v. HEW, 396 F. Supp. 203 (S.D. Ohio 1975), *rev'd and remanded on other grounds*, 532 F.2d 1070 (6th Cir. 1976).

28. This last innovation reflected a recognition that the state of the art in test measurement really could not provide the type of "objective" tests contemplated by the regulations.

29. For a more detailed discussion of faculty desegregation law and

its relation to the law on student desegregation issues, see Rebell and Block, "Faculty Desegregation: The Law and Its Implementation," ERIC/CUE Urban Diversity Series, Teachers College, Columbia University Monograph No. 86 (Fall 1983).

1. Clune and Lindquist, "What Implementation Isn't: Toward a General Framework for Implementation Research," 1981 Wisc. L. Rev. 1044, 1045.
2. J. Pressman and A. Wildavsky, Implementation xviii (2d ed. 1973).
3. Although most implementation analyses begin with or assume a clear statutory goal as a starting point, many statutory schemes like Title VI, in fact, delegate ambiguous policy goals to the administrative agencies. See, e.g., J. Mashaw, Bureaucratic Justice: Managing Social Security Disability Claims 52 (1983) (statute is ambiguous in defining "disability" and in permitting simultaneous emphasis on fiscal caution and on generosity in the handling of claims); M. Derthick, Uncontrollable Spending for Social Service Grants (1975) (statute providing grants in aid to states for social services "loosely" defines "services" and criteria for matching grants); Bickel and Wellington, "Legislative Purpose and the Judicial Process: The Lincoln Mills Case," 71 Harv. L. Rev. 1, 16 n.66 (1957) (two key phrases of the Civil Rights Act of 1957 were not thoroughly defined by its drafters).
4. See supra chapter 4, note 1.
5. See the discussion in chapter 3.
6. There was also agreement in September 1977 on a "Lau Plan" to improve services for language-minority children. This plan, however, added little to the board's existing obligations under a federal court decree in the ASPIRA case. In any event, the additional requirements never were implemented (Whitney interview).
7. In Chicago, extensive negotiations led to agreement on a faculty assignment plan involving mandatory transfers and on extensive bilingual educational programming. As in New York, agreement also was reached on student ability grouping issues; the other Big City Review issues essentially were dropped. In Philadelphia, after agreement was reached on a similar mandatory faculty transfer plan and bilingual issues, the other student services items (on many of which extensive evidence had been gathered) were not followed up. In Los Angeles, OCR again concentrated on a faculty assign-

ment plan and bilingual issues, and in this instance it did not even commence an investigation on any of the other issues.

Gerry testified in *Caulfield* that one pressure for adding the assignment issues in New York City was that their omission here undermined his position in Los Angeles and Chicago, where school officials asked him why OCR was not taking action on these issues in New York (No. 77 Civ. 2155 [E.D.N.Y. May 15, 1979] [testimony of Martin Gerry, trial transcript, at 617-18]).

8. Of course, the very fact that an administrative policy initiative is substantially dependent on the personality and presence of a single individual reveals a significant lack of "staying power."

9. In New York, but not in the other three cities, OCR's efforts also were deflected from the initial student services issues to a heavy concentration on the hiring procedures under the Board of Examiners licensing system. Considerations of prudence (confrontation with the teachers' union and the need to invalidate state law) and marshalling of evidence (the difficulties of proving test validation) had argued against pressing these issues. The strikingly disproportionate number of minorities hired in New York City had strongly impressed both Gerry and Tatel, especially since such patterns did not exist in the other large cities. But it appears that both OCR directors were also influenced in their decision to persist with these issues by the clear policy standard against the use of unvalidated tests having disproportionate impact on minority job seekers, which had been established by Congress in Title VII and by the Supreme Court in Griggs v. Duke Power Co., 401 U.S. 424 (1971). Essentially, OCR sought to apply these well-established Title VII policy standards to the more nebulous Title VI compliance process.

10. The precise manner in which the faculty integration and ability grouping standards actually came into the process and filled the goal ambiguity "void" was, of course, a function of organizational processes and politics. Note, for example, that the complaint procedures given priority by the *Adams* decree and the well-established investigative methods for examining teacher assignment patterns were "standard operating procedures" that had more staying power than the policy agenda Gerry tried to substitute into the Title VI void.

11. *See*, e.g., Pressman and Wildavsky, *supra* note 2, at 107-109; G. Bardach, The Implementation Game (1977).

12. On the other hand, Gerry remained in a position to conceptualize

and oversee the implementation of his project for over four years, giving the project an unusually long continuity of committed leadership.

13. 414 U.S. 563 (1974).
14. 401 U.S. 424 (1971).
15. 413 U.S. 189 (1973).
16. 418 U.S. 717 (1974).
17. 426 U.S. 229 (1976).
18. The first letter did not even allege "intent" to discriminate. Also, in his testimony at the *Caulfield* trial, Gerry argued that the *Davis* constitutional standard actually was no less stringent than the *Griggs* Title VII standard (Gerry, *supra* note 7, at 777-79).
19. Note in this regard that OCR's extensive collection of data on the issue of teachers with less experience being assigned to minority schools was scathingly rejected by the administrative law judge in Chicago (In the Matter of Chicago Public School District No. 299 et al., No. S-120 [February 15, 1977]).
20. The interesting amalgamation of Title VI and ESAA standards was even more dramatic in Los Angeles and Philadelphia, where the school districts had applied for substantial amounts of ESAA funding at the very time that OCR's Big City Reviews were being mounted. In those cities, OCR's letters of findings, on their face, dealt simultaneously with Title VI and ESAA issues, and it was virtually impossible to determine where allegations of noncompliance under one statute terminated and allegations under the other began. (*See*, e.g., letter from Floyd L. Pierce, Director, OCR Region IX, to William J. Johnston, Superintendent of Schools, Los Angeles Unified School District [April 7, 1975].) Henry E. Boas, program planning coordinator for the Los Angeles School District, thought that as a matter of conscious strategy OCR decided to "use their biggest guns, the stringent requirements of the ESAA to cover everything." Boas stated further that a high OCR official had admitted to him that "once you file for ESAA, you come under a different category for review of your practices. ESAA criteria are much tougher."
21. The extent of Senator D'Amato's political intervention was unprecedented. Although Senators Javits and Moynihan had kept abreast of developments throughout the years of the New York City Review, neither had directly or publicly involved themselves in the negotiations. Even Senator Moynihan's controversial speech on the Senate floor objecting to aspects of the 1977 Agreement

had not been followed up by any substantive effort to overturn the agreement.

22. Schonhaut interview. A good account of the political power of the UFT, and its impact on organizational processes of the New York City Board of Education in other contexts, is provided in J. Viteritte, Across the River: Politics and Education in the City (1983).

23. Healey interview.

24. Conrad Harper, the private attorney who was conducting the negotiations in Chicago for OCR, noted that at one critical point during the negotiations the union threatened to pull out all the stops and block the agreement. "They stood firm, hinted at strikes, and tried to approach Carter through the back door." According to Harper, all of a sudden, shortly after this confrontation, the union "took a dive; they just went away." He attributed this turnaround to the fact that President Carter passed the buck on this issue to Califano and Tatel, who stood firm in backing him.

Robert Healey, the union president in Chicago, related an incident that occurred in 1978, one year after the agreement had been reached and as OCR was pushing for midyear transfers to ensure immediate compliance with the agreed ratios. When Healey got to see Secretary Califano, "through the offices of Shanker," he found out that Califano's mother was a schoolteacher in New York City. Said Healey, "He knew what we meant. He agreed to put off these transfers to September." By the next September, with new appointments, there no longer was a substantial compliance problem, and no further mandatory transfers were necessary.

25. In Chicago, from the outset, the board of education officials briefed union officials on developments on a regular basis, although the union representatives never were permitted personally to sit at the table. In New York, by way of contrast, the union quickly got impatient with its initial background role and insisted that Shanker's chief assistant, Sandra Feldman, actively take part in the deliberations.

26. The United Teachers of Los Angeles was the largest teachers' union in Los Angeles at the time, but, under California's "meet and confer" statute, it was not an exclusive bargaining agent. UTLA was considered the most liberal of the teachers' unions and had a large minority constituency among its membership. The other Los Angeles teachers' unions tended to be more conservative and took a strong position in opposition to the agreement. (One

of the other unions, the Professional Employees of Los Angeles, commenced a litigation against the agreement which was dismissed by the courts. *See* Zaslawsky et al. v. Board of Education, 610 F.2d 661 [9th Cir. 1979].)

In Philadelphia, school district officials admitted that they were surprised by the union's "amiability" in agreeing to talk immediately about implementation. These officials attributed the union's attitude to a psychological "softening up" after having lived with integration pressures for over 10 years and, more specifically, to a fear of layoffs if federal funds were actually terminated. In addition, the officials remarked that the union was eager to obtain the additional jobs that were likely to come with ESAA funding. John Ryan, the union president at the time, said that his cooperative stance was informed both by a fear of federal funding cutoffs and by ongoing contract negotiations. (The racial balance issue became just an additional aspect of an exceedingly complex and difficult situation the union faced with fiscal problems, layoffs, enrollment declines, and transfers.) Ryan was subsequently defeated in a reelection bid, and he, as well as the school district officials, believed that his conciliatory stance on the teacher transfer issue was a major factor in his defeat.

27. Assistant Superintendent Joan Raymond, who was the main representative of the Chicago Board of Education in its faculty assignment negotiations with OCR, also spoke of that system's sensitivity to charges of civil rights violations. She said that the school system took very seriously the fact that it was being accused by the United States government of being in violation of the Constitution, and she indicated that this sensitivity had a direct impact on the final outcome.

28. Personalities in this context are also reflections of organizational roles, that is, the distinctions in the behavior of careerists, politicians, and professionals in agencies. *See* Schuck, "The Politics of Regulation," 90 Yale L.J. 702, 718 (1982).

29. The present discussion focuses on the direct implementation issues as they relate to adherence to the terms of the two agreements; it leaves for further consideration in chapter 10 the broader evaluative issues of whether OCR's intervention in New York City should be considered positive or negative, successful or unsuccessful. The term "success," when used in this chapter, is meant to connote no more than a substantial degree of compliance with the specific terms of the agreements.

30. *See* Yudof, "Implementation Theories and Desegregation Realities," 32 Ala. L. Rev. 441, 463 (1981).
31. In Chicago, initially, letters went out informing 1,706 teachers that they were slated for mandatory transfers. Nine hundred and eighty-four appeals were filed and, of these, 349 were successful, leading to the necessity for a "second pass" and the assignment of additional mandatory transfers to reach the agreed-upon compliance figures. Chicago Public Schools Plan for the Implementation of Title VI of the Civil Rights Act of 1964 Related to Integration of Faculties, Assignment Patterns of Principals, and Bi-lingual Education Programs (October 1977). In Philadelphia, where a larger number of teachers were transferred on even shorter notice, even more mistakes appear to have been made. The union there brought a major arbitration proceeding, claiming that in a substantial number of cases seniority had been miscalculated and the wrong people transferred. As a result of the union victory in this arbitration, many of the transfers had to be reassessed in February.
32. Raymond clearly took professional umbrage at having been compelled by OCR to rush through full implementation on only several months' notice. She said she had warned the agency that it "would destroy the system. In the end, many scars were left." She thought the operation an unnecessary upheaval, because the results could have been achieved on a phase-in basis.
33. Kresner interview.
34. Memorandum from Robert Searle to Bill Lucas (April 20, 1981). Although the teacher transfer plan in Philadelphia also had a substantial detrimental effect on teacher morale, school board officials there expressed less continuing resentment years after the process had begun than was true in Los Angeles. In fact, Murray Bookbinder, executive director of the Philadelphia Board of Education's Office of Personnel and Labor Relations, volunteered the sentiment that "in the long run, this may have been a plus." He believed that attitudes toward integration of a large number of teachers had been favorably changed with the passing of time and the stabilization of the transfer system. He acknowledged, however, that not all teachers had changed their attitude, especially those white teachers with substantial seniority who had been compelled to transfer to black schools in "bad" areas.
35. Continuing compliance has been most successful in Philadelphia, where both OCR and school district officials agreed that even without an active monitoring presence by OCR the district has

remained in compliance. Michael Aaronson, assistant to the executive director of the Philadelphia Board of Education's Office of Personnel and Labor Relations, took pride in noting that, after the first year, the Office of Personnel "got the bugs out of the system" and now has the methods for calculating seniority and transfer rights "down to a science. . . . It all works rather automatically now."

In Chicago, OCR informed the district on several occasions that they were out of compliance in specific schools. These problems were dealt with sporadically for several years. Finally, in 1979, as part of the overall ESAA negotiations, the basic agreement was modified to allow certain substitute teachers to be counted in computing ratios, and it was agreed that the system would then be in compliance (Letter from Patricia Roberts Harris to Joseph P. Hannon [September 15, 1979] Attachment, at 3). Robert Healey, president of the Chicago Teachers' Union, reported that a small number of teachers also had to be transferred in September of 1981, because layoffs resulting from the board's fiscal crisis had upset the established ratios. Similar compliance problems in certain schools developed in Los Angeles in recent years, and on several occasions the board of education requested a broadening of the ratio ranges. However, these modification requests were rejected by OCR.

36. Similarly, the major provisions of the examination system reforms also had not been effected. The board (and the UFT) had failed to secure legislative enactment of amendments to the laws pertaining to eligible list exhaustion and rank order appointment, and they had failed to initiate "appropriate litigation" to achieve these ends. The labor pool study, which was to establish parameters for the basic affirmative action hiring plan, also was yet to be finalized.

37. Although an injunction against enforcement of aspects of the agreement, which was in effect for approximately one year in the *Caulfield* case, might be said to have delayed the date of full compliance, it cannot explain the extensive pattern of noncompliance more than two years after the anticipated target date, especially since the final result of that case was to uphold the validity of the agreement.

38. The New York City Board of Education had planned to achieve compliance through assignments resulting from the rehiring process, as the system was rebuilt after the massive layoffs caused by the 1976 fiscal emergency. It turned out, however, that many fewer

vacancies occurred than had been expected, and there was a shortage of teachers willing to accept assignments in minority schools.

39. It is ironic, but fully understandable in this light, that talk of possible teacher transfers in New York City aroused more intense publicity and political intervention (led by Democratic Senator Moynihan at one point and Republican Senator D'Amato at another) than did the actual fact of massive teacher transfers on a proportionately larger scale in Chicago, Los Angeles, and Philadelphia.

40. It was also clear that OCR's monitoring operations were plagued by problems of poor organization, lack of follow-through, and inconsistent political commitment. Lines of authority between the Washington headquarters and the regional offices were often unclear. Responses to board of education compliance reports or queries were delayed many months. A failure to renew the Delta Research Corporation's contract for data processing services in the 1980-1981 school term denied OCR staff the data base needed to continue compliance monitoring. These problems were exacerbated by a lack of continuity in OCR leadership. Between 1977 and 1982, OCR had six directors (Gerry, Tatel, Stewart, Brown, Thomas, and Singleton) and two acting directors (Hamlin and Cioffi), and OCR was totally reorganized as its education branch moved to the new Department of Education.

41. The extent of actual compliance with the student suspension provisions is difficult to gauge because of the incompleteness of OCR's data gathering and analysis in this area.

42. Note, however, that if these statistics had indicated a perpetuation or increase in the number of racially isolated classes, it probably would have been impossible for OCR to sort out the various justifications for the suspect assignments. In other words, OCR's monitoring function was manageable mainly because there was compliance and because no extensive follow-up analysis or intervention was required.

43. And how does one calculate the additional price paid in terms of teacher morale and educational instability in Chicago, Los Angeles, and Philadelphia?

44. It is arguable that the New York City faculty integration agreement, despite its failure to achieve fully the original promised integration ratios, was "successful" because a lesser, but still significant, measure of integration was achieved without the turmoil and confrontation experienced in the other cities. Note, however,

that although five of the nine OCR/government respondents to
our questionnaire thought OCR's intervention "improved" hiring
and faculty assignment, only one of seven board of education
respondents agreed as to hiring and two as to assignment. Only
one of six interest group respondents responded positively on either
issue.

It is also arguable that, even without the full execution of an
agreement, OCR's actions in raising many of the issues may have
positively influenced some future developments. About half of the
OCR/government respondents to our questionnaire thought that
OCR's mere intervention had helped improve opportunities for
female faculty, and one-third of them saw improvements in comparability of resources. However, none of the board of education
or interest group respondents agreed that OCR's involvement had
affected resource allocations, and only three out of thirteen thought
there had been some favorable impact on job opportunities for
female supervisors.

<h2 style="text-align:center">NOTES TO CHAPTER NINE</h2>

1. D. Yates, Bureaucratic Democracy 115 (1983).
2. M. Rebell and A. Block, Educational Policy Making and the
   Courts: An Empirical Study of Judicial Activism (1982) [herein-
   after cited as EPAC].
3. See EPAC, supra note 2, at chaps. 2 and 10, for a fuller discussion
   of these points. For an analysis of how broader social trends are
   expanding the domain of constitutional principle, see also Rebell,
   "Judicial Activism and the Courts' New Role," 12 Soc. Pol'y, No.
   4, 24 (1982). The EPAC study utilized the following definitions:

   > "*Principle*: A statement establishing a right of an indi-
   > vidual against the state or against another individual (or, less
   > frequently, the right of an institution to maintain the integrity
   > of its legally defined prerogatives). A principle is expressed as
   > a general rule that should be enforced whenever applicable,
   > regardless of social welfare consequences, except when it is
   > outweighed by a countervailing principle" (EPAC, *supra* note
   > 2, at 23).

   > "*Policy*: A statement concerning collective goals. Policy
   > arguments consider the relative importance or desirability of
   > particular methods for achieving such goals. A policy state-
   > ment is normally expressed in more specific terms than is a

principle, and in a particular context it may be subordinated to competing policy claims that are determined to be better able to serve collective goals more effectively" (EPAC, *supra* note 2, at 24).

4. For a further discussion of these distinctions, see EPAC, *supra* note 2, at 208. The concept of partisan mutual adjustment decision-making is developed in C. Lindblom, The Intelligence of Democracy (1965).

5. As indicated in the Introduction, note 35, the administrative law literature tends to emphasize the importance of formal rule-making procedures, adversary procedures, and judicial review mechanisms for ensuring the accountability of agency policymaking. Title VI, in theory, would appear to have provided such strong procedural restraints: HEW was granted rule-making authority, subject to formal presidential approval; individual case enforcement had to pass scrutiny in adversary procedures before an administrative law judge; and all of HEW's enforcement powers were subject to judicial review under the Administrative Procedure Act (with the specific proviso that Title VI sanctions were *not* decisions committed to agency discretion). Any final decision to wield the ultimate funding termination sanction was subject to additional political scrutiny by both the president and Congress.

The major policy decision in the Big City Reviews ostensibly involved investigation and application of preexisting compliance standards to a new geographical setting and subject area. In fact, however, the application of result-oriented desegregation guidelines and ESAA regulations to northern cities and to new student services issues without prior findings of *de jure* or intentional segregation constituted a major policy decision. The indirect manner of this decision-making through an investigative and negotiating process tended to nullify the accountability protections established by the formal procedural mechanisms.

6. Compare in this regard the EEOC, which, in its enforcement of Title VII of the 1964 Civil Rights Act, was limited to individual case investigation, conciliation, and referral of enforcement issues to the courts. Unlike OCR, EEOC had no independent adjudicating responsibilities, sanctioning authority, or rewarding capabilities. *See* J. Freedman, Crisis and Legitimacy: The Administrative Process and American Government chap. 8 (1978). *See also* Blumrosen, "Anti-Discrimination Laws in Action in New Jersey: A Law-Sociology Study," 19 Rutgers L. Rev. 191 (1965); Urban League of

Rochester, New York, Inc., The Effectiveness of the New York State Division of Human Rights as a Civil Rights Enforcement Agency (1977).

7. In chapter 19 of The Intelligence of Democracy, *supra* note 4, Lindblom discusses the applicability of mutual adjustment processes to administrative decision making. *But cf.* Yates, *supra* note 1, at 118-19. For an example of an open-ended mutual adjustment development of social policy in the administrative implementation process, see M. Derthick, Uncontrollable Spending for Social Services Grants (1975).

8. The insulation of the negotiations in New York and Chicago from political pressures was further enhanced by the use of independent outside counsel as OCR's chief negotiators.

9. "Bureaucratic" decision making generally is assumed to be rational-analytic, especially when systems analysis and other sophisticated planning strategies are utilized. See C. Lindblom, The Policy Making Process chap. 1 (1968). *See also* Rabkin, "Office for Civil Rights," in The Politics of Regulation 331-32 (J. Wilson ed. 1980), for a detailed discussion of further implications of OCR's national rule-making perspective.

10. In this sense, OCR's posture might better be compared to that of a prosecutor than to that of a disinterested judge. OCR probably was perceived by the board of education as being more confrontational than would plaintiffs or their attorneys in a civil rights litigation. (Note in this regard OCR's consistent rejection of the NTE alternative hiring system, which plaintiffs in the previous court cases were willing to accept.) Plaintiffs can, of course, bring strongly honed arguments to a litigation, and they can assert extreme or even radical interpretations of applicable legal principles. But private attorneys lack OCR's aura of governmental legitimacy and its power to impose substantial sanctions even before administrative or judicial review has been invoked. Under these circumstances, principled positions taken by OCR clearly have intensified impact.

11. Rabkin, *supra* note 9, at 331.

12. *See* EPAC, *supra* note 2, at 210-12, for a discussion of the manner in which the parties substantially participate in the formulation of judicial remedial decrees in such cases. In some court cases, negotiation of a consent decree may take place before the court has issued a final or even a preliminary liability decision. *See,* e.g., Pennsylvania Association of Retarded Children v. Commonwealth

of Pennsylvania, 334 F. Supp. 1257 (E.D. Pa. 1971), *modified*, 343 F. Supp. 279 (E.D. Pa. 1972); United States v. Board of Education of the City of Chicago, 554 F. Supp. 912 (D. Ill. 1983). In such situations, the negotiated consent decree may be more reflective of the "pragmatic-analytic" decision-making mode characteristic of the administrative process discussed in the text.

13. 269 F. Supp. 401 (D.D.C. 1967), *aff'd sub nom.* Smuck v. Hobson, 408 F.2d 175 (D.C. Cir. 1969).

14. Diver, "Policy Making Paradigms in Administrative Law," 95 Harv. L. Rev. 393 (1981).

15. *See* EPAC, *supra* note 2, at chaps. 3 and 10.

16. Representatives of the Board of Examiners also managed to participate in the discussions on the hiring issues.

17. There did not appear to be any basis in principle for including the union but not other groups in the New York City deliberations (or for including the union in New York but not in the other cities). Clearly, the UFT gained access because of its extensive political influence. The fact that the UFT was accorded this privileged status heightened skepticism about the agreement among many of the advocacy groups in New York City and made them suspicious of the compromises OCR accepted on many key points.

18. OCR's lack of sustained involvement with its minority constituencies and its apparent failure to reflect their priorities was also evident in Chicago, where the faculty assignment ratios it insisted upon would have the result of guaranteeing a white faculty majority in every school in the city. Black community groups and leaders such as Jesse Jackson reportedly spoke out against this result (Healey interview).

19. Four of six interest group representatives responding to our questionnaire said that OCR did not adequately consider their views, and three of five (one did not respond to this question) felt that the board did not. Twelve of twenty-two respondents to our questionnaire indicated that a number of organizations, especially AFC and the PEA, had attemped to participate in the review process and the negotiations, but they were rebuffed.

20. Caulfield v. Board of Education, 449 F. Supp. 1203, 1207 (E.D.N.Y.), *rev'd*, 583 F.2d 605 (2d Cir. 1978).

21. 449 F. Supp. at 1206.

22. Although Judge Weinstein's order requiring greater participation in the administrative process was reversed, he clearly practiced what he preached in terms of allowing full participation in the

follow-up court proceedings in *Caulfield*. The original parties to the suit were six community school boards and individual teachers and supervisors who claimed that the first agreement violated their rights. Defendants were the board of education, HEW, and the state commissioner of education. The court granted motions to intervene on behalf of the UFT, the Council of Supervisors and Administrators, three additional community school boards, the Coalition of Concerned Black Educators, and four individual black teachers. In addition, friend of the court briefs were permitted to be filed by the American Jewish Congress, the Anti-Defamation League of B'Nai B'Rith, and an individual.

23. Eisenberg interview. Professor Richard Stewart, in his classic article, "The Reformation of American Administrative Law," 88 Harv. L. Rev. 1667 (1978), considers at length recent trends to expand interest group representation in the rule-making process as an accountability mechanism that might legitimize the trend toward broad delegation of policymaking authority to administrative agencies. He concludes that interest group representation is ineffective for this purpose because of problems such as the difficulty of ensuring that all interests are adequately represented and the delay and indeterminacy that expanded participation adds to the rule-making process. However, Stewart's findings may be less relevant to an investigative-negotiating process like the New York City Review, in which the number of affected interests is more limited, the issues are more clearly defined, and the modes of possible participation are more flexible.

24. Compare in this regard Beryl Radin's suggestion that minority group representatives be accorded a formal participatory role in negotiated settlements of Title VI charges. To ensure proper representation, she proposes creating a procedure for designating a class representative. *See* B. Radin, Implementation, Change, and the Federal Bureaucracy: School Desegregation Policy in HEW, 1964-1968 138 (1977).

25. David Tatel noted that minority advocacy groups were very helpful in monitoring OCR agreements pertaining to desegregation of colleges and universities. Note in this regard the important role played by AFC in monitoring the discipline component of the second New York City agreement.

26. *Caulfield* initially was brought by community school board representatives who had not participated in the negotiations on the First Agreement and strongly opposed its contents. In Los Angeles,

also, litigation was commenced by individual teachers and splinter teacher union groups who were not affiliated with the main teachers' group that participated in the process, at least in its later stages.

27. *See* EPAC, *supra* note 2, at chaps. 4 and 10.

28. The magnitude and complexity of the data gathering tasks which Martin Gerry set out for the project were enormous. The foundation for the New York City investigation was to be an extensive data bank. OCR had identified two thousand "attributes"—these were labels for discrete pieces of information that had to be obtained in order to test all of its hypotheses about discrimination. Thousands of pages of documents containing the necessary information would be transformed into microfiche records (or into entries on computer tapes) and then painstakingly indexed according to relevant attributes. Theoretically, OCR would be able to back up its factual conclusions to the most minute particular by retrieving source of the data virtually at the push of a button.

If the data bank was the heart of the investigation, the "data analysis plan" was its brain. This plan was a complex guide linking the hypotheses set out in the Issues Outline to the attribute cells in the data base. For example, the hypothesis that minority children were given "less expensive human resources" would first be broken down into sub-questions and then cross-referenced against the client groups involved, types of resources, and information needed. The plan was like a cookbook: it told one what ingredients were needed to establish a particular finding, where to get them, and how to combine them.

In the midst of all this complexity, there was one important respect in which the data operation was comparatively simple. Because of OCR's legal and administrative ability to obtain complete information regarding most attributes—such as the race of every principal in the entire school system—the statistical analyses could be based on relatively simple correlations. In other words, OCR had the full "universe" of data and did not need to engage in complex, abstract mathematical formulas to establish the validity of a sample or the statistical significance of correlations within the sample.

29. 45 C.F.R. § 80.6 (1973). In New York City, OCR received extensive support from central school system officials in its data gathering efforts. When some community school districts refused to cooperate in the collection of certain racial data, Chancellor Anker (albeit somewhat reluctantly) acted to supersede them pur-

suant to his powers under N.Y. Educ. Law § 2590-1. Ultimately, despite the chancellor's cooperation, OCR needed a court order to obtain the desired data.

30. A valid issue that might be raised, however, is whether such extensive data gathering can reach a saturation point beyond which principals and teachers who feel overburdened with data requests will not make the effort to provide accurate or complete information. Henry Boas indicated that this point may have been reached in Los Angeles, even though that city did not experience a full-scale investigation like New York's.

Another major question that should be raised is how representative the New York City investigation was of administrative fact-finding in general or even of major OCR compliance investigations. The extent of the resource commitment here was enormous, and it is not clear whether OCR is in a position to undertake such complete fact-finding in "normal investigations." Its Big City Reviews process in Los Angeles, for example, did not even purport to engage in such extensive data processing functions. Moreover, in addition to questions of resource availability and commitment, there may be political and legal limitations on OCR's ability to replicate massive investigations of this type. The Big City Reviews operation in Philadelphia illustrates the problems involved. There, although school district officials in all other ways were probably more cooperative with OCR than were New York's school representatives, from the beginning they took a strong line on limiting OCR's "burdensome" data gathering requests. Superintendent Michael Marcase sent detailed letters to Secretary Califano, Philadelphia congressmen, and Pennsylvania senators, complaining that OCR's data requests would cost the district up to $2 million. *See*, e.g., letter from Michael P. Marcase to Joseph Califano (February 7, 1977) and letter from Michael P. Marcase to Joshua Eilberg (February 7, 1977). Shortly thereafter, many of the data requests were withdrawn (*see* letter from Albert T. Hamlin to Michael P. Marcase [February 17, 1977]).

Philadelphia also attacked OCR's data gathering on legal grounds. It claimed that OCR was not a regulatory agency and, therefore, in the absence of specific complaints, it did not have authority to seek wide-ranging information from the school district. In addition, Philadelphia officials alleged that OCR violated the Federal Reports Act, because it had not obtained clearance from the Office of Management and Budget before using survey protocols. OMB officials agreed that there had been a violation of the Act and asked OCR to submit its forms for clearance. (*See* letter from Joseph W. Duncan to Martin M. Gerry [February 13, 1976]). The delay attendant upon this clearance process apparently led OCR to withdraw its data gathering attempts in certain areas, especially discipline (Penry, Wilson interviews).

There were also indications that at one point Gerry agreed to pay Philadelphia for the extra administrative costs involved in meeting the data requests, but, in fact, such payments never materialized (Wilson interview).

31. Boas interview. (Boas, besides being program planning coordinator for the Los Angeles Unified School District, also served as chairman of the Committee on Evaluation and Information Systems for the National Council of Chief State School Officers.) When asked to respond to these charges, John Palomino, chief of the Education Branch, OCR, Region IX, agreed that OCR personnel are basically attorneys and statisticians. "If we had mainly educators, we would never have desegregation. Hard statistics are necessary to put educational rationales in perspective."

32. Judge Jack Weinstein was a professor at Columbia Law School and a scholar on issues of evidence and procedure before coming to the bench. Of course, Judge Weinstein did not define his task as determining whether OCR had actually proven that the board had violated Title VI or the Constitution. Rather, because the case arose as a claim that the board and OCR had violated the law by entering into a settlement agreement providing for racially defined remedies, the standard he applied was whether the parties "could have reasonably believed a violation of the Constitution or the statutes could be shown" (486 F. Supp. 862, 885). He found that OCR's legal arguments and factual proofs passed this test.

33. In Chicago, after an administrative enforcement hearing in which the school district chose not to participate, the law judge concluded that OCR had not proven its case on comparability. OCR prevailed on its other allegations (In the Matter of Chicago Public School District No. 299 et al., No. S-120 [February 15, 1977]).

34. See EPAC, *supra* note 2, at chaps. 5 and 10. In 41 cases in which remedial orders were issued, only 15 involved extensive reform decrees requiring ongoing judicial involvement in school district affairs.

35. Attorneys interviewed in these 41 cases indicated there was "full

compliance" with court orders in 32, partial compliance in 9, in no instance was token or "no" compliance indicated.

36. *See,* e.g., difficulties experienced by both the plaintiffs and the school board defendants when they jointly sought to modify the "permanent plan" in the *Chance* case (EPAC, *supra* note 2, at chap. 6). *But see* Block, "Enforcement of Title VI Compliance Agreements by Third Party Beneficiaries," 18 Harv. C.R.-C.L. L. Rev. 1, 21, n. 63 (1983) (in some circumstances, beneficiaries of Title VI agreements need protection from inappropriate modification of agreements).

37. And, of course, as we noted in chapter 8, the longer it takes an implementation process to unfold, the greater the number of complicating variables that will intervene.

38. The survey responses to our statement, "In general, the courts seemed to interfere with day to day school operations more than did OCR," were: strongly agree-6; moderately agree-11; moderately disagree-3; strongly disagree-0. At the same time, however, 15 of the respondents thought that court decrees were implemented more successfully than the OCR agreements, and only 3 disagreed.

39. If OCR had included local constituency groups as partners in the process, it is possible that a mechanism might have been included in these agreements that would have given these groups some monitoring role in the implementation process. Any such role, however, was not likely to have been as extensive as that of a party in a court case.

40. Interestingly, although OCR did not pursue this option in New York City, some blacks and Puerto Ricans have commenced an enforcement suit claiming, *inter alia,* that they are third party beneficiaries of the agreement between OCR and the board of education (New York Association of Black Educators II v. United States Department of Education, No. 77 C. 2531 (E.D.N.Y.). *See also* Block, *supra* note 36.

41. Note that in Los Angeles and Philadelphia, where the basic agreements could be said to have been "ESAA-driven," the yearly ESAA funding cycle provided an automatic reopening of the case, somewhat comparable to ongoing judicial proceedings. Compliance in those cities has been more substantial than in either New York or Chicago.

42. As indicated above, OCR also has the option of asking the Justice Department to bring an injunctive suit against a fund recipient to perform its obligations under the assurances it executed as part of

its funding contract, but this option, which makes OCR dependent upon decisions by the Justice Department and the courts, has not been invoked frequently. Additionally, pursuant to Title IV of the 1964 Civil Rights Act, OCR can refer desegregation cases to the Justice Department for prosecution of constitutional violations. This procedure has been used. *See* Brown v. Weinberger, 417 F. Supp. 1215, 1222 (D.D.C. 1976); United States v. Chicago, *supra* note 12.

43. *See* the discussion in chapter 4. *See also* H. R. Rodgers and C. Bullock, Coercion to Compliance (1976); G. Orfield, Reconstruction of Southern Education (1969). In most of these situations, there was a strong political consensus supporting prompt action, the school district violations were beyond dispute, and the advent of numerous new federal education programs facilitated utilization of the deferral sanction.

44. J. Califano, Governing America: An Insider's Report from the White House and the Cabinet 253 (1981). For example, John Palomino, chief of OCR's education branch in Region IX, noted in the course of his interview that he was sure the Los Angeles School District attorneys would have advised the board that, in the last 10 years, funds actually had been cut off in only one district and that consequently there was little real likelihood of a Title VI funding cutoff in Los Angeles. For an insightful discussion of the implementation realities relevant to "sanction theory," see Clune, "A Political Model of Implementation and Implications of the Model for Public Policy, Research, and the Changing Roles of Law and Lawyers," 69 Iowa L. Rev. 47, 78ff. (1983) [hereinafter cited as A Political Model of Implementation].

45. The deferral approach permitted graduated pressure in more modest and, therefore, politically viable degrees, but by the late 1970s there were too few new federal programs to make deferral regularly available.

46. In some situations, the relatively small ESAA grant could indirectly be given added force by outside pressures. For example, in Los Angeles and Philadelphia, ESAA monies were counted on to fund desegregation activities otherwise required by civil rights orders of state courts. Thus, the loss of the federal grant could set off a chain reaction of sanctions throughout other agencies.

An additional advantage of the ESAA sanction was that the grant process was built into a yearly refunding cycle which permitted ongoing monitoring and compliance follow-up. Furthermore, the application process proceeded on specific time schedules. An applicant declared ineligible (and not granted a waiver) would forever lose its earmarked funds; thus, the deprivation of funding was at least as immediate as Title VI deferral, but it constituted a final, and not an interim, denial.

47. The final faculty assignment provisions were negotiated prior to the emergence of the CETA deferral threat in August. However, the complete agreement may never have been accepted by the board in September were it not for the CETA pressure on both the union and the board. In our survey, 15 of the 16 responses received from federal and board of education officials (and former officials) agreed that the CETA deferral sanction "gave OCR significant leverage to obtain concessions from the Board of Education during the negotiation of the first agreement." All 16 of these respondents gave a similar answer regarding ESAA, and 11 responded this way regarding the Title VI cutoff. Our respondents also were asked to name the single most important sanction. Out of the 16 OCR and board of education respondents, 9 singled out CETA deferral, 2 stressed ESAA, and 2 named Title VI termination. (One respondent listed both ESAA and CETA.) Similarly, key negotiators Tatel, Flannery, and Schonhaut put great emphasis on CETA as a major factor—perhaps a necessary one—for concluding an agreement.

Although the Title VI funding termination sanction had little real credibility among school district officials, it did continue to affect the overall process in an unforeseen and fascinating way. While the 16 OCR and board of education respondents in our survey (those "in the know") overwhelmingly listed the CETA threat as OCR's most effective sanctions, all four of the interest group respondents who answered this question thought that the Title VI termination threat was the most formidable. This response was consistent with statements made to us by Los Angeles union officials, who said that, although they realized Title VI funding cutoffs were not likely, the population at large tended to believe that all federal funding might really be terminated. This general perception facilitated their public relations efforts; it allowed them to justify acceptance of mandatory transfers to the membership by indicating that, if it fought the agreement, the district might potentially lose millions of dollars in total federal funding.

In New York City, similar general perceptions also had some significance. The OCR agreement was reached at a time of great uncertainty about the city's credit-worthiness, heightened by Securities and Exchange Commission allegations that the city may have misrepresented its financial condition on its bond prospectus. Hence, even if the Title VI funding termination threat was not credible to knowledgeable city officials, it might deter wary investors in city bonds (Schonhaut interview).

48. From this perspective, the repeal of the ESAA by the Education Consolidation and Improvement Act of 1981, 20 U.S.C. § 3832(3), (7) (which placed desegregation aid in a general block grant appropriation), would impede OCR's future ability to obtain prompt, effective compliance orders.

49. Arguably, the substance of the agreements in Chicago, Los Angeles, and Philadelphia would support such a view.

50. Specific constitutional provisions call for "blending" in many areas, as with the president's "legislative authority" to veto congressional enactments, the Senate's "executive authority" to ratify presidential appointments, and Congress's "judicial authority" to impeach the president. These blendings led Richard Neustadt to argue that the classic model might more accurately be called "a government of separated institutions sharing power" (R. Neustadt, Presidential Power 101 [1976]). For a more detailed discussion of "blending," see Sharp, "The Classical American Doctrine of 'The Separation of Powers,' " 2 U. Chi. L. Rev. 385, 427 (1935). Sharp maintains that the constitutional convention explicitly rejected James Wilson's call for a rigid model of separation of powers (Ibid. at 412). See also Montesquieu, The Spirit of the Laws 160 (Hafner ed. 1949).

51. "Today . . . injustices are readily perceived, their tractability is widely assumed and collective intervention by legal rule appears to be our remedy of choice. As our perception of imperfection has grown, our tolerance for it has diminished. These attitudes no doubt reflect a complex evolution in morality, ideas and politics. Whatever their cultural sources, they have fused in a melioristic, not to say, utopian, ambition to reform a disagreeable social reality through the affirmative application of public power. That impulse has virtually obliterated the moral, constitutional and political boundaries that once contained it, and the social consensus that once domesticated it" (Schuck, "The Politics of Regulation," 90 Yale L.J. 702, 725 [1981]). For insightful discussions of the roles of courts and administrative agencies under the circumstances of the "activist state," see also Ackerman, "Foreword: Law in an

Activist State," 92 Yale L.J. 1083 (1983); Mashaw, "Rights in the
Federal Administrative State," 92 Yale L.J. 1129 (1983).

52. Most contemporary discussions of the separation of powers doctrine mesh specific judicial review issues with the broader questions
of the proper division of responsibilities among all three branches,
tending to imply that a significant legitimacy issue arises only in
regard to the role of the courts. Indeed, some of those who write
extensively on judicial policymaking believe that the division of
policymaking responsibilities between the legislative and executive
branches is relatively inconsequential, especially when there is
agreement between these branches on their roles. *See*, e.g.,
M. Perry, The Constitution, the Courts and Human Rights chap.
2 (1982); J. Choper, Judicial Review and the National Political
Process: A Functional Consideration of the Supreme Court chap.
5 (1980).

These approaches overlook, however, the critical problem of
reconceptualizing institutional roles under the conditions of the
activist state, in which all three branches have undertaken expanded functions which differ dramatically from traditional assumptions. Therefore, substantial legitimacy issues affect the functioning of all three branches, and the legitimacy of the courts'
judicial review functions cannot be considered in isolation from
the changing legislative and executive functions. The fact that in
many instances Congress has acquiesced in the delegation of policymaking power to the executive branch or to an administrative
agency—and, indeed, in many cases, affirmatively entrusts the
courts and the agencies with fundamental policymaking authority—cannot be the end of the legitimacy inquiry; on the contrary,
it is the beginning, since in the post–New Deal era, "there are no
practical limitations on the potential scope of agency authority"
(Rabin, "Legitimacy Discretion and the Concept of Rights" 92
Yale L.J. 1174, 1181 [1983]).

For a discussion of the key legitimacy issues in the judicial activism debate, and especially of the distinctions between "inter-
pretivist" approaches emphasizing the importance of close adherence to the literal constitutional text and "non-interpretivist"
approaches which justify reasonable adoptions in light of major
changes in historical and social conditions, *see* Perry, *supra*; J. Ely,
Democracy and Distrust (1980); Grey, "Do We Have an Unwritten
Constitution?" 27 Stan. L. Rev. 703 (1975). *Compare* Bickel, "The
Original Understanding and the Segregation Decision," 69 Harv.

L. Rev. 1, 59-65 (1955), *with* R. Berger, Government by Judiciary (1977).

53. Even critics of judicial and administrative activism realize the importance of comparative institutional analysis. Note in this regard Chief Justice Burger's recent statement in Immigration and Naturalization Service v. Chadha, 103 S. Ct. 2765, 2784 (1983): "Although not 'hermetically' sealed from one another, Buckley v. Valeo, *supra*, 424 U.S. at 121, the powers delegated to the three Branches are *functionally identifiable*" (emphasis added).

54. 79 Mich. L. Rev. 1350 (1981). *See also* Komesar, "Taking Institutions Seriously: Introduction to a Strategy for Constitutional Analysis," 51 Chi. L. Rev. 366 (1984); Fletcher, "The Discretionary Constitution: Institutional Remedies and Judicial Legitimacy," 91 Yale L.J. 635 (1982) (judicial remedial activism is justified only by serious, chronic defaults of other branches); Scharpf, "Judicial Review and the Political Question: A Functional Analysis," 75 Yale L.J. 517 (1966) (functional theory of the political questions doctrine). *Cf.* Bickel and Wellington, "Legislative Purpose and the Judicial Process: The Lincoln Mills Case," 71 Harv. L. Rev. 1 (1957). For a comparative analysis of legislative and judicial competence in promoting open government communications, see M. Yudof, When Government Speaks chap. 10 (1983).

55. Komesar, *supra* note 54, at 1350.

56. *Ibid.* Komesar compares the field of comparative institutional analysis with the "new law and economics" school, which considers issues pertaining to relative institutional efficiency in resource allocation. *See*, e.g., Posner, "Some Uses and Abuses of Economics in Law," 46 U. Chi. L. Rev. 281 (1979); R. Posner, Economic Analysis of Law (1977); G. Calabresi, The Costs of Accidents (1970).

57. Komesar, *supra* note 54, at 1391.

58. EPAC, *supra* note 2, at 215.

59. Clune, "Courts and Legislatures as Arbitrators of Social Change," 93 Yale L.J. 763 (1984) [hereinafter cited as Courts and Legislatures]. Professor Yudof, in his essay review of our book, appears to agree with our cautious approach to the legitimacy issues, and he emphasizes the difficulties of assessing the comparative advantages or disadvantages of legislative and judicial decision-making modes (Yudof, "Plato's Ideal and the Perversity of Politics," 81 Mich. L. Rev. 730 [1983]). *See also* Fishman, "Book Review: Educational Policy Making and the Courts: An Emprical Study of

Judicial Activism," 4 Pace L. Rev. 195 (1983); Levine, "Book Review: Educational Policy Making and the Courts: An Empirical Study of Judicial Activism," 34 Hastings L.J. 1325 (1983).

60. Clune develops his attack on "formalism" in greater detail in another recent work which sets forth a political model of implementation that views the functioning of all three branches of government, and indeed the entire legal system, as a complex interrelated process of ongoing organizational interaction, with no ascertainable formal boundaries (A Political Model of Implementation, *supra* note 44.

61. For discussions of the analogous problems in determining when minorities have been denied "fair access" to the legislative process, see J. Ely, *supra* note 52; Sandalow, "Judicial Protection of Minorities," 75 Mich. L. Rev. 1162 (1977); Choper, *supra* note 52.

62. Courts and Legislatures, *supra* note 59, at 769. Clune does not specifically define *formalism*, and his approach may be based on an assumption that contemporary formal legal doctrines are a veneer to cover a fundamentally political decision-making process; from such a perspective, courts would be subject to more, rather than less, constraint by Clune's proposed comparative institutional perspective. Any such assumption, however, would need substantial theoretical and empirical validation. Our own research leads in a contrary direction, since it indicates that contemporary legitimacy doctrines emphasizing the weight of precedent and a limited policymaking role for the judiciary do significantly constrain judges' decisions (*see* EPAC, *supra* note 2, at 31).

63. Fiss, "Objectivity and Interpretation," 34 Stan. L. Rev. 739, 756-57 (1982). *See also* R. McClosky, The Supreme Court (1960).

64. "Once established power structures are stripped of their presumptively legitimate status, how is the law to check a political elite from using a momentary electoral victory as a mandate for the totalitarian overhaul of our basic institutions?" (Ackerman, *supra* note 51, at 1124).

65. 103 S. Ct. at 2791 n.7. The Supreme Court has endorsed a similar approach in other areas of constitutional law which required fundamental reconceptualization. For example, Justice Rehnquist, writing for the majority in Mueller v. Allen, 103 S. Ct. 3062, 3069 (1983), stated: "We find it useful . . . to compare the attenuated financial benefits flowing to parochial schools from the section to the evils against which our Establishment Clause was designed to protect." *See also* Everson v. Board of Education, 330 U.S. 1, 14-

15 (1947); School District of Abington Township v. Schempp, 374 U.S. 203, 236 (1963) (Brennan, J., concurring).
66. The Federalist No. 47, at 302-303 (J. Madison) (C. Rossiter ed. 1961). *See also* T. Jefferson, Notes on the State of Virginia 195 (1787) ("The concentrating of these in the same hands is precisely the definition of despotic government"); G. Wood, The Creation of the American Republic 446-53 (1969). Note also the consistency of the approach put forward here with the "blending approach" articulated by Madison in The Federalist Nos. 47-51 and written into the Constitution. *See also* Strauss, "The Place of Agencies in Government: Separation of Powers and the Fourth Branch," 84 Colum. L. Rev. 574 (1984). (The Constitution intended undefined rivalries and tensions among the branches to prevent irreversible domination by any one body.)

It is somewhat ironic that contemporary critics of judicial and administrative activism emphasize the centrality of legislative supremacy, when it is clear that fear of excessive legislative power was the framers' main concern. *See*, e.g., The Federalist Nos. 48, 78 (C. Rossiter ed. 1961). Berns, "Judicial Review and the Rights and Laws of Nature," 1982 S. Ct. Rev. 49, 77-79; Sharp, *supra* note 50, at 412-13; Levi, "Some Aspects of the Separation of Powers," 76 Colum. L. Rev. 371, 372-75 (1976).

67. The Supreme Court has not directly confronted the fundamental separation of powers issue raised in the text. The majority decision in *Chadha*, *supra* note 53, which invalidated the legislative veto mechanism by which the House of Representatives sought to oversee administrative policymaking powers, clearly reflects a lack of sympathy for mechanisms which would permit extensive delegation of policymaking powers with specific congressional oversights. Although the facts in that case involved a one-house veto of a deportation decision made by the attorney general, a situation which had few general policy implications, the majority decision indicates that legislative vetoes of more substantial delegated policymaking authority—and legislative vetoes requiring action by both houses of Congress—would also be considered unconstitutional. Still, the Court's major pronouncements on separation of powers issues are sufficiently broad that there is room for continued debate and experimentation in this area. *See*, e.g., Youngstown Sheet & Tube Co. v. Sawyer, 343 U.S. 579 (1952); Buckley v. Valeo, 424 U.S. 1 (1976); Nixon v. Administrator of General Services, 433 U.S. 425 (1977); Dames & Moore v. Regan, 453

326326326326326 NOTES TO CHAPTER TEN

U.S. 654 (1981). *See also* Elliott, "INS v. Chadha: The Administrative Constitution, the Constitution, and the Legislative Veto," 1983 S. Ct. Rev. 125.
68. See the congressional modifications of Title VI cited in chapter 3, note 19. Note that Title VI also provided for significant judicial oversight.
69. *See* E. Bardach and R. Kagan, Going By the Book: The Problems of Regulatory Unreasonableness (1982); Mashaw, "Regulatory Logic and Ideology," 3 Regulation 44 (1979) (the legislature delegates policy issues to administrative agencies to devise solutions in light of concrete experience, but agencies, over time, tend to generalize and overextend their regulatory authority). For a discussion of potential problems of overextension of the courts' role in institutional reform litigations, see Fiss, "The Bureaucratization of the Judiciary," 90 Yale L.J. 473 (1981).
70. *See* A. Bickel, The Least Dangerous Branch (1962). *See also* Yudof, *supra* note 59, at 741-44.

NOTES TO CHAPTER TEN

1. 103 S. Ct. 3221 (1983).
2. "The Supreme Court, 1982 Term," 97 Harv. L. Rev. 70, 245 (1983).
3. The intent/impact distinction proved not to be critical to the Supreme Court's actual disposition of this case since, despite differences on this point, a majority of the justices upheld the lower court's order on a number of alternate grounds, including the proposition that Title VI does not provide a private right of action, and that a private plaintiff can recover only injunctive, non-compensatory relief for an unintentional violation of Title VI.
4. 103 S. Ct. at 3254-55. Justice Stevens's opinion was joined by Justices Brennan and Blackmun. Justices White and Marshall interpreted the Title VI statute itself to impose an impact standard, but Justice White also agreed that, even in the absence of an impact standard in the statute, the higher standard could be imposed by the administrative regulations (103 S. Ct. at 3226-27).
5. 103 S. Ct. at 3228. Justice Powell agreed with Justice O'Connor's position and added further: "I do not question the view that the Court should sustain a reasonable administrative interpretation even if we would have reached a different result had the question initially risen in a judicial proceeding . . . but I know of no precedent whatever for asserting that this deference to administrative

NOTES TO CHAPTER TEN                                    327

interpretation is proper *after* this Court already has issued a definitive—and contrary—construction of its own" (103 S. Ct. at 3237 n.5).

6. The complexity of the Title VI intent/impact issues in the *Guardians* case arose from the fact that in Regents of the University of California v. Bakke, 438 U.S. 265 (1978), four of the justices who supported a race-conscious affirmative action admissions policy (Justices Brennan, Marshall, White, and Blackmun) joined Justice Powell in arguing that Congress intended in Title VI to incorporate the constitutional equal protection standard as articulated by the Supreme Court, no more and no less. Having taken this stand in *Bakke* to support a position in favor of affirmative action, these same justices were then confronted, in *Guardians*, with a major problem, because incorporation of the established constitutional standard (which, under Washington v. Davis, 426 U.S. 229 [1976], is an intent standard) would preclude upholding the affirmative action position there. Faced with this dilemma, Justice White attempted to distinguish the facts and therefore the implications of the precedents in *Bakke* and *Guardians* (103 S. Ct. at 3226). Justice Marshall stated, "I frankly concede that our reasoning in *Bakke* was broader than it should have been" (103 S. Ct. at 3243-44). Justices Brennan and Blackmun acknowledged the force of precedent in the position they had taken in *Bakke*, and they joined Justice Stevens in setting forth the novel position discussed in the text, which would uphold administrative regulations inconsistent with the Court's interpretation of congressional intent in the underlying statute.

   In a recent decision, a *unanimous* Court reiterated the impact holding of *Guardians*, stating that ". . . we held [in Guardians] that Title VI had delegated to the agencies in the first instance the complex determination of what sorts of disparate impacts upon minorities constituted sufficiently significant social problems . . . to warrant altering the practices of the federal grantees. . . ." Alexander v. Choate, 83 L. Ed. 2d 661 (1985).

7. A suggested formulation of such a doctrine was set forth in "The Supreme Court, 1982 Term," *supra* note 2, at 249, as follows: "A better solution would have been to rule that Title VI itself adopts neither an intent role nor an impact standard, but rather delegates the authority to establish the applicable standard to the federal agencies responsible for particular programs." In support of this proposal, its authors cited Professor Abernathy's article, "Title VI and the Constitution: A Regulatory Model for Defining Discrim-

ination," 70 Geo. L.J. 1 (1981), which argued that in 1964 Congress actually intended to delegate the key egalitarian policymaking role to the administrative agencies. We have already noted in chapter 3 that we disagree with this reading of the legislative history. However, our overall findings in this study do support the view that the delegation approach may be suitable for egalitarian policy situations; therefore, it should be explicitly recognized rather than indirectly invoked by Congress in the future.

In *Guardians* itself, we think a sounder justification for the result would have been to acknowledge congressional intent to defer the intent/impact issue for further judicial development, and then to carve out an exception to the Washington v. Davis intent standard for this area where the Court had, over a 19-year period (*see*, e.g., Lau v. Nichols), acknowledged the need for pragmatic-analytic policymaking by the administrative agencies.

8. *See*, e.g., G. Orfield, Must We Bus? 300-301 (1978); Letter from 57 civil rights and civic organizations to HEW Secretary David Mathews (December 10, 1975), discussed in chapter 4, note 51.

9. "OCR's study of expenditure patterns, in-school tracking systems and many other school operations in New York consumed more than three years of effort on the part of its New York regional office—during which time it devoted only peripheral attention to possible civil rights violations in all other school districts of New York and New Jersey. And after all of this effort, OCR in the end backed away from its threat to cut off funds to financially stricken New York, settling for only minor changes in the city's pattern of student services" (Rabkin, "Office for Civil Rights," in The Politics of Regulation 304, 346 [J. Wilson ed. 1980]). *See also* B. Radin, Implementation, Change and the Federal Bureaucracy: School Desegregation Policy in HEW, 1964-1968 208 (1977).

10. The comparative case studies of Chicago, Los Angeles, and Philadelphia also demonstrated that more "successful" implementation of the provisions of a compliance agreement can be achieved when the administrative/regulatory agency has strong sanctions available to it, and when the agreement requires immediate, statistically verifiable institutional changes. The "success" of prompt, thoroughgoing compliance, however, must be weighed against the substantial administrative disruption and possible detrimental long-term effects on morale. The comparative institutional perspective also cautions us to consider the extent to which the strengthening of an agency's sanctioning power might upset the

negotiating equilibrium which, in New York City, led to ideologically balanced agreements.

11. As indicated above, civil rights advocates have tended to take a skeptical view of comprehensive compliance reviews; indeed, for most of the past decade, the civil rights organizations have fought to improve the individual complaint and investigation process, using the legal leverage gained in the *Adams* and *Brown* cases (*see supra* chapter 4). However, this strategy may have created an overemphasis on individualized complaints as compared to the system-wide issues. (All system-wide reviews, of course, need not involve the extensive marshalling of resources that took place in the New York Review.)

We note in this regard that statistics on OCR's complaint load indicated a bias toward "middle-class" issues (such as special education and sex discrimination) at the expense of traditional racial discrimination concerns. In a current 2⅓-year period, 63 percent of the complaints that were resolved with corrective action dealt with issues of handicapped children. The second largest category was sex discrimination, at 21 percent. Only 15 percent of the corrective action responded to complaints of racial and language minorities. (Source: OCR computer printout of complaints. FY 1980-1982 [through April 30, 1982], supplied to the authors pursuant to a Freedom of Information Act request.)

12. *See*, e.g., Block, "Enforcement of Title VI Compliance Agreements by Third Party Beneficiaries," 18 Harv. C.R.-C.L. L. Rev. 1 (1983).

13. *See* Clune, "A Political Model of Implementation and Implications of the Model for Public Policy, Research, and the Changing Roles of Law and Lawyers," 69 Iowa L. Rev. 47, 91-93 (1983). *See also* Days, "Seeking a New Civil Rights Consensus," 112 Daedalus No. 4, 197, 213-14 (1983).

14. If institutional restructuring should indeed encourage further ideological reconciliations of opportunity/result controversies in a wider number of geographical locales and in regard to a broader array of specific issues, ultimately it may be possible to perceive a developing overall moral consensus that could be articulated as a consistent fundamental constitutional principle. Articulation of such a fundamental principle would ultimately be the province of the courts. *See* M. Rebell and A. Block, Educational Policy Making and the Courts: An Empirical Study of Judicial Activism 215-16 (1982); Rebell, "Judicial Activism and the Court's New Role," Soc. Pol'y 24 (Spring 1982).

# INDEX

LIBRARY OF CONGRESS CATALOGING
IN PUBLICATION DATA

Rebell, Michael A.
  Equality and education.

  Bibliography: p.
  Includes index.
  1. Discrimination in education—Law and legislation—New York (N.Y.)
  2. Discrimination in education—Law and legislation—United States.
  3. New York (N.Y.)—Schools.   4. United States. Dept. of Health, Education, and Welfare. Office for Civil Rights.   I. Block, Arthur R.
  II. Title.
  KFX2065.R43   1985      344.747'0798      85-42700
  ISBN 0-691-07692-8      347.4704798

MICHAEL A. REBELL is a partner of Rebell and Krieger in New York City
and Visiting Lecturer in Law at The Yale Law School. He is also Chairman
of the Special Committee on Law and Education of the Association of the
Bar of the City of New York. ARTHUR R. BLOCK practices law in New York
City and is Lecturer in Law at Columbia Law School and Project Director
of "Lawyers as Social Reformers in the 1930s: Lessons from a Time of Crisis."
They are the coauthors of *Educational Policy Making and the Courts*
(Chicago).